An Introduction to Discourse

Discourse analysis considers how language, both spoken and written, enacts soc l and cultural perspectives and identities. Assuming no prior knowledge of l guistics, *An Introduction to Discourse Analysis* examines the field and pres nts James Paul Gee's unique integrated approach, which incorporates botl a theory of language-in-use and a method of research.

T   hird edition of this bestselling text has been extensively revised and ι   ed to include new material such as examples of oral and written   age, ranking from group discussions with children, adults, students, and ε   ers, to conversations, interviews, academic texts, and policy documents. ε it can be used as a stand-alone text, this edition has also been fully   referenced with the practical companion title *How to do Discourse* sis: A Toolkit, and together they provide the complete resource for ιts with an interest in this area.

γ structured and written in a highly accessible style, *An Introduction* ourse Analysis includes perspectives from a variety of approaches and ιines—including applied linguistics, education, psychology, anthro- ;, and communication—to help students and scholars from a range of ιounds to formulate their own views on discourse and engage in their iscourse analysis.

James Paul Gee is the Mary Lou Fulton Presidential Professor of Literacy Stuc s at Arizona State University. His many titles include *How to do Disc ιrse Analysis, Sociolinguistics and Literacies*, and *Situated Language and I :   ng*, all published by Routledge.

"Since it was first published in 1999, Gee's *An Introduction to Discourse Analysis* has become a classic in the field. Written in a refreshing and highly accessible style and full of interesting, contemporary examples, this book is useful not just for beginners seeking to understand the personal, practical and political implications of how we use language to communicate, but also for seasoned scholars seeking new ideas and inspiration. This new edition is substantially revised and reorganized, making it even more user-friendly, and includes a wealth of new, up-to-date examples and theoretical material, including material on images and multimodal texts."
Rodney Jones, *City University of Hong Kong, Hong Kong*

"This useful book provides an extensive set of tools for systematically analyzing language use. The book reflects Gee's broad and deep grasp of relevant fields, drawing on insights not only about the social life of language but also about social theories of late capitalism, contemporary accounts of culture and sociocentric approaches to the mind. Earlier editions have proven their usefulness to both beginning and advanced students, and this new edition contains the useful original material together with nice additions like more extensive sample analyses and a primer on analyzing multimodal texts."
Stanton Wortham, *University of Pennsylvania, USA*

"Wonderful entrance point, engaging, well-grounded in the literature, and full of analytical insights, this book offers helpful, interesting, and practical examples across different aspects of discourse analysis. Gee's accessible and engaging writing style and his openness to difference encourages scholars to begin or continue exploring the ways in which discourses operate as practices and activities in the world. This book stimulates various analytical, theoretical, and conceptual conversations among students, researchers, and practitioners."
Mirka Koro-Ljungberg, *University of Florida, USA*

An Introduction to Discourse Analysis

Theory and method

Third Edition

James Paul Gee

Routledge
Taylor & Francis Group

NEW YORK AND LONDON

First published in the USA and Canada 1999
Second edition published 2005
Third edition published 2011
by Routledge
270 Madison Ave, New York, NY 10016

Simultaneously published in the UK
by Routledge
2 Park Square, Milton Park, Abingdon, Oxon OX14 4RN

Routledge is an imprint of the Taylor & Francis Group, an informa business

© 1999, 2005, 2011 James Paul Gee

Typeset in ITC Berkeley Oldstyle Std Medium 10/12pt by Fakenham Photosetting Limited
Printed and bound by Edwards Brothers, Inc.

British Library Cataloguing in Publication Data
A catalogue record for this book is available from the British Library

Library of Congress Cataloging in Publication Data
Gee, James Paul.
An introduction to discourse analysis: theory and method / James Paul Gee. — 3rd ed.
   p. cm.
1. Discourse analysis. I. Title.
   P302.G4 2010
   401'.41—dc22
                         2010001121

ISBN10: 0-415-58569-4 (hbk)
ISBN10: 0-415-58570-8 (pbk)
ISBN10: 0-203-84788-1 (ebk)

ISBN13: 978-0-415-58569-9 (hbk)
ISBN13: 978-0-415-58570-5 (pbk)
ISBN13: 978-0-203-84788-6 (ebk)

Contents

CHAPTER ONE
Introduction

Language as Saying, Doing, and Being

What is language for? Many people think language exists so that we can "say things" in the sense of communicating information. However, language serves a great many functions in our lives. Giving and getting information is by no means the only one. Language does, of course, allow us to inform each other. But it also allows us to do things and to be things, as well. In fact, saying things in language never goes without also doing things and being things.

Language allows us to do things. It allows us to engage in actions and activities. We promise people things, we open committee meetings, we propose to our lovers, we argue over politics, and we "talk to God" (pray). These are among the myriad of things we do with language beyond giving and getting information.

Language allows us to be things. It allows us to take on different socially significant identities. We can speak as experts—as doctors, lawyers, anime aficionados, or carpenters—or as "everyday people." To take on any identity at a given time and place we have to "talk the talk," not just "walk the walk." When they are being gang members, street-gang members talk a different talk than do honor students when they are being students. Furthermore, one and the same person could be both things at different times and places.

In language, there are important connections among saying (informing), doing (action), and being (identity). If I say anything to you, you cannot really understand it fully if you do not know what I am trying to do and who I am trying to be by saying it. To understand anything fully you need to know *who* is saying it and *what* the person saying it is trying to do.

Let's take a simple example. Imagine a stranger on the street walks up to you and says "Hi, how are you?" The stranger has said something, but you do not know what to make of it. Who is this person? What is the stranger doing?

Imagine you find out that the person is taking part in a game where strangers ask other people how they are in order to see what sorts of reactions they get. Or imagine that the person is a friend of your twin and thinks you are your sibling (I have a twin and this sort of thing has often happened to me). Or imagine the person is someone you met long ago and have long forgotten, but who, unbeknownst to you, thinks of you as a friend. In one case, a gamer is playing; in another case, a friend of your sibling's is mistakenly being friendly; and, in yet another case, someone who mistakenly thinks he is a friend of yours is also being friendly. Once you sort things out, everything is clear (but not necessarily comfortable).

My doctor, who also happens to be a friend, tells me, as she greets me in her office: "You look tired." Is she speaking to me as a friend (*who*) making small talk (*what*) or is she speaking to me as a doctor (*who*) making a professional judgment (*what*) about my health? It makes quite a big difference whether a friend (*who*) is playfully insulting (*what*) his friend in a bar or a hard-core biker (*who*) is threatening (*what*) a stranger. The words can be the same, but they will mean very different things. Who we are and what we are doing when we say things matters.

This book is concerned with a theory of how we use language to say things, do things, and be things. It is concerned, as well, with a method of how to study saying, doing, and being in language. When I talk about "being things," I will use the word "identity" in a special way. I do not mean your core sense of self, who you take yourself "essentially" to be. I mean different ways of being in the world at different times and places for different purposes; for example, ways of being a "good student," an "avid bird watcher," a "mainstream politician," a "tough cop," a video-game "gamer," a "Native American," and so on and so forth through a nearly endless list.

Language and Practices

One of the best ways to see something that we have come to take too much for granted (like language) is to look at an example of it that makes it strange again. So consider *Yu-Gi-Oh!*, a popular-culture activity, but one whose use of language will seem strange to many.

Here are some facts about *Yu-Gi-Oh!*: *Yu-Gi-Oh!* is a card game that can be played face-to-face or in video games. There are also *Yu-Gi-Oh!* television shows, movies, and books (in all of which characters act out moves in the card game). There are thousands of *Yu-Gi-Oh!* cards. Players choose a deck of 40 cards and "duel" each other. The moves in the game represent battles between the monsters on their cards. Each card has instructions about what moves can be made in the game when that card is used. *Yu-Gi-Oh!* is a form of Japanese "anime," that is, animated ("cartoon") characters and their stories shown in "mangas" (comic books), television shows, and movies. Japanese anime is now a worldwide phenomenon. If this all seems strange to you, that is all to the good.

Below I print part of the text on one card:

> When this card is Normal Summoned, Flip Summoned, or Special Summoned successfully, select and activate 1 of the following effects: Select 1 equipped Equip Spell Card and destroy it. Select 1 equipped Equip Spell Card and equip it to this card.

What does this mean? Notice, first of all, that you, as a speaker of English, recognize each word in this text. But that does you very little good. You still do not really know what it means if you do not understand *Yu-Gi-Oh!*.

So how would you find out what the text really means? Since we are all influenced a great deal by how school has taught us to think about language, we are liable to think that the answer to this question is this: Look up what the words mean in some sort of dictionary or guide. But this does not help anywhere as much as you might think. There are web sites where you can look up what the words and phrases on *Yu-Gi-Oh!* cards mean, and this is the sort of thing you see if you go to such web sites:

> **Equip Spell Cards** are Spell Cards that *usually* change the ATK and/or DEF of a Monster Card on the field, and/or grant that Monster Card special abilitie(s). They are universally referred to as **Equip Cards**, since Equip Cards can either be Equip Spell Cards, or Trap Cards that are treated as Equip Cards after activation. When you activate an Equip Spell Card, you choose a face-up monster on the field to equip the card to, and that Equip Spell Card's card's effect applies to that monster until the card is destroyed or otherwise removed from the field. When the equipped monster is removed from the field or flipped face-down, all the Equip Spell Cards equipped to that monster are destroyed. A fair few Equip Spell Cards are representations of weapons or armour. (http://yugioh.wikia.com/wiki/Equip_Spell_Cards)

Does this really help? If you do not understand the card, you do not understand this much better. And think how much more of this I would have to give you to explicate the whole text on the *Yu-Gi-Oh!* card, short though it is.

Why didn't it help? Because, in general, if you do not understand some words, getting yet more of the same sorts of words does not help you know what the original words mean. In fact, it is hard to understand words just by getting definitions (other words) or other sorts of verbal explanations. Even if we understand a definition, it only tells us the range of meanings a word has, it does not really tell us how to use the word appropriately in real contexts of use.

So if you had to learn what "*Yu-Gi-Oh!* language" actually meant, how would you go about it? You probably would not choose to read lots of texts like the one above from the web site. Even if you did, I assure you that you would still be lost if you had actually to play *Yu-Gi-Oh!*.

The way you could best learn what the language on the card meant would be to learn to play the game of *Yu-Gi-Oh!*, not just read more text. How would you do this? You would watch and play games, let other players mentor you, play *Yu-Gi-Oh!* video games which coach you on how to play the game, watch *Yu-Gi-Oh!* television shows and movies which act out the game, and, then, too, read things.

Why is this the best way to learn what the card means? Because, in this case, it is pretty clear that the language on the card gets its meaning from the game, from its rules and the ways players play the game. The language is used—together with other actions (remember language itself is a form of action)—to play (to enact) the game as an activity or practice in the world.

The language on *Yu-Gi-Oh!* cards does not get its meaning first and foremost from definitions or verbal explanations, that is, from other words. It gets its meaning from what it is used to do, in this case, play a game. This is language as doing.

However, *Yu-Gi-Oh!* is an activity—a way of doing things (in this case, playing a game)—because certain sorts of people take on certain sorts of identities, in this case identities as gamers and enthusiasts of certain sorts (here, fans of anime and anime card games like *Pokémon* and *Yu-Gi-Oh!* and others). This is language as being.

If there were no anime gamers/fans (being), then there would be no anime games and gaming (doing). If there were no anime gamers/fans and no anime games and gaming, then the words on the cards would be meaningless, there would be no saying (information). Saying follows, in language, from doing and being.

Is this *Yu-Gi-Oh!* example just strange and untypical? In this book I want to argue that it is actually typical of how language works. Its very strangeness allows us to see what we take for granted in examples of language with which we are much more familiar and where we have forgotten the role of doing and being in language and remember only the role of saying and communicating.

In the case of the language on the *Yu-Gi-Oh!* card, we said that the language on the card got its meaning, not from dictionaries or other words, but from a game and its rules and the things players do. In a sense all language gets its meaning from a game, though we don't typically use the word "game." We use the more arcane word "practice."

A game is composed of a set of rules that determines winners and losers. Other activities, like taking part in a committee meeting, a lecture, a political debate, or "small talk" among neighbors, are not games, but they are conducted according to certain "rules" or conventions. These "rules" or conventions do not determine winners and losers (usually), but they do determine who has acted "appropriately" or "normally" or not, and this in society can, indeed, be a type of winning and losing.

These sorts of activities—things like committee meetings, lectures, political debates, and "small talk"—are often called "practices," though we could just as well use the word "games" in an extended sense. This book will argue that all language—like *Yu-Gi-Oh!* language—gets its meaning from the games or practices within which it is used. These games or practices are always ways of saying, doing, and being.

Language and "Politics"

If you break the rules of *Yu-Gi-Oh!* either you are playing the game incorrectly or you are attempting to change the rules. This can get you into trouble with the other players. If you follow the rules, you are playing appropriately and others will accept you as a *Yu-Gi-Oh!* player, though not necessarily as a good one. If you follow the rules—and use them well to your advantage—you may win the game often and others will consider you a good player.

If you care about *Yu-Gi-Oh!* and want to be considered a player or even a good player, then having others judge you as a player or a good player is what I will call a "social good." Social goods are anything some people in a society want and value. Being considered a *Yu-Gi-Oh!* player or a good *Yu-Gi-Oh!*

player is a social good for some people. In that case, how they play the game and how others accept their game play is important and consequential for them.

Above I said that just as *Yu-Gi-Oh!* language is used to enact the game of *Yu-Gi-Oh!*, so, too, other forms of language are used to enact other "games" or practices. Consider, for example, the practice ("game") of being a "good student" in elementary school. In different classrooms and schools this game is played somewhat differently. And this game changes over time. What made someone a "good student" in the seventeenth century in the United States— how "good students" talked and behaved—is different than what makes someone a "good student" today.

However, in each case there are conventions (rules) about how "good students" talk and behave ("good students" here being the ones teachers and school personnel say are "good students," that is why the phrase is in quotes). Many children want to be accepted in this identity, just as some people want to be accepted as good *Yu-Gi-Oh!* players. Many parents want their children to be accepted as "good students" as well. So being accepted as a "good student" is, for these people, a social good.

In this sense, even though practices like being a "good student" are not really games—their "rules" or conventions are usually much less formal—there are, in these practices, in a sense, "winners" and "losers." The winners are people who want to be accepted as a "good student" and gain such acceptance. The "losers" are people who want such acceptance, but do not get it.

There are, as we have said, different practices—different "games"—about how good students talk and act in different classrooms and schools. There are also people, like in the case of *Yu-Gi-Oh!*, who want to interpret the "rules" differently or change them altogether. For example, should it be a "rule" that "good students" always closely follow the teacher's instructions or should "good students" sometimes innovate and even challenge teachers? Is a student who asks a teacher how she knows something she has claimed to know being a "good student" or a "problem student"?

You may not want to be accepted as a *Yu-Gi-Oh!* player and maybe you resisted being a "good student" in school. Then these are not social goods for you. But some things are social goods for you. Perhaps, being accepted as an "acceptable" ("normal," "good," "adequate") citizen, man or woman, worker, friend, activist, football fan, educated person, Native American, religious person, Christian, Jewish person, or Islamic person, or what have you, is a social good for you.

The "games" or practices where you want to "win" (be accepted within them as "acceptable" or "good") are cases where social goods are at stake for you. In these cases, how you use language (and more generally how you say, do, and be) and how people respond to you are deeply consequential to you and for you. If you get accepted—"win" the game—you gain a social good. If you do not get fully accepted—"lose" the game—you lose a social good.

People fight over the rules of *Yu-Gi-Oh!* in terms of what they really mean and how exactly they should be applied. People try sometimes to change the rules or agree to play by somewhat different rules. So, too, with practices in society. People fight over what the "rules" for being a "good student" ought to be. They sometimes seek to change them or to agree to a new set of "rules." They fight over these things because important social goods are at stake.

Let's take a dramatic case to make the point clear. Marriage is a practice. There are formal and informal laws and conventions (rules) about how married people talk and act and how others talk and act in regard to marriage as an institution. Today, people fight over whether it is appropriate to talk about gay people being married to each other, whether they can rightly say they are married, and whether such marriages should be recognized in law or in church.

For many gay people, a failure to use the language of marriage for their union with each other is to deny them a social good. They fight to interpret the rules—or change the rules—of marriage in ways that will allow them this social good. For many gay people, a different term, like "legal union," even if it gives all the same legal protections as marriage, is still unacceptable.

All forms of language—like *Yu-Gi-Oh!* language or the language we use around the practice of marriage—get their meaning from the games or practices they are used to enact. These games or practices determine who is "acceptable" or "good"—who is a "winner" or "loser"—in the game or practice. "Winning" in these practices is often, for many people, a social good. Thus, in using language, social goods are always at stake, at least for some people. If no one cared about a game or practice anymore—no one saw being accepted as "acceptable" or "good" in the game or practice as important anymore—the game or practice would no longer have any social goods to offer and would cease to exist.

Thus, in using language, social goods are always at stake. When we speak or write, we always risk being seen as a "winner" or "loser" in a given game or practice. Furthermore, we can speak or write so as to accept others as "winners" or "losers" in the game or practice in which we are engaged. In speaking and writing, then, we can both gain or lose and give or deny social goods. Gay people who say they are married to their partners are bidding for a social good. How we act out the "game" of the marriage practice in our society can give or deny them this social good. And how people talk about marriage or anything else is never just a decision about saying (informing), it is a decision about doing and being, as well.

Social goods are the stuff of politics. Politics is not just about contending political parties. At a much deeper level it is about how to distribute social goods in a society: who gets what in terms of money, status, power, and acceptance on a variety of different terms, all social goods. Since, when we use language, social goods and their distribution are always at stake, language is always "political" in a deep sense.

Two Forms of Discourse Analysis: Descriptive and "Critical"

Discourse analysis is the study of language-in-use. There are many different approaches to discourse analysis (see Readings section at the end of this chapter). Some of them look only at the "content" of the language being used, the themes or issues being discussed in a conversation or a newspaper article, for example. Other approaches pay more attention to the structure of language ("grammar") and how this structure functions to make meaning in specific contexts. These approaches are rooted in the discipline of linguistics. This book is about one such approach.

Different linguistic approaches to discourse analysis use different theories of grammar and take different views about how to talk about meaning. The approach in this book looks at meaning as an integration of ways of saying (informing), doing (action), and being (identity), and grammar as a set of tools to bring about this integration. To take an example, consider the two sentences below:

1. Hornworms sure vary a lot in how well they grow.
2. Hornworm growth exhibits a significant amount of variation.

Sentence 1 is in a style of language (called the "vernacular") we use when we want to talk as an "everyday person," not as a specialist of any kind. This is the identity (being) it expresses. It is a way to express an opinion based on one's own observations (of hornworms in this case). This is an action (doing). The sentence can be used to do other actions as well, such as show surprise or entice someone to grow hornworms. The sentence is about hornworms, which are cute green caterpillars with little yellow horns. This is a part of what the sentence says (informing).

Sentence 2 is in a specialist style of language, one we would associate with biology and biologists. It expresses one's identity (being) as being such a specialist. It is not just expressing an opinion based on one's observations of hornworms, it is making a claim based on statistical tests of "significance" that are "owned" and "operated" by the discipline of biology, not any one person, including the speaker or writer. This is an action (doing). The sentence is not about hornworms, but "hornworm growth," an abstract trait of hornworms (much less cute than hornworms). This is part of what the sentence says (informing).

The grammar (structure) of the two sentences is very different. In sentence 1, the subject of the sentence—which names the "topic" of the sentence—is the noun "hornworms." But in sentence 2, the subject is the noun phrase "hornworm growth." "Hornworm growth" is a noun phrase that expresses a whole sentence's worth of information ("Hornworms grow") and is a much more complex structure than the simple noun "hornworms." It is a way to talk about an abstract trait of hornworms, and not the hornworms themselves. It is also part of what makes this language "specialist" and not "everyday."

The phrase "significant amount of variation" in sentence 2 uses an abstract noun ("variation") rather than the verb "vary" in sentence 1 and combines this noun with "significant amount." So a process (varying) has been turned into an abstract thing ("variation") that can be quantified using statistics ("significant amount"). This, too, is, again, now a way to talk about abstract things rather than more concrete things and processes in the world. It is also, again, part of what makes this language "specialist" and ties it to tools (like statistical tests of significance) in a discipline and not just to an individual's observations in the world.

So the grammar of the two sentences offers us different ways to say things that amount to different ways of doing (actions) and being (identity). Looking closely at the structure of language as it is being used can help us uncover different ways of saying things, doing things, and being things in the world.

But why would we want to do this? Some approaches to discourse analysis, which we can call "descriptive," answer this question by saying that their goal is to describe how language works in order to understand it, just as the goal of the physicist is to describe how the physical world works in order to understand it. In both cases—the discourse analyst and the physicist—their hope may also be to gain deep explanations of how language or the world works and why they work that way. Though their work may have practical applications in the world, these discourse analysts and physicists are not motivated by those applications.

Some other approaches to discourse analysis, which we can call "critical" as in "critical discourse analysis," answer this question differently. Their goal is not just to describe how language works or even to offer deep explanations, though they do want to do this. They also want to speak to and, perhaps, intervene in, social or political issues, problems, and controversies in the world. They want to apply their work to the world in some fashion.

People who take a descriptive approach often think that a critical approach is "unscientific" because the critical discourse analyst is swayed by his or her interest or passion for intervening in some problem in the world. People who take a critical approach often think that a purely descriptive approach is an evasion of social and political responsibility.

My view—the view in this book—is that all discourse analysis needs to be critical, not because discourse analysts are or need to be political, but because language itself is, as we have discussed above, political. I have argued that any use of language gains its meaning from the "game" or practice of which it is a part and which it is enacting. I have argued, as well, that such "games" or practices inherently involve potential social goods and the distribution of social goods, which I have defined as central to the realm of "politics." Thus, any full description of any use of language would have to deal with "politics."

Beyond this general point, language is a key way we humans make and break our world, our institutions, and our relationships through how we deal with social goods. Thus, discourse analysis can illuminate problems and controversies in the world. It can illuminate issues about the distribution of social goods, who gets helped, and who gets harmed.

So, as an example, consider again sentences 1 and 2 and the variant in sentence 3 below. Note that it is odd—a bit funny—to say something like sentence 3:

3. Hornworm growth sure exhibits a significant amount of variation.

Why is this odd? It mixes "everyday language" ("sure") with specialist language. "Sure" in sentence 1 is a way to express one's attitude and emotion about what one has observed about hornworms. The speaker is impressed and a bit surprised. Perhaps, the speaker is even showing enthusiasm for the hornworms he or she has raised. But the "voice" of science—the "voice" behind sentence 2 and most of sentence 3—is not supposed to show attitude and emotion. It is supposed to be dispassionate, the voice of "reason." That is one of the "rules" of the game of science.

Describing these "rules"—explaining why sentence 3 is odd—is part of the job of any discourse analyst dealing with language like that in sentences 1–3. But, then, we can also ask, in specific cases, is this claim to being "dispassionate" being used for authentic scientific progress or as an evasion for one's own personal responsibility?

Later in this book, in fact, we will see a case where such specialist language does, indeed, appear to be a way to hide and evade the ethical and emotional dilemmas of what was done in an experiment. Since this is part of the saying, doing, being going on in specific language-in-use, it is our responsibility as discourse analysts to study it, even though we are then having to make judgments with consequences in the world. In this sense, all discourse analysis is critical discourse analysis, since all language is political and all language is part of the way we build and sustain our world, cultures, and institutions. So, then, too, all discourse analysis is "practical" or "applied," since it uncovers the workings—for good or ill—of this world building.

About this Book: Theory and Method

Now it is time to turn to some "truth in lending" disclaimers. This book is an introduction to *one* approach to discourse analysis. There are many different approaches to discourse analysis, none of them, including this one, uniquely "right." Different approaches fit different issues and questions better or worse than others. And, too, different approaches sometimes reach similar conclusions though they use different tools and terminologies connected to different "micro-communities" of researchers.

Furthermore, the approach to discourse analysis taken in this book is not "mine." No set of research tools and no theory belongs to a single person, no matter how much academic style and our own egos sometimes tempt us to write that way. I have freely begged, borrowed, and patched together. If there is any quality in my work, it is primarily in the "taste" with which I have raided others' stores and in the way I have adapted and mixed together the ingredients and, thereby, made the soup. Some will, of course, not recognize the ingredient they have contributed, or, at least, not want to admit they do after they taste my soup. If there are occasional inventions, their only chance for a full life is that someone else will borrow them and mix them into new soup.

This book is partly about a method of research. However, I hasten to point out that the whole issue of research "methods" is, as far as I am concerned, badly confused. First of all, any method always goes with a *theory*. Method and theory cannot be separated, despite the fact that methods are often taught as if they could stand alone. Any method of research is a way to investigate some particular domain. In this case, the domain is language-in-use. There can be no sensible method to study a domain unless one also has a theory of what that domain is. Thus, this book offers, as it must, a theory about the nature of language-in-use. In fact, you have already heard part of this theory: language-in-use is about saying-doing-being and gains its meaning from the "game" or practice it is part of and enacts.

People with different theories about a domain will use different methods for their research. The reason this is so is because a research method is made up of various "tools of inquiry" and strategies for applying them. Tools of inquiry are designed to describe and explain what the researcher takes to exist and to be important in a domain. Thus, when theories about a domain differ—for instance, a theory about what language-in-use is or about what evolution is—tools of inquiry will differ as well.

Besides seeing that methods change with theories, it is important, as well, to see that research, whether in physics, literary criticism, or in discourse analysis, is not an algorithmic procedure; it is not a set of "rules" that can be followed step-by-linear-step to get guaranteed results. There is no "scientific method," even in the "hard" sciences, if by this we mean such a set of rules to follow. Rather, research adopts and adapts specific tools of inquiry and strategies for implementing them. These tools and strategies ultimately reside in a "community of practice" formed by those engaged in such research.

Such tools and strategies are continually and flexibly adapted to specific issues, problems, and contexts of study. They are continually transformed as they are applied in practice. At the same time, new researchers in an area are normed by examples of research that more advanced researchers in the area take (for the time) to be "prototypical" examples of that area's tools and strategies in operation. Methods are through and through social and communal.

This book will introduce various tools of inquiry for discourse analysis and strategies for using them. It will give a number of examples of the tools in action, as well. But the reader should keep in mind that these tools of inquiry are not meant to be rigid definitions. Rather, they are meant to be "thinking devices" that guide inquiry in regard to specific sorts of data and specific sorts of issues and questions. They are meant to be adapted for the reader's own purposes. They are meant, as well, to be transformed as the reader adapts them to his or her own theory of the domain. Of course, if the reader's theory gets too far away from my theory of the domain, the tools will be less and less easily or sensibly adaptable and useful.

Finally, let me say that in the approach to discourse analysis taken in this book, I am not interested in specific analyses of data just in and for themselves. For me, a discourse analysis must have a point. I am not interested in simply describing data so that we can admire the intricacy of language, though such intricacy is indeed admirable. Rather, I am interested, beyond description, in a method that can do two things: a) illuminate and gain us evidence for our theory of the domain, a theory that helps to explain how and why language works the way it does when it is put into action; and b) contribute, in terms of understanding and intervention, to important issues and problems in some area that interests and motivates us as global citizens.

Thanks to the fact that, for me, discourse analyses must have a "point," this book will have relevance to "applied" issues throughout, though these issues are not always in the foreground of attention. In discourse analysis, any idea that applications and practice are less prestigious, or less important, or less "pure" than theory has no place. Such a notion has no place, because, as the reader will see, the theory of language in this book is that *language has meaning only in and through social practices*, practices which often leave us morally complicit with harm and injustice unless we attempt to transform them. It is a tenet of this book that any proper theory of language is a theory of practice—or, as we have seen, of the "games" we humans play.

More about this Book

This book is directed at three audiences. It is meant to introduce students and researchers in other areas to one form of discourse analysis that I hope they can use and experiment with as they learn other forms of discourse analysis and come up with their own ideas. It is meant, as well, for people interested in language, culture, and institutions, but who have not focused their own work on discourse analysis. Finally, it is meant for my colleagues in discourse studies, so that they can compare and contrast their own views to those developed here, and so that, together, we can advance our common enterprise of understanding how language works in society to create worlds, institutions, and human relationships.

The book is structured as follows: The "method" is fully sketched out in Chapter 8. Each of Chapters 2–7 discusses, with many examples, specific tools of inquiry that are part of the overall method and strategies for using them. These tools and strategies are fully embedded in a theory of language-in-use in culture and society. Thus, that theory is also laid out in Chapters

2–7. Chapter 7 briefly recapitulates our tools of inquiry and places them in the framework of an overall approach to discourse analysis. I also discuss the issue of validity for discourse analysis in this chapter.

Chapter 9 deals with some linguistic details (various aspects of grammar and discourse) that play an important role in discourse analysis. Here issues about how speech is planned and produced are taken up. These linguistic details will, hopefully, make more sense once the "big picture" is made clear in Chapters 2–8, and will give readers some additional tools with which to deal with the empirical details of discourse analysis. Chapters 10–12 are extended examples of discourse analysis using some of the tools and strategies developed earlier in the book. These chapters are not meant to be a step-by-step "how to" manual (for that see my book *How to do Discourse Analysis*, Routledge, 2011); they are simply meant to exemplify in practice a few of the tools discussed in this book. The book ends with an appendix and a glossary. The appendix discusses how the approach to discourse analysis discussed in the book can apply to images and multimodal texts (texts composed of images and words), both forms of communication that are ever more crucial in our digital age. The glossary defines key terms used in the book so readers can consult this list if they have forgotten where the term was introduced.

My analyses throughout this book do not assume any specific theory of grammar or, for that matter, any great depth of knowledge about grammar. However, readers may want to supplement their reading of this book with some additional reading about grammar, preferably grammar as it functions in communication and social interaction. The best-known such "functional" approach to grammar is that developed by M. A. K. Halliday. Good introductory secondary sources exist on Halliday's approach to grammar. See the Readings at the end of this chapter for references.

Since this book is meant to be an "introduction," I have tried not to clutter up the chapters with long lists of interpolated references. I leave references and suggested readings to the Readings section at the end of each chapter. The downside of this policy is that I will have to leave out references to the more specialized work of many colleagues whose work I value greatly. The upside is that people new to discourse analysis may actually read some of the material I cite and will have good places to start their further investigations. The material I do cite is, in most cases, replete with further references to the literature.

Finally, let me explain the connection between this book and my book *How to do Discourse Analysis* mentioned above. *How to do Discourse Analysis* contains some of the same material as this book but is a more step-by-step guide on how to do discourse analysis. It leaves a good deal for readers to do in the way of working with data and engaging with their own discourse analyses. Those who prefer more explanation and explication may well prefer this book, and those who want to work through a lot of the issues for themselves or in collaboration with others may well prefer the other book.

Readings

Chafe, W. (1994). *Discourse, consciousness, and time: The flow and displacement of conscious experience in speech and writing*. Chicago: University of Chicago Press. [An important and influential approach to discourse analysis rooted in the flow of ideas in the mind and in speech]

Duranti, A. (1997). *Linguistic anthropology*. Cambridge: Cambridge University Press. [Excellent overview of discourse analysis within a cultural framework]

Fairclough, N. (2003). *Analyzing discourse: Textual analysis for social research*. London: Routledge. [Fairclough offers his well-known and widely used approach to "critical discourse analysis"]

Gee, J. P. (2004). *Situated language and learning: A critique of traditional schooling*. London: Routledge. [Discusses popular culture activities like *Yu-Gi-Oh!* and video gaming and the complex sorts of language and literacy they often involve today]

Gee, J. P. (2007). *Social linguistics and literacies: Ideology in discourses*. Third Edition. London: Taylor & Francis. [This book applies some of the ideas about discourse analysis in this book to issues in education]

Gumperz, J. J. (1982). *Discourse strategies*. Cambridge: Cambridge University Press. [A classic approach to discourse from an anthropological linguist]

Halliday, M. A. K. & Hasan, R. (1989). *Language, context, and text: Aspects of language as a social-semiotic perspective*. Oxford: Oxford University Press. [A classic on the theoretical background of Halliday's Systemic Functional Grammar]

Halliday, M. A. K. & Matthiessen, C. M. I. M. (2004). *An introduction to functional grammar*. Third Edition. London: Hodder Arnold. [The most detailed and best-known functional approach to grammar]

Hutchby, I. & Wooffitt, R. (2008). *Conversational analysis*. Malden, MA: Polity Press. ["CA"—which stands for "conversational analysis"—is a widely used approach to analyzing face-to-face conversations based in sociology]

Schiffrin, D., Tannen, D., & Hamilton, H. E., Eds. (2001). *The handbook of discourse analysis*. Malden, MA: Blackwell. [A good handbook with many articles representing different approaches to and areas in discourse analysis]

Thompson, G. (2004). *Introducing functional grammar*. Second Edition. London: Hodder Arnold. [A good secondary introductory source on Halliday's functional approach to grammar]

Van Dijk, T. A., Ed. (1997). *Discourse as social interaction*. London: Sage. [This and the book below are both good collections of articles detailing different approaches to and areas in discourse analysis]

Van Dijk, T. A. (1997). *Discourse as structure and process*. London: Sage.

Van Dijk, T. A. (2008). *Discourse and power*. New York: Palgrave/Macmillan [Van Dijk has done a great deal of work on using his own style of discourse analysis to deal with important social and political issues]

CHAPTER TWO
Building Tasks

Building Things through Language

In Chapter 1 we argued that language-in-use is about saying, doing, and being. We argued, as well, that by saying, doing, and being we enact certain "games" or "practices" (e.g., committee meetings, a *Yu-Gi-Oh!* play session, an argument in court, a turf battle between gangs, teaching reading to a first-grade class, "small talk" with a neighbor, asking someone out on a date) which, in turn, give meaning to our saying, doing, and being. These "games" or practices always belong to social groups (e.g., street-gang members, lawyers, anime fans), cultures (e.g., Americans, African-Americans, Native Americans), or institutions (e.g., universities, schools, governments). So when we enact these "games" or practices, we also sustain these social groups, cultures, and institutions.

Different cultures have different conventions about how to make music. But within any culture, each musical performer makes music that both fits those conventions (and, thus, is old) and is unique, played according to the talent and style of that performer (and, thus, is new). The same is true of language. We use the term "grammar" for conventions about how to speak and write. Each time a person uses language, that person does so in ways that fit the conventions (are "grammatical") and that, at the same time, are unique, expressing what that person has to say and how they have chosen to say it. Like music, what we do with language is always both old and new.

It is pretty clear what it means to make music, but we use language to make meaning, and it is not clear what that means. In the broadest sense, we make meaning by using language to say things that, in actual contexts of use, amount, as well, to doing things and being things. These things we do and are (identities) then come to exist in the world and they, too, bring about other things in the world. We use language to build things in the world and to engage in world building.

It is as if you could build a building by simply speaking words. While we cannot build a building by simply speaking words, there are, indeed, things we can build in the world by speaking words that accomplish actions and enact identities.

Let's take a very simple example. An umpire in a baseball game says "Strike!" and a "strike" exists in the game. That is what the rules of the game allow to happen. It is a strike if the umpire says it is. Similarly, the rules of marriage allow a marriage to actually happen in the world when a properly ordained minister or a judge says "I now pronounce you man and wife." Umpires actually make strikes happen and ministers actually make marriages happen.

These are what we can call "direct speech acts." Saying something makes it so, as long as one has said it in the right circumstances (so, "promise" is also a direct speech act, since saying "I promise" in the right settings—e.g., not on a stage as part of a play—makes a promise happen). But there are also things we make happen in the world through language that do not actually require language, but which are much easier to do with language than without it. I can most certainly threaten you through gestures and behavior, but it is often easier to do it in language.

We make or build things in the world through language. Not just strikes, marriages, and threats, but many things. For example, I can make (or break) a relationship with other people through language. If I talk to you in an informal, bonding sort of way, I am "bidding" to have you accept me as a friend, someone with whom you are comfortable. If you talk that way back to me, that sort of relationship becomes "real" (at least for that time and place) and has consequences in the world (e.g., it is now harder for you to turn down my invitation for you to come to my house for dinner).

Whenever we speak or write, we always (often simultaneously) construct or build seven things or seven areas of "reality." Let's call these seven things the "seven building tasks" of language. In turn, since we use language to build these seven things, a discourse analyst can ask seven different questions about any piece of language-in-use. Below, I list the seven building tasks and the discourse analysis question to which each gives rise:

1. **Significance**

   There are things in life that are, by nearly everyone's standards, significant (for example the birth or death of a child). But for many things, we need to use language to render them significant or to lessen their significance, to signal to others how we view their significance.

   "Hornworms sure vary a lot in how well they grow" signals that the speaker takes the variation in the hornworms to be significant by the use of the adverb "sure." This is a marker of attitude or feeling. "Hornworm growth exhibits a significant amount of variation" signals that the speaker takes the variation in the hornworms to be significant by the use of the phrase "significant amount of variation." This use of the word "significant" here is a technical term and refers to the statistical tools of an academic discipline.

   Discourse Analysis Question: How is this piece of language being used to make certain things significant or not and in what ways?

2. **Practices (Activities)**

   We have already talked a lot about practices. By a "practice" I mean a socially recognized and institutionally or culturally supported endeavor that usually involves sequencing or combining actions in certain specified ways. Encouraging a student is an action, mentoring the student as his or her advisor in a graduate program is a practice. Telling someone something about linguistics is an action (informing), lecturing on linguistics in a course is a practice. Sometimes the term "activity" is used for what I am calling a practice.

   We use language to get recognized as engaging in a certain sort of practice or activity. For example, I talk and act in one way and I am engaged in formally opening a committee meeting; I talk and act in another way and I am engaged in "chit-chat" before the official start of the meeting.

When we think about practices, we confront a significant "chicken and egg" sort of question. What we say, do, and are in using language enacts practices. At the same time, what we say, do, and are would have no meaning unless these practices already existed.

Which comes first then: A practice like committee meetings or the language we use to carry out committee meetings, our committee ways of talking and inter-acting? Is this a "committee meeting" *because* we are speaking and acting this way, or are we speaking and acting this way *because* this is a committee meeting? The practice of committee meetings gives meaning and purpose to our language in the meetings and our language in the meetings enacts the committee meeting and makes it exist.

The answer to this chicken and egg question is this: Language and practices "boot strap" each other into existence in a reciprocal process through time. We cannot have one without the other.

This does, of course, raise the question of how new practices arise. Often new practices are variants of old ones, ones people have changed or transformed. At other times, new practices start by people borrowing elements of their other older practices to make something new. That is why computer interfaces look like and are talked about as "desktops." We use something old to understand and build something new.

Discourse Analysis Question: What practice (activity) or practices (activities) is this piece of language being used to enact (i.e., get others to recognize as going on)?

3. Identities

We use language to get recognized as taking on a certain identity or role, that is, to build an identity here and now. For example, I talk and act in one way and I am speaking and acting as "chair" of the committee; at the next moment I speak and talk in a different way and I am speaking and acting as one peer/colleague speaking to another. Even if I have an official appointment as chair of the committee, I am not always taken as acting as the chair, even during meetings. I have to enact this identity at the right times and places to make it work.

We often enact our identities by speaking or writing in such a way as to attribute a certain identity to others, an identity that we explicitly or implicitly compare or contrast to our own. We build identities for others as a way to build ones for ourselves. For example, it is impossible to enact a racist identity for oneself without building in speech or writing some sort of inferior identity for people of another "race."

Discourse Analysis Question: What identity or identities is this piece of language being used to enact (i.e., get others to recognize as operative)? What identity or identities is this piece of language attributing to others and how does this help the speaker or writer enact his or her own identity?

4. Relationships

We use language to signal what sort of relationship we have, want to have, or are trying to have with our listener(s), reader(s), or other people, groups, or institutions about whom we are communicating. We use language to build social relationships. For example, in a committee meeting, as chair of the committee, I say "Prof. Smith, I'm very sorry to have to move us on to the next agenda item" and signal a relatively formal and deferential relationship with Prof. Smith. On the other hand, suppose I say, "Ed, it's time to move on." Now I signal a relatively informal and less deferential relationship with the same person.

Discourse Analysis Question: What sort of relationship or relationships is this piece of language seeking to enact with others (present or not)?

5. **Politics (the distribution of social goods)**

We use language to convey a perspective on the nature of the distribution of social goods, that is, to build a perspective on social goods. For example, if I say "Microsoft loaded its operating system with bugs," I treat Microsoft as purposeful and responsible, perhaps even culpable. I deny them a social good. If I say, on the other hand, "Microsoft's operating system is loaded with bugs," I treat Microsoft as less purposeful and responsible, less culpable. I am still denying them a social good, but I have mitigated this denial. If I say, "Like all innovative pieces of software, Microsoft's operating system has bugs," I grant Microsoft a social good (being innovative) and even make the bugs a sign of this, rather than a problem. How I phrase the matter has implications for social goods like guilt and blame, legal responsibility or lack of it, or Microsoft's bad or good motives.

Social goods are potentially at stake any time we speak or write so as to state or imply that something or someone is "adequate," "normal," "good," or "acceptable" (or the opposite) in some fashion important to some group in society or society as a whole. In Chapter 1, I defined perspectives on the distribution of social goods as "politics."

Discourse Analysis Question: What perspective on social goods is this piece of language communicating (i.e., what is being communicated as to what is taken to be "normal," "right," "good," "correct," "proper," "appropriate," "valuable," "the ways things are," "the way things ought to be," "high status or low status," "like me or not like me," and so forth)?

6. **Connections**

We use language to render certain things connected or relevant (or not) to other things, that is, to build connections or relevance. For example, I can talk or write so as to connect Christian fundamentalism in the United States to Islamic fundamentalism in the Middle East, or talk and write as if they are not connected and are very different sorts of things. Of course, using the term "fundamentalism" already is a way of connecting them. Things are not always inherently connected or relevant to each other. Often, we have to make such connections. Even when things seem inherently connected or relevant to each other, we can use language to break or mitigate such connections.

Discourse Analysis Question: How does this piece of language connect or disconnect things; how does it make one thing relevant or irrelevant to another?

7. **Sign Systems and Knowledge**

There are many different languages (e.g., Spanish, Russian, English). There are many different varieties of any one language (e.g., the language of lawyers, the language of biologists, the language of hip-hop artists). There are communicative systems that are not language (e.g., equations, graphs, images). These are all different sign systems.

Furthermore, we humans are always making knowledge and belief claims within these systems. We can use language to make certain sign systems and certain forms of knowledge and belief relevant or privileged, or not, in given situations, that is, to build privilege or prestige for one sign system or way of knowing over another. For example, I talk and act so as to make the knowledge and language of lawyers relevant (privileged), or not, over "everyday language" or over "non-lawyerly academic language" in our committee discussion of facilitating the admission of more minority students. We also use language to create, change, sustain, and revise language itself and other sign systems and their ways of making knowledge claims about the world. This is an important function, but one I will leave aside in this book.

Discourse Analysis Question: How does this piece of language privilege or disprivilege specific sign systems (e.g., Spanish vs. English, technical language vs. everyday language, words vs. images, words vs. equations, etc.) or different ways of knowing and believing or claims to knowledge and belief (e.g., science vs. the Humanities, science vs. "common sense," biology vs. "creation science")?

An Example

We turn now to an example of discourse analysis using the questions generated by the seven building tasks above. It is important, at the outset, however, to keep several things in mind. First, since we will only be dealing with a small piece of data, taken from a much larger corpus, we will be formulating *hypotheses* about this data. These hypotheses would need to be confirmed further by looking at more data and, perhaps, engaging in the collection of additional data.

Much of discourse analysis—much of science, in general—is about formulating and gaining some confidence in hypotheses which must be further investigated, rather than gaining any sort of "definitive proof," which really does not exist in empirical investigations. We must always be open, no matter how confident we are in our hypotheses, to finding evidence that might go against our favored views.

Second, discourse analysis is always a movement from context to language and from language to context. We have not yet talked about "context," an extremely important notion in discourse analysis. Right now we will just use the term in an informal way for the actual setting in which a piece of language is used. In doing discourse analysis, we gain information about a context in which a piece of language has been used and use this information to form hypotheses about what that piece of language means and is doing. In turn, we closely study the piece of language and ask ourselves what we can learn about the context in which the language was used and how that context was construed (interpreted) by the speaker or writer and listener(s) or reader(s). In this brief example, we can only engage in this two-way process in a quite limited way.

The data comes from a project where a university history professor (I will refer to her as "Sara Vogel," not her real name) wanted to work with middle-school teachers to have their students engage in oral history. She wanted the children to interview their relatives and neighbors to gain information about the history of their local neighborhoods and the city in which they lived. These oral histories were intended eventually to inform an exhibit in the city's historical museum.

The university at which the professor taught—which I will call "Woodson"—was a small elite private university that was over a hundred years old. The city in which the university resided—which I will call "Middleview"—was largely a working-class industrial city. The teachers that the professor dealt with were public school teachers with working-class origins. There were historic town–gown tensions between the university and the city and, in particular, tensions between people who taught at the university and people who taught in the public schools, tensions over status and commitment to the city. The university faculty were not, by and large, born in the city and often did not stay there, moving on to other jobs in other cities; the public school teachers were invariably born there and intended to stay there.

The data printed below comes from the first meeting of the group that was going to work on the oral history project in two schools. The meeting, held at one of the two schools to be involved in the project, was attended by four teachers from the two schools, the university professor and two of her research assistants, and a representative of a group that was helping to fund the joint work of the professor and the teachers. There were a few other people there, as well. The speaker is one of the teachers (I will call her "Karen"). She has been asked by the person chairing the meeting (the representative of the funding agency) to give those at the meeting some background on what had transpired prior to this first official meeting.

The history professor had called the curriculum coordinator at Karen's school—a woman we will refer to as "Mary Washington"—to ask for help on her project and to gain access to the school. The "Summer Institute" Karen refers to was a workshop on research collaborations between university educators and local school teachers sponsored by the Education program at the university. The funders of the oral history project, who were also helping to support the Summer Institute, had hoped that Prof. Vogel and the teachers she was going to work with would attend the Institute.

So, at last, here's the data. To make matters clearer, I leave out many details from the transcript, things like pausing and hesitation, details which are, of course, themselves also meaningful and would be included in any fuller analysis. I capitalize words that were said with particular emphasis:

1. Last year, Mary Washington, who is our curriculum coordinator here, had a call from Sara at Woodson
2. And called me and said:

3. "We have a person from Woodson who's in the History Department
4. And she's interested in doing some research into Black history in Middleview
5. And she would like to get involved with the school
6. And here's her number
7. Give her a call"
8. And I DID call her
9. And we BOTH expected to be around for the Summer Institute at Woodson
10. I DID participate in it
11. But SARA wasn't able to do THAT

While not all building tasks will be as readily apparent in all pieces of data, we can always ask questions about each one to see what we get. One device that helps us think about what something means is to ask in what other ways it could have been said or written. Once we see what alternatives existed, we can ask why the person said or wrote it as they did and not in some alternative way. So let's look at each of the building tasks in turn:

1. Significance

How does Karen make the fact that Sara wasn't at the Summer Institute significant? This event could have been treated as unimportant, of little significance. However, Karen treats it as a significant happening.

Karen uses her words to create a clear contrast between herself and Sara. Sara's failure to attend the Summer Institute takes on significance in terms of this contrast. Karen portrays herself as responsible and as someone who did what she was told to do. She stresses this by saying "I DID call her," instead of just "I called her." She says that both (stressing "both") she and Sara "expected" (intended) to be "around for the Summer Institute," implying, perhaps, that Sara may have "been around," but, nonetheless, not bothered to come. She then stresses that she herself did participate (note, again, "I DID participate in it" instead of "I participated" or just "I went").

Karen concludes "But SARA wasn't able to do THAT." Here she uses "but" to create a contrast between her own behavior and Sara's. She stresses both "Sara" and "that," thereby emphasizing the contrast between herself and Sara yet more. And she focuses on Sara's "ability" ("wasn't able to do"), rather than just saying "But Sara didn't come" or "Sara couldn't come."

All these details make us see that Sara's absence from the Institute is treated by Karen as a significant or meaningful fact. She does not say exactly what she finds significant about this fact, but leaves this to be inferred by her listeners.

2. Practices (Activities)

What social practice or activity is Karen enacting in her language? She is at an "official" project meeting and has been asked to "catch people up" on what has gone on before the meeting. She is giving the "history" of the project—a powerful role, since how things happened in the past and how we construe them can have implications for how things will go in the future. So, we can say her activity here or the practice in which she is engaging is giving a history—or telling the "origins story"—of the project. Some such practice is not at all uncommon in such projects.

Karen tells this history in terms of a certain hierarchy, which she, in turn, tries to undo. Sara went to an administrator in Karen's school. In turn, the administrator ordered Karen to call Sara. In this chain, Karen is at the bottom. However, Karen goes on to contrast her proactive and responsible behavior in a project that she didn't ask to be on with Sara's less proactive and responsible behavior and lesser commitment to a project she herself had requested and set in motion.

This is the first meeting of the project and Karen is seeking to position herself and others in terms of how they have in the past and will in the future be viewed and function within the project. Note the pattern: I DID …, we BOTH expected …, I DID …, But SARA wasn't able to do THAT …" Karen sets herself up as a "do-er" and Sara as not a "do-er."

Of course, Karen could have formulated her language quite differently had she wanted to. She could, for example, have said something like: "I called Sara and, while we both had expected to be around for the Summer Institute, I was able to attend, but Sara couldn't make it." This formulation does not emphasize doing on Karen's part by using "did" and it formulates Sara's lack of attendance in a way that stresses not her inability to come, but makes it sound as if something came up over which she had less control ("couldn't make it"). This alternative way still does not, of course, completely mitigate the contrast, but it softens it, nonetheless.

The point here is that a practice like "catching us up," giving the "history," telling the "origin story" (whatever we call it) is an opportunity to engage in a good deal of social work. Karen is telling a "story" in which, though she was ordered to do things (and, thus, was lower in the hierarchy), she has been, in fact, a do-er and leader on the project (and, thus, higher in the hierarchy). She is "bidding," as well, to change the hierarchy and power relations on the project. As the project unfolded it was clear that Karen and the other teachers on the project wanted to be seen as "equals" and, in respect to their own classrooms, as the "bosses" (not the administrators or professors).

3. Identities

What identity is Karen trying to take on or enact? We have already seen how Karen enacts in her language an identity as a proactive and responsible do-er on a project she did not ask for, but was "ordered" to get involved with. We have also seen how Karen uses an identity she attributes to others (in this case, Sara as less proactive and responsible) to enact, in comparison, her own identity.

4. Relationships

What relationship is Karen trying to enact in regard to Sara and the project as a whole? From what we have said so far, it is clear that Karen is enacting a distanced but not particularly deferential relationship to Sara. The contrast of herself as "do-er" and Sara as not a "do-er" that she creates accomplishes this, but so does the fact that she uses Sara's first name both in her introduction to her dialogue with the curriculum coordinator and in her concluding remark that "Sara wasn't able to do that."

Note, too, that in her portrayal of the dialogue with the curriculum coordinator, Karen uses the phrase "a person from Woodson who's in the History Department," rather than something like "a Woodson history professor" or "a professor from Woodson's History Department." We should note, too, that these references to the historian are made while the historian herself is sitting at a small table with the rest of the group, waiting for her turn to talk. We could ask, as well, about what sort of relationship Karen is attempting to create with the group as a whole and with the project they are embarking on.

5. Politics

What sorts of implications for the distribution of social goods does Karen's language have? Of course, one social good at stake here is Karen's and Sara's reputations as responsible, trustworthy people. Another is their reputations as "do-ers" or people who fail to do what is needed.

Yet another social good at stake—one that is not readily apparent to anyone who does not know the situation better—is who has "rights" to school children. At a much later meeting of the group, the other teacher from Karen's school (and her close friend) eventually makes it clear that the teachers feel that they "own" their children (e.g., she says "In a sense we OWN the kids") and that researchers like Sara should go through teachers (contact them directly) to gain access to their children, not go through an authority figure like the curriculum coordinator.

While this became clear only in a later meeting, it helps explain some of how Karen's language is designed in the short excerpt we are dealing with here. The other teachers in the room well knew that the way in which the professor (albeit inadvertently) caused the curriculum coordinator to "order" Karen to call her in order to get access to Karen's class was a breach of protocol and they can clearly hear this in her language.

It is clear that the way in which Karen is using language here is fully caught up with the "politics" of schools and universities. Social goods and hierarchies of status and power (themselves social goods) are at stake.

6. Connections

How is Karen connecting things or making them relevant to each other? How is she disconnecting them or making them not relevant to each other? It is clear by now how Karen renders her attendance at the Institute and Sara's lack of attendance connected and relevant to each other ("I DID..., we BOTH expected, I DID, but SARA wasn't able to do THAT"). Furthermore, she implies that this contrast is relevant to the initial call Sara made to the school in the way in which she directly juxtaposes Sara setting the project in motion with that phone call (without Karen's own initiative) only to fail to attend the initial event that was meant to facilitate the project and Karen's involvement.

7. Sign Systems and Knowledge

How is Karen privileging or disprivileging specific sign systems (languages, styles of language, non-verbal sign systems) or specific ways of or claims to know and believe? This short excerpt is really the beginning of a long struggle enacted in and through language as to whether teacher knowledge or university-professor knowledge in regard to history, teaching history, classrooms, children, and the community is to be privileged—and when, where, and why. This process already starts with the contrast between the use of the curriculum coordinator's first and last name (Mary Washington) and the professor's first name only. It is hinted at in the way in which the curriculum coordinator is depicted as saying "a person from Woodson" and "interested in doing some research into Black history in Middleview." Both descriptions are vague.

"A person from Woodson" makes it sound like the curriculum coordinator does not really know the professor and does not cede her the authority of her rank and title. "Some research into Black history in Middleview" makes it sound like either the professor is vague about what research she wants to do ("some research on Black history") or the coordinator doesn't know or care much what it is exactly (and, it just so happens, the curriculum coordinator is an African-American).

In fact, everyone knew from the outset that the professor wanted to do oral history with children studying their own neighborhoods and families—that is, in fact, why Karen was involved, since she already did oral histories with the children in her class. We should keep in mind that what the curriculum coordinator says in Karen's story is Karen's depiction—with Prof. Vogel sitting there—of what was said, not necessarily what actually was said.

It is clear that all the building tasks are integrally linked to each other and often mutually and simultaneously supported by the same words and phrases. We have generated some hypotheses from this small piece of data, based on mutual considerations of context and language-in-use. In turn, these hypotheses would guide our search through additional data. Our confidence in these hypotheses will rise if we look through more and more talk from this same group of people in this and subsequent meetings and we gain more and more evidence for our hypotheses—more and more examples that appear to be best explained by our hypotheses.

If we see these hypotheses further confirmed in other sorts of data— perhaps in other encounters among university professors and teachers in this and other cities—then our confidence will rise yet more. If, in the end, no equally good competing hypotheses are available, then we accept our hypotheses, at least until disconfirming evidence appears, and work on their basis. This is just how all empirical research works. Unlike mathematics, there are no hard "proofs" to be had here.

Our hypotheses make predictions about what we expect to find in further data or in a closer look at our original data. For example, by the end of our excerpt at line 11, we certainly have evidence that Prof. Vogel could have heard this excerpt as a criticism of herself. She could have heard line 11 as implying she did not have good reasons for not attending the Summer Institute. We would certainly want to look closely at Prof. Vogel's reaction at this point, both verbally and non-verbally (which is why it is good to video tape and not just audio tape data).

When we go back and look further at our recordings, we see, from both verbal and non-verbal cues, that Prof. Vogel attempts to interrupt Karen at just the point Karen stresses the word "that" at the end of line 11. The professor gives a small laugh and says, in a low voice, "I heard ... how did you get." Karen speaks right through the attempted interruption, cutting it off, saying, "Well, so Sara and I talked a little bit about what her plans were and sort of what our expectations were." We don't know, of course, what the professor wanted to say, but it is clear that she had heard the end of line 11 as a point at which she wanted to stop Karen and interject something.

In the end, in the research from which this data came, the hypotheses we have begun to formulate here were richly supported by more and more data as the project went on. These hypotheses, in turn, helped discourse researchers understand how and why the project, at various points, was failing and allowed them to help make things work a bit better. Could they make it "perfect"? Of course not. Some of the problems and issues (largely to do with status, power, and institutional conflicts) our hypotheses point to are entrenched problems in the real world and would require substantive social and institutional changes to remove. But that doesn't mean we can't do anything and it doesn't mean we can't start on the process of institutional change.

In Chapter 8, I will elaborate further on the seven "building tasks" I have introduced here and their relevance for discourse analysis. But in the next four chapters, I want to develop several "tools of inquiry." These are ways of looking at language-in-use that will help us study how the building tasks are carried out and with what social and political consequences.

Readings

Austin, J. L. (1975). *How to do things with words*. Second Edition. Cambridge, MA: Harvard University Press. [A classic philosophical work on how language is as much about doing as saying and that, in fact, saying is a form of doing]

Hanks, W. F. (1995). *Language and communicative practices*. New York: Westview. [A wonderful and deep book on language as practice—we will discuss this book in a later chapter]

Searle, J. (1979). *Expression and meaning: Studies in the theory of speech acts*. Cambridge: Cambridge University Press. [The classic book on "speech acts"]

CHAPTER THREE
Tools of Inquiry and Discourses

Tools

In the last chapter we looked at seven "building tasks," seven areas or things that we use language to enact or build in the world. We now turn to some tools we can use to analyze the workings of these building tasks in specific instances of language-in-use. The tools of inquiry I introduce in this chapter are primarily relevant to how people build identities and practices and recognize identities and practices that others are building around them. However, the tools of inquiry introduced here are most certainly caught up with all the other building tasks we discussed in the last chapter, as well, and we will see this progressively throughout this book.

The tools of inquiry to be discussed in this chapter are:

a) **Social languages.** People use different styles or varieties of language for different purposes. They use different varieties of language to enact and recognize different identities in different settings; they also use different varieties of language to engage in all the other building tasks discussed in the last chapter. I will call each such variety a "social language."

For example, a student studying hornworms might say in everyday language, a variety of language often referred to as "vernacular language," something like "Hornworms sure vary a lot in how big they get," while the same student might use a more technical variety of language to say or write something like "Hornworm growth exhibits a significant amount of variation." The vernacular version is one social language and the technical version is another. Investigating how different social languages are used and mixed is one tool of inquiry for engaging in discourse analysis.

b) **Discourses.** People build identities and activities not just through language, but by using language together with other "stuff" that isn't language. If you want to get recognized as a street-gang member of a certain sort you have to speak in the "right" way, but you also have to act and dress in the "right" way, as well. You also have to engage (or, at least, behave as if you are engaging) in characteristic ways of thinking, acting, interacting, valuing, feeling, and believing. You also have to use or be able to use various sorts of symbols (e.g., graffiti), tools (e.g., a weapon), and objects (e.g., street corners) in the "right" places and at the "right" times. You can't just "talk the talk," you have to "walk the walk" as well.

The same is true of doing/being a corporate lawyer, Marine sergeant, radical feminist, or a regular at the local bar. One and the same person might talk, act, and interact in such a way as to get recognized as a "street-gang member" in one context and, in another context, talk, act, and interact in quite different ways so as to get recognized as a "gifted student." And, indeed, these two identities, and their concomitant ways of talking, acting, and interacting, may well conflict with each other in some circumstances (where different people expect different identities from the person), as well as in the person's own mind.

I use the term "Discourse," with a capital "D," for ways of combining and integrating language, actions, interactions, ways of thinking, believing, valuing, and using various symbols, tools, and objects to enact a particular sort of socially recognizable identity. Thinking about the different Discourses a piece of language is part of is another tool for engaging in discourse analysis.

c) **Conversations.** Sometimes when we talk or write, our words don't just allude or relate to someone else's words (as in the case of intertextuality), but they allude or relate to themes, debates, or motifs that have been the focus of much talk and writing in some social group with which we are familiar or in our society as a whole. These themes, debates, or motifs play a role in how language is interpreted. For example, how do you know that when I tell you "Smoking is associated with health problems" that I mean to say that smoking leads to health problems and not that health problems lead people to smoke because, say, their health problems are making them nervous and they are smoking in order to calm themselves down (the most probable meaning for a sentence like "Writing a will is associated with health problems")? You know this because you are well aware of the long-running discussions in our society over the ill-effects of smoking.

I refer to all the talk and writing that has gone on in a specific social group or in society at large around a major theme, debate, or motif as a "Conversation" with a capital "C," using the term metaphorically, of course. Most of us today are aware of the societal Conversations going on around us about things like abortion, creationism, global warming, terrorism, and so on and so forth through many other issues. To know about these Conversations is to know about the various sides one can take in debates about these issues and what sorts of people are usually on each side. As members of various social groups and of our society as a whole we are privy (know something about) a great many such Conversations. People interpret our language—and we interpret theirs—partly through such knowledge. Thinking about the different Conversations a piece of language impinges on or relates to is another tool for engaging in discourse analysis.

d) **Intertextuality.** When we speak or write, our words often allude to or relate to, in some fashion, other "texts" or certain types of "texts," where by "texts" I mean words other people have said or written. For example, *Wired* magazine once printed a story with this title: "The New Face of the Silicon Age: Tech jobs are fleeing to India faster than ever. You got a problem with that?" (February 2004). The sentence "You got a problem with that?" reminds us of "tough guy" talk we have heard in many movies or read in books. It intrigues us that such talk occurs written in a magazine devoted to technology. This sort of cross-reference to another text or type of text I will refer to as "intertextuality." In instances of intertextuality, one spoken or written text alludes to, quotes, or otherwise relates to another one.

Discourses: *Whos* and *Whats*

Let's start by trying to get at the notion of a "big D" Discourse. A Discourse is a characteristic way of saying, doing, and being. When you speak or write anything, you use the resources of English to project yourself as a certain kind of person, a different kind in different circumstances. You also project yourself as engaged in a certain practice or activity. If I have no idea who you are and what you are doing, then I cannot make sense of what you have said, written, or done.

You project a different identity at a formal dinner party than you do at the family dinner table. And, though these are both dinner, they are nonetheless different practices or activities (different "games"). The fact that people have differential access to different identities and practices, connected to different sorts of status and social goods, is a root source of inequality in society. Intervening in such matters can be a contribution to social justice. Since different identities and activities are enacted in and through language, the study of language is integrally connected to matters of equity and justice.

An oral or written "utterance" has meaning, then, only if and when it communicates a *who* and a *what* (see Wieder & Pratt 1990). What I mean by a "who" is a *socially situated identity*, the "kind of person" one is seeking to be and enact here and now. What I mean by a "what" is a *socially situated practice* or *activity* that the utterance helps to constitute. Such identities and practices are, of course, two of the building tasks we discussed in Chapter 2.

Lots of interesting complications can set in when we think about identity enacted in and through language. *Whos* can be multiple and they need not always be people. The President's Press Secretary can issue an utterance that is, in fact, authored by a speech writer and authorized (and even claimed) by the President. In this case, the utterance communicates a sort of overlapping and compound *who*. The Press Secretary, even if she is directly quoting the speech writer, must inflect the remark with her own voice. In turn, the speech writer is both "mimicking" the President's "voice" and creating an identity for the President.

Not just individuals, but also institutions, through the "anonymous" texts and products they circulate, can author or issue "utterances." For example, we will see below that the warning on an aspirin bottle actually communicates multiple *whos*. An utterance can be authored, authorized by, or issued by a group or a single individual.

Finally, we can point out that *whos* and *whats* are not really discrete and separable. You are *who* you are partly through *what* you are doing, and *what* you are doing is partly recognized for what it is by *who* is doing it. So it is better, in fact, to say that utterances communicate an integrated, though often multiple or "heteroglossic," *who-doing-what*.

"Real Indians"

Though I have focused on language, thus far, it is important to see that making visible and recognizable *who* (identity) we are and *what* (practice) we are doing always requires more than language. It requires, as well, that we act, think, value, and interact in ways that together with language render *who* we are and *what* we are doing recognizable to others (and ourselves). In fact, to be a particular *who* and to pull off a particular *what* requires that we act, value, interact, and use language *in sync with* or *in coordination with* other people and with various objects ("props") in appropriate locations and at appropriate times.

To see this wider notion of language as integrated with "other stuff" (other people, objects, values, times, and places), we will briefly consider Wieder and Pratt's fascinating work on how Native Americans recognize each other as "really Indian" (their work is based on a variety of different groups, though no claim is made that it is true of all Native American groups). Wieder and Pratt point out that real Indians "refer to persons who are 'really Indian' in just those words with regularity and standardization" (p. 48—all page references are to Wieder & Pratt 1990). Wieder and Pratt's work will also make clear how the identities (the *whos*) we take on are flexibly negotiated in actual contexts of practice.

The term "real Indian" is, of course, an "insiders' term." The fact that it is used by some Native Americans in enacting their own identity work does not license non-Native Americans to use the term. Thus, though it may clutter the text, I will below always place the term "real Indian" in scare quotes to make clear that I am talking about the term and not claiming that I have the "right" to actually use it of anyone. Finally, let me say that I am not discussing Native Americans here because I think they are "esoteric." In fact, I am using this example because I think it is a clear and dramatic example of what we *all* do all the time, though in different ways.

The problem of "recognition and being recognized" is very consequential and problematic for Native Americans. While, in order to be considered a "real Indian," one must be able to make some claims to kinship with others who are recognized as "real Indians," this by no means settles the matter. People with such (biological) ties can fail to get recognized as a "really Indian," and people of mixed kinship can be so recognized.

Being a "real Indian" is not something one can simply be. Rather, it is something that one becomes or is *in the doing* of it, that is, in the performance. Though one must have certain kinship ties to get into the "game," beyond this entry criterion, there is no being (once and for all) a "real Indian," rather there is only *doing being-or-becoming-a-"real-Indian."* If one does not continue to "practice" being a "real Indian," one ceases to be one.

Finally, "doing" being-and-becoming-a-"real-Indian" is not something that one can do all by oneself. It requires the participation of others. One cannot be a "real Indian" unless one appropriately recognizes other "real Indians" and gets recognized by others as a "real Indian" in the practices of doing being-and-becoming-a-"real-Indian." Being a "real Indian" also requires appropriate accompanying objects (props), times, and places.

There are many ways one can do being-and-becoming-a-"real-Indian." Some of these are (following Wieder and Pratt): "Real Indians" prefer to avoid conversation with strangers, Native American or otherwise. They cannot be related to one another as "mere acquaintances," as some "non-Indians" might put it. So, for "real Indians," any conversation they do have with a stranger who may turn out to be a "real Indian" will, in the discovery of the other's "Indianness," establish substantial obligations between the conversational partners just through the mutual acknowledgment that they are "Indians" and that they are now no longer strangers to one another.

In their search for the other's "real Indianness" and in their display of their own "Indianness," "real Indians" frequently engage in a distinctive form of verbal sparring. By correctly responding to and correctly engaging in this sparring, which "Indians" call "razzing," each participant further establishes cultural competency in the eyes of the other.

"Real Indians" manage face-to-face relations with others in such a way that they appear to be in agreement with them (or, at least, they do not overtly disagree); they are modest and "fit in." They show accord and harmony and are reserved about their own interests, skills, attainments, and positions. "Real Indians" understand that they should not elevate themselves over other "real Indians." And they understand that the complex system of obligations they have to kin and other "real Indians" takes priority over those contractual obligations and pursuit of self-interest that some "non-Indians" prize so highly.

"Real Indians" must be competent in "doing their part" in participating in conversations that begin with the participants exchanging greetings and other amenities and then lapsing into extended periods of silence. They must know that neither they nor the others have an obligation to speak—that silence on the part of all conversants is permissible.

When they are among "Indians," "real Indians" must also be able to perform in the roles of "student" and "teacher" and be able to recognize the behaviors appropriate to these roles. These roles are brought into play when the appropriate occasion arises for transmitting cultural knowledge (i.e., things pertinent to being a "real Indian"). Although many "non-Indians" find it proper to ask questions of someone who is instructing them, "Indians" regard questions in such a situation as being inattentive, rude, insolent, and so forth. The person who has taken the role of "student" shows attentiveness by avoiding eye contact and by being silent. The teaching situation, then, as a witnessed monologue, lacks the dialogical features that characterize some Western instruction.

While the above sort of information gives us something of the flavor of what sorts of things one must do and say to get recognized as a "real Indian," such information can lead to a bad mistake. It can sound as if the above features are necessary and sufficient criteria for doing being-and-becoming-a-"real-Indian." But this is not true.

These features are not a test that can be or ever is administered all at once, and once and for all, to determine who is or is not a "real Indian." Rather, the circumstances under which these features are employed by "Indians" emerge over the course of a developing history among groups of people. They are employed always in the context of actual situations, and at different times in the life history of groups of people. The ways in which the judgment, "He (or she) is (or is not) a 'real Indian,'" is embedded within situations that motivate it make such judgments intrinsically provisional. Those now recognized can spoil their acceptance or have it spoiled and those not now accepted can have another chance, even when others are reluctant to extend it.

The same thing applies, in fact, in regard to many other social identities, not just being "a real Indian." There are no once and for all tests for who is a "real" feminist, gang member, patriot, humanist, cutting-edge scientist, "yuppie," or "regular" at the local bar. These matters are settled provisionally and continuously, in practice, as part and parcel of shared histories and ongoing activities.

Different social identities (different *whos*) may seriously conflict with one another. For instance, Scollon and Scollon 1981 point out that for the Native Americans they studied (Athabaskans in Canada and the U.S.), writing essays, a practice common in school, can constitute a crisis in identity. To produce an essay requires the Athabaskan to produce a major self-display, which is appropriate to Athabaskans only when a person is in a position of dominance in relation to the audience (in the case of school, this is the teacher, not the student).

Furthermore, in essayist prose, the audience and the author are "fiction-alized" (not really me and you, but decontextualized and rather generic "types" of readers and writers) and the text is decontextualized from specific social networks and relationships. Where the relationship of the communi-cants is decontextualized and unknown, Athabaskans prefer silence.

The paradox of prose for Athabaskans, the Scollons point out, is that if it is communication between known author and audience it is contextualized and compatible with Athabaskan values, but not good essayist prose. To the extent that it becomes decontextualized and thus good essayist prose, it becomes uncharacteristic of Athabaskans to seek to communicate. What is required to do and be an Athabaskan is in large part mutually exclusive with what it is required to do and be a writer of school-based essayist prose. This doesn't mean Athabaskans cannot do both (remember, we are all multiple), it simply means that they may face very real conflicts in terms of values and identity. And, as the Scollons point out, many other groups of people have similar or related "identity issues" with essayist literacy.

Discourses (with a Big "D")

So how does someone get recognized as a "real Indian" (a *who*) engaged in verbal sparring of the sort "real Indians" do (a *what*)? Such matters are consequential, as we said above. By correctly engaging in this sparring (which "Indians" call "razzing") participants establish their cultural competency to and for each other. This is a problem of "recognition and being recognized."

The problem of "recognition and being recognized" is very consequential, not only for Native Americans, but for all of us all the time. And, as we saw above, making visible and recognizable *who* we are and *what* we are doing always involves a great deal more than "just language." Think of about how someone gets recognized as a "good student," a "good cook," a "gang member," a "competent lawyer," a "real basketball fan," or a "real Catholic." These all involve acting-interacting-thinking-valuing-talking-(sometimes writing-reading) in the "appropriate way" with the "appropriate" props at the "appropriate" times in the "appropriate" places.

"Good cooks" cannot just talk a good game. They have to be able to use recipes, utensils, and ingredients in a sort of "dance" of coordinating everything together. They also have to value certain things (e.g., presentation of food, combinations of tastes, pairings of food and wine) in certain ways.

How do we know a young child is becoming part of a literate Discourse (being-doing literacy of a certain sort)? We test that the child can turn a book right side up, knows what books are for, can interact with a parent appropriately while being read too, can engage in pretend book readings (i.e., "talk like a book"), and values books enough not to tear them apart. We test all this before a child can actually decode print (it is all part of what we call "emergent literacy," by which we mean a child is emerging into a "literate" sort of person).

Such socially accepted associations among ways of using language, of thinking, valuing, acting, and interacting, in the "right" places and at the "right" times with the "right" objects (associations that can be used to identify oneself as a member of a socially meaningful group or "social network"), I will refer to as "Discourses," with a capital "D." I will reserve the word "discourse," with a little "d," to mean language-in-use or stretches of language (like conversations or stories). "Big D" Discourses are always language *plus* "other stuff."

There are innumerable Discourses in any modern, technological, urban-based society: for example, (enacting) being something as general as a type of African-American or Anglo-Australian or something as specific as being a type of modern British young second-generation affluent Sikh woman. Being a type of middle-class American, factory worker, or executive, doctor or hospital patient, teacher, administrator, or student, student of physics or of literature, member of a club or street gang, regular at the local bar, or, as we have just seen, "real Indian" are all Discourses. Discourses are about being different "kinds of people."

The key to Discourses is "recognition." If you put language, action, interaction, values, beliefs, symbols, objects, tools, and places together in such a way that others *recognize* you as a particular type of *who* (identity) engaged in a particular type of *what* (activity), here and now, then you have pulled off a Discourse (and thereby continued it through history, if only for a while longer). Whatever you have done must be similar enough to other performances to be recognizable. However, if it is different enough from what has gone before, but still recognizable, it can simultaneously change and transform Discourses. If it is not recognizable, then you're not "in" the Discourse.

Discourses are always embedded in a medley of social institutions, and often involve various "props" like books and magazines of various sorts, laboratories, classrooms, buildings of various sorts, various technologies, and a myriad of other objects from sewing needles (for sewing circles) through birds (for bird watchers) to basketball courts and basketballs (for basketball players). Think of all the words, symbols, deeds, objects, clothes, and tools you need to coordinate in the right way at the right time and place to "pull off" (or recognize someone as) being a cutting-edge particle physicist or a Los Angeles Latino street-gang member or a sensitive high-culture humanist (of old).

It is sometimes helpful to think about social and political issues as if it is not just us humans who are talking and interacting with each other, but, rather, the Discourses we represent and enact, and for which we are "carriers." The Discourses we enact existed before each of us came on the scene and most of them will exist long after we have left the scene. Discourses, through our words and deeds, have talked to each other through history, and, in doing so, form human history.

Think, for instance, of the long-running and ever-changing historical interchange in the U.S. and Canada between the Discourses of "being an Indian" and "being an Anglo" or of the different, but equally long-running, historical interchange in New Zealand between "being a Maori" and "being an Anglo" (or, for that matter, think of the long-running interchange between "being a British Anglo" and "being an American Anglo"). Think of the long-running and ever-changing interchange between creationists and biologists. Think of the long-running and ever-changing interchange in Los Angeles between African-American teenage gang members and the L.A. police (some of whom, for instance, are leading experts, even academically speaking, on the "grammar" of gang graffiti, which varies significantly, by the way, between African-American gangs and Latino gangs). Intriguingly, we humans are very often unaware of the history of these interchanges, and, thus, in a deep sense, not fully aware of what we mean when we act and talk.

When we discussed being a "real Indian," we argued that "knowing how" to be a "real Indian" rests on one's being able to be in sync with other "real Indians" and with objects (e.g., the material items of the culture) in the appropriate times and places. Recent studies of science suggest much the same thing is true for scientists.

For example, these studies argue that the physics that the experimental physicists "know" is, in large part, *not* in their heads. Rather, it is spread out (distributed), inscribed in (and often trapped in) scientific apparatus, symbolic systems, books, papers, and journals, institutions, habits of bodies, routines of practice, and other people. Each domain of practice, each scientific Discourse—for example, a specific area within physics or biology—*attunes* actions, expressions, objects, and people (the scientists themselves) so that they become "workable" *in relation* to each other and in relation to tools, technologies, symbols, texts, and the objects they study in the world. They are "in sync."

Just as there are verbal and non-verbal ways to be a "real Indian," there are verbal and non-verbal ways to be a "real experimental physicist." Being an experimental physicist or being a "real Indian" are ways with words, feelings, values, beliefs, emotions, people, actions, things, tools, and places that allow us to display and recognize characteristic *whos* doing characteristic *whats*. They are both, then, Discourses.

The scientist's "know-how" is the ability to *coordinate and be coordinated by* constellations of expressions, actions, objects, and people. In a sense, the scientist is *both* an actor (coordinating other people and various things, tools, technologies, and symbol systems) and a *patient* (being coordinated by other people and various things, tools, technologies, and symbol systems). Scientists become *agent-patients* "in sync with," "linked with," "in association with," "in coordination with," however we want to put it, other "actants" (adapting a term from Latour 2005), such as particular forms of language, other people, objects (e.g., scientific equipment, atoms, molecules, or birds), places (e.g., labs or fields), and non-verbal practices.

In the end a Discourse is a "dance" that exists in the abstract as a coordinated pattern of words, deeds, values, beliefs, symbols, tools, objects, times, and places and in the here and now as a performance that is recognizable as just such a coordination. Like a dance, the performance here and now is never exactly the same. It all comes down, often, to what the "masters of the dance" (the people who inhabit the Discourse) will allow to be recognized or will be forced to recognize as a possible instantiation of the dance.

Discourses are not "Units" with Clear Boundaries

The notion of Discourses will be important throughout this book. It is important, therefore, to make some points clear to avoid some common misunderstandings. Imagine I freeze a moment of thought, talk, action, or interaction for you, in the way in which a projector can freeze a piece of film. To make sense of that moment, you have to recognize the identities and practices (activities) involved in it. Perhaps for this frozen moment you can't do so, so you move the film back and forward enough until you can make such a recognition judgment.

"Oh, now I see," you say. "It's a 'real Indian' razzing another 'real Indian'," or "It's a radical feminist berating a male for a crass patriarchal remark" or "It's a laboratory physicist orienting colleagues to a graph" or "It's a first-grader in Ms X's class starting a sharing time story." Perhaps if you now move the film backwards and forwards a bit more, you will change your judgments a little, a lot, or not at all.

Perhaps you are not sure. You and I even argue about the matter. You say that "It's a skinhead sending intimidating glances to a passing adult on the street" and I say, "No, it's just a wanna-be trying to act tough." You say, "It's a modern classroom teacher leading a discussion" and I say, "No, it's a traditional teacher giving a hidden lecture in the guise of a series of known-answer questions to the students."

This is what I call "recognition work." People engage in such work when they try to make visible to others (and to themselves, as well) who they are and what they are doing. People engage in such work when they try to recognize others for who they are and what they are doing. People engage in such work within interactions, moment by moment. They engage in such work when they reflect on their interactions later. They engage in such work, as well, when they try to understand human interaction as researchers, practitioners, theoreticians, or interventionists of various sorts.

Sometimes such recognition work is conscious, sometimes it is not. Sometimes people have labels they can articulate for the *whos* and *whats* they recognize, sometimes they don't. Sometimes they fight over the labels, sometimes they don't. And the labels change over time.

Thanks to the fact that we humans engage in recognition work, Discourses exist in the world. For example, there is a way of being a kindergarten student in Ms X's class with its associated activities and ways with words, deeds, and things. Ms X, her students, her classroom, with its objects and artifacts, and characteristic practices (activities), are all in the Discourse she and her students create. These same people and things, of course, can be in other Discourses, as well.

Recognition work and Discourses out in the world go hand-in-hand. Ms X and her students engage in recognition work, for example, when a certain sort of sharing time ("show and tell") story isn't recognized as "acceptable" in this class and another type is. That recognition work creates a Discourse, that is, ways with words, actions, beliefs, emotions, values, interactions, people, objects, tools, and technologies that come to constitute "being and doing a student in Ms X's class." In turn, this Discourse renders recognition work possible and meaningful. It's another "chicken and egg" question, then: Which comes first, recognition work or Discourses? Neither. They are reflexively related, such that each creates the other.

Discourses have no discrete boundaries because people are always, in history, creating new Discourses, changing old ones, and contesting and pushing the boundaries of Discourses. You, an African-American male, speak and act here and now in an attempt to get recognized as a "business manager coaching a project team." If you get recognized as such, then your performance is *in the Discourse* of business management. If you don't, it isn't.

If your performance has been influenced, intentionally or not, by another one of your Discourses (say, your membership in the Discourse of doing and being a jazz fan or your membership in a certain version of African-American culture as a Discourse), and it gets recognized in the business management Discourse, then you just, at least for here and now, "infected" one Discourse with another and widened what "counts" in the new capitalist management Discourse. You pushed the boundaries. In another time and place they may get narrowed.

You can get several of your Discourses recognized all at once. You (thinking of one my esteemed friends and colleagues at a university where I previously worked) "pull off" being here and now, in a class or meeting, for example, "a British, twice-migrant, globally oriented, traditional and modern, fashionable, female, Sikh, American professor of cultural studies and feminist postmodern anthropology" by weaving strands of your multiple Discourses together. If this sort of thing gets enacted and recognized enough, by enough people, then it will become not multiple strands of multiple Discourses interleaved, but a single Discourse whose hybridity may ultimately be forgotten. The point is *not* how we "count" Discourses; the point is the performance, negotiation, and recognition work that goes into creating, sustaining, and transforming them, and the role of language (always with other things) in this process.

Let me make several other brief, but important points about Discourses:

1. Discourses can split into two or more Discourses. For example, medieval "natural philosophy" eventually split into philosophy and physics and other sciences.
2. Two or more Discourses can meld together. For example, after the movie *Colors* came out, many years ago now, mixed Latino, African-American, and white gangs emerged. Prior to that, Latinos, African-Americans, and whites had quite separate ways of being and doing gangs, as they still do in the case of segregated gangs.
3. It can be problematic whether a Discourse today is or is not the same as one in the past. For example, modern medicine bears little similarity to medicine before the nineteenth century, but, perhaps, enough to draw some important parallels for some purposes, though not for others.
4. New Discourses emerge and old ones die all the time. For example, some years ago, in Palmdale, California (a desert community outside Los Angeles), and I assume other places, as well, an anti-racist skinhead Discourse was dying out because people, including the police, tended to confuse its members with a quite separate, but similar looking, racist Neo-Nazi skinhead Discourse.
5. Discourses are always defined in relationships of complicity and contestation with other Discourses, and so they change when other Discourses in a society emerge or die. For example, the emergence of a "new male" Discourse in the 1970s (ways of doing and being a "new male") happened

in response to various gender-based Discourses (e.g., various sorts of feminism) and class-based Discourses (the baby-boom middle class was too big for all young males to stay in it, so those who "made it" needed to mark their difference from those who did not), and, in turn, changed the meanings and actions of these other Discourses.

6. Discourses need, by no means, be "grand" or large scale. I used to eat regularly at a restaurant with a long bar. Among regulars, there were two different Discourses at opposite ends of the bar, that is, different ways of being and doing at each end of the bar. One involved young men and women and a lot of male-dominated sexual bantering; the other involved older people and lots of hard-luck stories. The restaurant assigned different bartenders to each end (always a young female at the young end) and many of the bartenders could fully articulate the Discourse at their end of the bar and their role in it.

7. Discourses can be hybrids of other Discourses. For example, the school yards of many urban middle and high schools are places where teenagers of different ethnic groups come together and engage in what I have elsewhere called a "borderland Discourse" of doing and being urban teenager peers, when they cannot safely go into each other's neighbor-hoods and when they each have their own neighborhood peer-based Discourses. The borderland Discourse is quite manifestly a mixture of the various neighborhood peer Discourses, with some emergent properties of its own.

8. There are limitless Discourses and no way to count them, both because new ones, even quite non-grand ones, can always emerge and because boundaries are always contestable.

9. Discourses are out in the world and history as coordinations ("a dance") of people, places, times, actions, interactions, verbal and non-verbal expression, symbols, things, tools, and technologies that betoken certain identities and associated activities. Thus, they are material realities. But Discourses exist, also, as work we humans do to get ourselves and things recognized in certain ways and not others. They are also the "maps" in our heads by which we understand society. Discourses, then, are social practices and mental entities, as well as material realities.

Discourses as "Kits"

If you are having trouble understanding the notion of "big D" Discourses, maybe this will help. Think for a minute of all the stuff you would put into the "Barbie doll" Discourse, restricting ourselves for the moment just to Barbie dolls and their accoutrements. How do you recognize something as in the "Barbie doll" world or Discourse, even if it hasn't got the Barbie logo on it? Girl and boy (e.g., Ken) Barbie dolls look a certain way (e.g., their bodies have certain sorts of shapes and not others). They have characteristic sorts of clothes and accessories. They talk and act in certain ways in books, games, and television shows. They display certain sorts of values and attitudes. This configuration of words and things is the Barbie doll Discourse. You interpret everything Barbie within this frame. It is a sort of kit made of words, things, clothes, values, attitudes, and so forth, from which one could build Barbie doll meanings. Even if you want to demean the Barbie doll Discourse by making a parody Barbie doll (such as Australia's "feral Cheryl"), you have to recognize the Discourse in the first place.

Now imagine real people wanted to enact a Barbie Discourse. We know what they would have to look, act, interact, and talk like. We know what values and attitudes they would have to display. We know what sorts of objects, accessories, and places they would associate themselves with. They would draw these out of their now real-world Barbie kit. In fact, young people sometimes talk about someone, usually a girl, as being or trying to be a Barbie doll type of person.

The workings of society and history have given rise to innumerable kits with which we can live out our social lives as different and multiple kinds of people, different for different times and places—hopefully not as Barbie dolls, but as men, women, workers, students, gamers, lovers, bird watchers, environmentalists, radicals, conservatives, feminists, African-Americans, scientists, bar members (lawyers or drinkers) of different types, and so on and so forth through an endless and changing list.

Note

The term "Discourse" (with a big "D") is meant to cover important aspects of what others have called: discourses (Foucault 1966); communities of practice (Lave & Wenger 1991); cultural communities (Clark 1996); discourse communities (Bizzell 1992); distributed knowledge or distributed systems (Hutchins 1995); thought collectives (Fleck 1979); practices (Bourdieu 1990); cultures (Geertz 1973); activity systems (Engeström, Miettinen, & Punamäki 1999); actor-actant networks (Latour 2005), collectives (Latour 2004); and (one interpretation of) "forms of life" (Wittgenstein 1958).

Discourses, for me, crucially involve: a) situated identities; b) ways of performing and recognizing characteristic identities and activities; c) ways of coordinating and getting coordinated by other people, things, tools, technologies, symbol systems, places, and times; d) characteristic ways of acting-interacting-feeling-emoting-valuing-gesturing-posturing-dressing-thinking-believing-knowing-speaking-listening (and, in some Discourses, reading-and-writing, as well).

A given Discourse can involve multiple identities. For example, a teacher, Ms X, and her kindergarten students can take on different situated identities, different from each other and different within different activities, within the "Ms X-and-her-students' classroom Discourse." For instance, in one second-grade classroom I visited, one African-American boy was referred to as "at risk" (for school failure), "one of my good readers" (good enough to be in a high reading group, but not to be pulled out during reading time to go to the gifted program for reading, despite the fact that both groups were reading at the same grade level), "well behaved," and "disaffiliated from the teacher." These are all identities that the teacher's classroom Discourse made available for this student. We can ask, of course, for each of these identities, and for other identities this child has within this classroom Discourse, which he is seeking to enact and which is being attributed to him based on behaviors that may, in fact, be bids for other identities.

Some people dislike the term "situated identity" and prefer, instead, something like "(social) position" or "subjectivity" (they tend to reserve the term "identity" for a sense of self that is relatively continuous and "fixed" over time). I use the term "identity" (or, to be specific, "socially situated identity") for the multiple identities we take on in different practices and contexts and would use the term "core identity" for whatever continuous and relatively (but only relatively) "fixed" sense of self underlies our contextually shifting multiple identities.

Readings

Bizzell, P. (1992). *Academic discourse and critical consciousness.* Pittsburgh, PA: University of Pittsburgh Press. [Excellent book in the field of "Composition and Rhetoric"]

Bourdieu, P. (1990). *In other words: Essays towards a reflexive sociology.* Stanford, CA: Stanford University Press. [Most accessible of Bourdieu's books—a major theorist on the role of practice in creating "status" in society]

Clark, H. H. (1996). *Using language.* Cambridge: Cambridge University Press. [Excellent discussion of the social aspects of language from a psychological perspective]

Engeström, Y., Miettinen, R. & Punamäki, R.-L., Eds. (1999). *Perspectives on activity theory.* Cambridge: Cambridge University Press [Engeström is the leading theorist in "activity theory" today]

Fleck, L. (1979 [1935]). *The genesis and development of a scientific fact.* Chicago: University of Chicago Press. [A little-known but classic "must read" book—best thing ever written on the social nature of thought]

Foucault, M. (1966). *The order of things: An archaeology of human sciences.* New York: Random House. [Foucault was the major theorist of how diverse aspects of a society and its institutions can at times represent similar values and themes]

Geertz, C. (1973). *The interpretations of cultures.* New York: Basic Books. [The leading work on culture by the twentieth century's outstanding anthropologist]

Hacking, I. (1986). Making up people, in T. C. Heller, M. Sosna, & D. E. Wellbery, with A. I. Davidson, A. Swidler, & I. Watt, Eds. *Reconstructing individualism: Autonomy, individuality, and the self in Western thought.* Stanford, CA: Stanford University Press, pp. 222–236. [Hacking's work on how different periods of history make being different "kinds of people" possible or impossible is deep and deeply important]

Hutchins, E. (1995). *Cognition in the wild.* Cambridge, MA: MIT Press. [A brilliant book on how thinking is accomplished through tools and collaboration]

Latour, B. (2004). *Politics of nature: How to bring the sciences into democracy.* Cambridge, MA: Harvard University Press. [An important book on how science does and can function in a democratic society, especially in regard to environmental issues]

Latour, B. (2005). *Reassembling the social: An introduction to actor-network-theory.* Oxford: Oxford University Press. [An overall summary and introduction to Latour's important and illuminating work on how humans enter into networks of things, tools, and other people in order to accomplish things in science and elsewhere]

Lave, J. & Wenger, E. (1991). *Situated learning: Legitimate peripheral participation.* New York: Cambridge University Press. [The classic work on "communities of practice"]

Scollon, R. & Scollon, S. W. (1981). *Narrative, literacy, and face in interethnic communication.* Norwood, NJ: Ablex. [The best book ever written on literacy and an outstanding discussion of the interactions between culture and discourse patterns]

Wieder, D. L. & Pratt, S. (1990). On being a recognizable Indian among Indians, in D. Carbaugh, Ed. *Cultural communication and intercultural contact.* Hillsdale, NJ: Lawrence Erlbaum, pp. 45–64. [An insightful discussion of how people get recognized as certain "kinds of people"]

Wittgenstein, L. (1958). *Philosophical investigations.* Oxford: Basil Blackwell. [Wittgenstein was perhaps the most important philosopher in the twentieth century. Wittgenstein's work on "language games" is crucial for anyone interested in language or discourse]

CHAPTER FOUR

Social Languages, Conversations, and Intertextuality

Whos-Doing-Whats in Language

This chapter will develop three of the tools of inquiry we introduced in the last chapter. First I discuss social languages, then Conversations, and then intertextuality. Social languages are different varieties of language that allow us to express different socially significant identities (e.g., talking and writing as a mathematician, doctor, or gang member) and enact different socially meaningful practices or activities (e.g., offering a proof in mathematics, writing a prescription in medicine, demonstrating solidarity with a fellow gang member).

"Conversations" (with a capital "C") are debates in society or within specific social groups (over focused issues like smoking, abortion, or school reform) that large numbers of people recognize, in terms of both what "sides" there are to take in such debates and what sorts of people tend to be on each side.

Intertextuality refers to cases where one oral or written text directly or indirectly quotes another text or alludes to another text in yet more subtle ways.

So, we turn now to the notion of social languages. The last chapter argued that to study language-in-use we need to study more than language alone, we need to study Discourses. Discourses are ways with and integrations of words, deeds interactions, thoughts, feelings, objects, tools, times, and places that allow us to enact and recognize different socially situated identities.

However, as linguistic discourse analysts, we often pay attention primarily to language and for a while, at least, we will leave non-language "stuff" out of consideration. When we do so, we are looking at how people communicate *who* they are and *what* they are doing through language. Of course, they are always also communicating via non-verbal elements like ways of acting, inter-acting, valuing, thinking, and using objects, but these can be left aside for a while—to be returned to later for a fuller analysis—while we concentrate first and foremost on language.

I will introduce the idea of social languages through an initial discussion of how *whos* and *whats* are communicated in language (keeping in mind that language alone is rarely enough and is always put together with "other stuff" to pull off a Discourse). Let me give an example to make my points about *whos-doing-whats* via language-in-use more concrete. Consider, then, the warning on an aspirin bottle, reprinted below (italics and capitals are on the warning):

> Warnings: *Children and teenagers should not use this medication for chicken pox or flu symptoms before a doctor is consulted about Reye Syndrome, a rare but serious illness reported to be associated with aspirin.* Keep this and all drugs out of the reach of children. In case of accidental overdose, seek professional assistance or contact a poison control center immediately. As with any drug, if you are pregnant or nursing a baby, seek the advice of a health professional before using this product. IT IS ESPECIALLY IMPORTANT NOT TO USE ASPIRIN DURING THE LAST 3 MONTHS OF PREGNANCY UNLESS SPECIFICALLY DIRECTED TO DO SO BY A DOCTOR BECAUSE IT MAY CAUSE PROBLEMS IN THE UNBORN CHILD

OR COMPLICATIONS DURING DELIVERY. See carton for arthritis use[+] and Important Notice.

My interpretation of this text is that there are two *who-doing-whats* in this warning, and they are interleaved. That is, there are two different answers to the question "Who is speaking to us?" and two corresponding answers to the question "What are they trying to do?" The first *who/what* combination is made up of the following sentences:

> *Children and teenagers should not use this medication for chicken pox or flu symptoms before a doctor is consulted about Reye Syndrome, a rare but serious illness reported to be associated with aspirin.* IT IS ESPECIALLY IMPORTANT NOT TO USE ASPIRIN DURING THE LAST 3 MONTHS OF PREGNANCY UNLESS SPECIFICALLY DIRECTED TO DO SO BY A DOCTOR BECAUSE IT MAY CAUSE PROBLEMS IN THE UNBORN CHILD OR COMPLICATIONS DURING DELIVERY.

Here things are referred to quite specifically ("children and teenagers," "this medication," "chicken pox," "flu," "Reye Syndrome," "aspirin," "last 3 months," "unborn child," "delivery"), doctors are called "doctor," and matters are treated emphatically (italics, capitals, "should not," "rare but serious," "especially important," "specifically directed"). We will see that this language enacts one type of *who* seeking to accomplish one type of *what*.

The second *who-doing-what* combination is made up of the following sentences, placed in the middle of the other two:

> Keep this and all drugs out of the reach of children. In case of accidental overdose, seek professional assistance or contact a poison control center immediately. As with any drug, if you are pregnant or nursing a baby, seek the advice of a health professional before using this product.

Here things are referred to more generally and generically ("this and all drugs," "any drug," and "this product," rather than "this medication" and "aspirin"; "children" rather than "children and teenagers," "pregnant" rather than "last 3 months of pregnancy"), doctors are not mentioned, rather the health profession is referred to more generally ("professional assistance," "poison control center," "health professional"), and matters are treated less stridently with the exception of the word "immediately" (here we get small print and the less strident phrases "keep out of the reach," "accidental overdose," "seek ... assistance," "seek ... advice," rather than the more direct "should not" and "important not to use" of the other part of the warning). This language enacts a different *who* seeking to accomplish a different *what*.

These two *who-doing-whats* "feel" different. They are authorized and issued by different "voices" to different purposes and effects. The first speaks with a lawyerly voice (*who*) responding to specific potential legal problems and court cases (*what*); the second speaks with the official voice of a caring, but authoritatively knowledgeable company (*who*) trying to protect and advise people, especially women and children, while still stressing that aspirin is not particularly special or dangerous compared to drugs in general (*what*).

Of course, this second *who-doing-what* sits in some tension with the first. By the way, the second *who-doing-what* on the aspirin bottle used to be the only warning on the bottle (with the order of the sentences a bit different). And, indeed, the warning has changed yet again on newer bottles.

This warning, like all utterances, reflects the company it has kept, or, to put the matter another way, it reflects the history that has given rise to it. In this case, presumably, the new sterner, more direct *who-doing-what* was added to the more general and avuncular one because the company got sued over things like Reye Syndrome.

The warning on the aspirin bottle is heteroglossic. That is, it is "double-voiced," since it interleaves two different *whos-doing-whats* together. Of course, in different cases, this sort of interleaving could be much more intricate, with the two (or more) *whos-doing-whats* more fully integrated, and harder to tease apart.

Social Languages

There is another term that it is useful in place of the cumbersome phrase "who-doing-what" as far as the language aspects of "who-doing-whats" are concerned (remembering that, in reality, language is caught up with "other stuff" in Discourses). This term is "social language." Each of the *who-doing-whats* we saw on the aspirin bottle are linguistically expressed in different "*social languages*" (different socially significant varieties of language). All languages, like English or French, are composed of many (a great many) different social languages. Social languages are what we learn and what we speak.

Keep in mind that "social languages" and "Discourses" are terms for different things. I will use the term "social languages" to talk about the role of language in Discourses. But, as I said above, Discourses always involve more than language. They always involve coordinating language with ways of acting, interacting, valuing, believing, feeling, and with bodies, clothes, non-linguistic symbols, objects, tools, technologies, times, and places.

Let me give a couple of examples of social languages at work, beyond the example of the two different social languages in the warning on the aspirin bottle, examples I have used over the years as particularly clear instances of different social languages. Consider, for instance, the following case of an upper-middle-class, Anglo-American young women named "Jane," in her twenties, who was attending one of my courses on language and communication. The course was discussing different social languages and, during the discussion, Jane claimed that she herself did not use different social languages in different contexts, but, rather, was consistent from context to context. In fact, to do otherwise, she said, would be "hypocritical," a failure to "be oneself."

In order to support her claim that she did not switch her style of speaking in different contexts and for different conversational partners, Jane decided to record herself talking to her parents and to her boyfriend. In both cases, she decided to discuss a story the class had discussed earlier, so as to be sure that, in both contexts, she was talking about the same thing.

In the story, a character named Abigail wants to get across a river to see her true love, Gregory. A riverboat captain (Roger) says he will take her only if she consents to sleep with him. In desperation to see Gregory, Abigail agrees to do so. But when she arrives and tells Gregory what she has done, he disowns her and sends her away. There is more to the story, but this is enough for our purposes here. Students in my class had been asked to rank-order the characters in the story from the most offensive to the least.

In explaining to her parents why she thought Gregory was the worst (least moral) character in the story, the young woman said the following:

> Well, when I thought about it, I don't know, it seemed to me that Gregory should be the most offensive. He showed no understanding for Abigail, when she told him what she was forced to do. He was callous. He was hypocritical, in the sense that he professed to love her, then acted like that.

Earlier, in her discussion with her boyfriend, in an informal setting, she had also explained why she thought Gregory was the worst character. In this context she said:

> What an ass that guy was, you know, her boyfriend. I should hope, if I ever did that to see you, you would shoot the guy. He uses her and he says he loves her. Roger never lies, you know what I mean?

It was clear—clear even to Jane—that Jane had used two very different forms of language. The differences between Jane's two social languages are everywhere apparent in the two texts.

To her parents, she carefully hedges her claims ("I don't know," "it seemed to me"); to her boyfriend, she makes her claims straight out. To her boyfriend, she uses terms like "ass" and "guy," while to her parents she uses more formal terms like "offensive," "understanding," "callous," "hypocritical" and "professed." She also uses more formal sentence structure to her parents ("it seemed to me that . . .," "He showed no understanding for Abigail, when . . .," "He was hypocritical, in the sense that . . .") than she does to her boyfriend (". . . that guy was, you know, her boyfriend," "Roger never lies, you know what I mean?").

Jane repeatedly addresses her boyfriend as "you," thereby noting his social involvement as a listener, but does not directly address her parents in this way. In talking to her boyfriend, she leaves several points to be inferred, points that she spells out more explicitly to her parents (e.g., her boyfriend must infer that Gregory is being accused of being a hypocrite from the information that though Roger is bad, at least he does not lie, which Gregory did in claiming to love Abigail).

All in all, Jane appears to use more "school-like" language to her parents. Her language to them requires less inferencing on their part and distances them as listeners from social and emotional involvement with what she is saying, while stressing, perhaps, their cognitive involvement and their judgment of her and her "intelligence." Her language to her boyfriend stresses, on the other hand, social and affective involvement, solidarity, and co-participation in meaning making.

This young woman is making visible and recognizable two different versions of *who* she is and *what* she is doing. In one case she is "a dutiful and intelligent daughter having dinner with her proud parents" and in the other case she is "a girlfriend being intimate with her boyfriend." Of course, I should add, that while people like Jane may talk at dinner this way to their parents, not all people do; there are other identities one can take on for one's parents, other social languages one can speak to them. And, indeed, there may well be others that Jane would use to her parents in different settings.

Let me give one more example of social languages at work, an example taken from Greg Myers' work (see Myers 1990; all page numbers below refer to this work). Biologists, and other scientists, write differently in professional journals than they do in popular science magazines. These two different ways of writing do different things and display different identities. The popular science article is *not* merely a "translation" or "simplification" of the professional article.

To see this, consider the two extracts below, the first from a professional journal, the second from a popular science magazine, both written by the same biologist on the same topic (p. 150):

> Experiments show that *Heliconius* butterflies are less likely to oviposit on host plants that possess eggs or egg-like structures. These egg-mimics are an unambiguous example of a plant trait evolved in response to a host-restricted group of insect herbivores. (Professional journal)

> *Heliconius* butterflies lay their eggs on *Passiflora* vines. In defense the vines seem to have evolved fake eggs that make it look to the butterflies as if eggs have already been laid on them. (Popular science)

The first extract, from a professional scientific journal, is about the *conceptual structure* of a specific *theory* within the scientific *discipline* of biology. The subject of the initial sentence is "experiments," a *methodological* tool in natural science. The subject of the next sentence is "these egg-mimics": note how plant-parts are named, not in terms of the plant itself, but in terms of the role they play in a particular *theory* of natural selection and evolution, namely "coevolution" of predator and prey (that is, the theory that predator and prey evolve together by shaping each other). Note also, in this regard, the earlier "host plants" in the preceding sentence, rather than the "vines" of the popular passage.

In the second sentence, the butterflies are referred to as "a host-restricted group of insect herbivores," which points simultaneously to an aspect of scientific methodology (like "experiments" did) and to the logic of a theory (like "egg-mimics" did). Any scientist arguing for the theory of coevolution faces the difficulty of demonstrating a causal connection between a particular plant characteristic and a particular predator when most plants have so many different sorts of animals attacking them. A central methodological technique to overcome this problem is to study plant groups (like *Passiflora* vines) that are preyed on by only one or a few predators (in this case, *Heliconius* butterflies). "Host-restricted group of insect herbivores," then, refers to both the relationship between plant and insect that is at the heart of the theory of coevolution and the methodological technique of picking plants and insects that are *restricted* to each other so as to "control" for other sorts of interactions.

The first passage, then, is concerned with scientific methodology and a particular theoretical perspective on evolution. On the other hand, the second extract, from a popular science magazine, is not about methodology and theory, but about *animals* in *nature*. The butterflies are the subject of the first sentence and the vine is the subject of the second. Further, the butterflies and the vine are labeled as such, not in terms of their role in a particular theory.

The second passage is a story about the struggles of insects and plants that are transparently open to the trained gaze of the scientist. Further, the plant and insect become "intentional" actors in the drama: the plants act in their own "defense" and things "look" a certain way to the insects, they are "deceived" by appearances as humans sometimes are.

These two examples replicate in the present what, in fact, is an historical difference. In the history of biology, the scientist's relationship with nature gradually changed from telling stories about direct observations of nature to carrying out complex experiments to test complex theories. Myers argues that professional science is now concerned with the expert management of uncertainty and complexity, and popular science with the general assurance that the world is knowable by and directly accessible to experts.

The need to "manage uncertainty" was created, in part, by the fact that mounting "observations" of nature led scientists, not to consensus, but to growing disagreement as to how to describe and explain such observations. This problem led, in turn, to the need to convince the public that such uncertainty did not damage the scientist's claim to professional expertise or the ultimate "knowability" of the world.

This example lets us see, then, not just that ways with words are connected to different *whos* (here the experimenter/theoretician versus the careful observer of nature) and *whats* (the professional contribution to science and the popularization of it), but that they are always acquired within and licensed by specific social and historically shaped practices representing the *values* and *interests* of distinctive groups of people.

So, it is clear now, I hope, that in using language what is at stake are *whos-doing-whats*. But, you cannot be any old *who* you want to. You cannot engage in any old *what* you want to. That is to say that *whos* and *whats* are creations in history and change in history, as we have just seen, in fact, in the examples from biology.

Two Aspects of Grammar

Each social language has its own distinctive grammar. However, two different aspects of grammar are important to social languages. One aspect is the traditional set of units like nouns, verbs, inflections, phrases, and clauses. The other aspect is the "rules" by which grammatical units like nouns and verbs, phrases and clauses, are used to create *patterns* which signal or "index" characteristic *whos-doing-whats-within-Discourses*. That is, we speakers and writers design our oral or written utterances to have patterns in them in virtue of which interpreters can attribute situated identities and specific activities to us and our utterances.

These patterns are called "collocational patterns" by linguists. This means that various sorts of grammatical devices "co-locate" with each other. The patterns I am trying to name here are "co-relations" (correlations) among different grammatical units. These correlations, in turn, also co-relate to (coordinate with) other non-language "stuff" to constitute (for historical, i.e., *conventional* reasons) *whos-doing-whats-within-Discourses*.

For example, in Jane's utterance to her boyfriend, "What an ass that guy was, you know, her boyfriend," note how informal terms like "ass" and "guy," the vague reference "that guy," the informal parenthetical device "you know," and the informal syntactic device of "right dislocation" (i.e., letting the phrase "her boyfriend" hang out at the end of the sentence) all pattern together to signal that this utterance is in an informal social language used to achieve solidarity.

The situation here is much like choosing clothes that go together in such a way that they communicate that we are engaged in a certain activity or are taking up a certain style connected to such activities. For example, consider how sandals, bathing suit, tank top, shades, and sun hat "co-locate" together to "signal" to us things like outdoor and water activities and the situated identities we take up in such situations.

An Example

Let me give you another example of these two aspects of grammar (traditional units like nouns and noun phrases and patterns we create out of these units). Consider the sentence below (adapted from Halliday & Martin 1993, p. 77):

1. Lung cancer death rates are clearly associated with an increase in smoking.

A whole bevy of linguistic features marks this sentence as part of a distinctive academic social language (though without more connected text we can't actually tell exactly which one). Some of these are: a heavy subject ("lung cancer death rates"), deverbal nouns ("increase," "smoking"), a complex compound noun ("lung cancer death rates"), a "low transitive" relational predicate ("are ... associated with"), passive or passive-like voice ("are ... associated"), the absence of agency (no mention of who does the associating), an abstract noun ("rates"), and an assertive modifier to the verb ("clearly").

No single grammatical feature marks the social language of this sentence. Rather, all these features (and a great many more if we took a larger stretch of text, including many discourse-level features) form a distinctive *configuration* (a correlation or, better, co-relation) that marks the social language.

I hasten to point out that the configuration of features that mark a social language are too complex and *too situated in the specific context they are helping to create* (after all, there is no such thing as a "general social science context") to be open to much generalized and rote learning. Linguistic relationships like these do not exist and are not learned outside the distinctive social practices (*whats*) of which they are an integral part. They *are* part and parcel of the very "voice" or "identity" (*whos*) of people who speak and write and think and act and value and live *that* way (e.g., as a social scientist) for a given time and place. To learn such relationships is part of what it means to learn to recognize the very social context one is in (and helping to create). This is not to say there is no role here for overt instruction (there is). It is only to say that there is no way we can leave out immersion in situated practices if we want to teach people new social languages.

It is sometimes said that what distinguishes "informal" social languages like the one Jane used to her boyfriend from more "formal" ones characteristic of literacy and "literate talk," like the social language Jane used to her parents, or the smoking example above, is that, in the "informal" case, "context" determines meaning and you just have to have been there to understand what was being said. In the more "formal" cases, it is held that the words and sentences mean in a more explicit, less contextual way. In fact, it is sometimes said that such language is "decontextualized." Some people in education claim that what many minority and lower socioeconomic children who do not succeed in school fail to know is how to use such "decontextualized language."

All this is seriously in error, and in ways that not only mislead us, but actually damage some people (e.g., the children just referred to). Consider sentence 1 again. This sentence is no more explicit than informal language. It is no less contextualized. It is simply inexplicit and contextualized in a different way.

Though we tend to think of writing, at least academic writing, as clear, unambiguous, and explicit in comparison to speech, sentence 1, in fact, has at least 112 different meanings! What is odder still is that anyone reading sentence 1 (at least anyone reading this book) hits on only *one* of these meanings (or but one of a select few) without any overt awareness that the other 111 meanings are perfectly possible.

There are theories in psycholinguistics that claim that what happens in a case like sentence 1 is that we unconsciously consider all 112 possible meanings and rule out all but one, but we do this so fast and so below the level of consciousness that we are completely unaware of it. Be that as it may, how can sentence 1 have so many meanings and why do we all, nonetheless, hit on one and, in fact, exactly the same one?

This fact is due to the grammar of the sentence. The subject of sentence 1 ("Lung cancer death rates") is a "nominalization" made up of a compound noun. Nominalizations are like trash compactors: they allow one to take a lot of information—indeed, a whole sentence's worth of information—and compact it into a compound word or a phrase. One can then insert this compacted information into another sentence (thereby making bigger and bigger sentences). The trouble is this: once one has made the compacted item (the nominalization), it is hard to tell what information exactly went into it. Just like the compacted trash in the trash compactor, you can't always tell exactly what's in it.

"Lung cancer death rates" could be a compaction of any of the following more expanded pieces of information:

2a.   [lung cancer] [death rates] = rates (number) of people dying from lung cancer = how many people die from lung cancer
2b.   [lung cancer] [death rates] = rates (speed) of people dying from lung cancer = how quickly people die from lung cancer
2c.   [lung] [cancer death] [rates] = rates (number) of lungs dying from cancer = how many lungs die from cancer
2d.   [lung] [cancer death] [rates] = rates (speed) of lungs dying from cancer = how quickly lungs die from cancer

The first two meanings (2a/b) parse the phrase "lung cancer death rates" as "lung-cancer (a disease) death-rates," that is "death-rates from lung-cancer," where "rates" can mean number of people dying or the speed of their death from the disease. The second two meanings (2c/d) parse the phrase "lung cancer death rates" as "lung cancer-death-rates," that is "cancer-death-rates for lungs," where, once again, "rates" can mean number of (this time) lungs dying from cancer or the speed with which they are dying from cancer. This way of parsing the phrase is analogous to the most obvious reading of "pet cancer death rates" (i.e., "cancer-death-rates for pets," that is, how many/how fast pets are dying from cancer). Of course, everyone reading this book interpreted "lung cancer death rates" to be a compaction of 2a. Our question is why?

Consider now the verbal phrase "are clearly associated with" in sentence 1. Such rather "colorless" relational predicates are typical of certain social languages. Such verbal expressions are ambiguous in two respects. In the first place, we cannot tell whether "associated with" indicates a relationship of *causation* or just *correlation*. Thus, does sentence 1 say that one thing causes another (e.g., smoking causes cancer) or just that one thing is correlated with another (smoking and cancer are found together, but, perhaps, something else causes both of them)?

In the second place, even if we take "associated with" to mean *cause*, we still cannot tell what causes what. You and I may know, in fact, that smoking causes cancer, but sentence 1 can perfectly mean that lung cancer death rates *lead to* increased smoking. "Perhaps," as Halliday and Martin remark, "people are so upset by fear of lung cancer that they need to smoke more in order to calm their nerves" (pp. 77–78). It is even possible that the writer did not want to commit to a choice between *cause* and *correlate*, or to a choice between smoking causing cancer or fear of cancer causing smoking. This gives us at least the following meaning possibilities for the verbal phrase "are clearly associated with":

3a.   cause
3b.   caused by
3c.   correlated with
3d.   writer does not want to commit herself

Now, let's finish with the phrase "increase in smoking." This is another nominalization, compacting information. Does it mean "people smoke more" (smokers are increasing the amount they smoke), or "more people smoke" (new smokers are being added to the list of smokers), or is it a combination of the two, meaning "more people smoke more"?

We can also ask, in regard to the death rates and the increased smoking taken together, if the people who are increasing their smoking (whether old smokers or new ones) are the people who are dying from lung cancer, or whether other people are dying as well (e.g., people who don't smoke, but, perhaps, are "associated with" smokers). Finally, we can ask of the sentence as a whole, whether it is representing a "real" situation ("*because* more people are smoking more people are dying") or just a hypothetical one ("*if* more people were to smoke we know more people would die")? This gives us at least seven more meaning possibilities:

4a.   increased smoking = people smoke more
4b.   increased smoking = more people smoke
4c.   increased smoking = more people smoke more
4d.   the same people are smoking and dying
4e.   the people smoking and dying are not all the same
4f.   the situation being talked about is real (*because*)
4g.   the situation being talked about is hypothetical (*if*)

We now have considered 4 possible meanings for the subject ("lung cancer death rates"), 4 possible meanings for the verbal phrase ("are clearly associated with") and 7 possibilities for the complement ("an increase in smoking"). Like an old-fashioned Chinese menu, you can take one from list A and another from list B and yet another from list C and get a specific combination of meanings. This gives us 4 times 4 times 7 possibilities, that is, 112 different possible meanings.

All of these meanings are perfectly allowed by the grammar of sentence 1. And, in fact, there are other possibilities I have not discussed, e.g., taking "rates" to mean "monetary costs" or "lung cancer death rates" to be the rates at which lung cancer is dying. And yet—here's our mystery again—everyone reading this book in a micro second hit on just one of these many meanings and the same one (or, at worst, consciously considered a very few of the possibilities). Why?

The answer to the mystery I am discussing here may be perfectly obvious to you, but I want to suggest that, nonetheless, it is important for how we view language and language learning. We all hit on only one (and the same one) of the 112 meanings because we have all been part of—we have all been privy to—the ongoing discussion in our society about smoking, disease, tobacco companies, contested research findings, warnings on cartons, ads that entice teens to smoke, and so on and so forth through a great many complex details.

Given this discussion as background, sentence 1 has one meaning. Without that discussion—with only the grammar of English in one's head—the sentence has more than 112 meanings. Obviously, however important grammar is, the conversation is more important. It leaves open one meaning (or a small number of possibilities, like allowing that sentence 1 also covers people getting lung cancer from secondary smoke).

A more technical way to put this point is this: meaning is not merely a matter of decoding grammar, it is also (and more importantly) a matter of knowing which of the many inferences that one can draw from an utterance are *relevant*. And "relevance" is a matter deeply tied to context, point of view, and culture. One knows what counts for a given group of people at a given time and place as "relevant" by having been privy to certain discussions those people have heretofore had. If there had been a major discussion about environmentally induced lung cancer in a nervous society, then sentence 1 could perfectly well have been taken to mean that the prevalence of lung cancer is causing many more people to turn to smoking to calm their nerves (2a + 3a + 4b).

So, we have concluded, we speak and write not in English alone, but in specific *social languages*. The utterances of these social languages have meaning—or, at least, the meanings they are, in fact, taken to have—thanks to being embedded in specific social discussions. Though I have established these points in regard to a single sentence (sentence 1 above), I take them to be generally true.

To teach someone the meaning of sentence 1—or any sentence for that matter—is to embed them in the conversational sea in which sentence 1 swims. To teach someone the sort of social language in which sentences like sentence 1 occur is to embed them in the discussions that have recruited (and which, in turn, continually reproduce) that social language.

Big "C" Conversations

Now it is time to become clearer about what I mean by the word "discussion" above when I said things like "The utterances of these social languages have meaning—or, at least, the meanings they are, in fact, taken to have—thanks to being embedded in specific social discussions." When we talk about things like the general societal discussion around issues like abortion or smoking, we are using the word "discussion" in a partly metaphorical way, of course. We are talking about the public debates that swirl around us in the media, in our reading, and in our interactions with other people, not any one specific discussion among specific people. On certain issues (e.g., abortion, smoking, gambling, feminism, affirmative action, etc.) you know what the "sides" are, how they are talked about, and what sort of people tend to be on specific sides. Some of these sorts of issues are known by nearly everyone in a society, others are known only by specific social groups (e.g., the ongoing big controversies in a given academic field). This knowledge is an ever-present background you can bring to interpret things you hear and read or in terms of which you can formulate your own talk and writing.

I will call such public debates, arguments, motifs, issues, or themes "Conversations" with a capital "C," speaking metaphorically as if the various sides in debates around issues like abortion or smoking were engaged in one big grand conversation (or debate or argument, whatever we want to call it). Of course, this big Conversation is composed of a myriad of interactional events taking place among specific people at specific times and places.

Let me give you an example of what I am trying to get at here. It is fashionable today for businesses to announce (in "mission statements") their "core values" in an attempt to create a particular company "culture" (see Collins & Porras 1994; examples below are from pp. 68–69). For instance, the announced core values of Johnson & Johnson, a large pharmaceutical company, include "The company exists to alleviate pain and disease" and "Individual opportunity and reward based on merit," as well as several others.

One might wonder, then, what the core values of a cigarette company might be. Given the Conversations that most of us are familiar with—about the U.S. and its history, as well as about smoking—we can almost predict what they will be. For example, the espoused core values of Philip Morris, a large company which sells cigarettes among a great many other products, include "The right to personal freedom of choice (to smoke, to buy whatever one wants) is worth defending," "Winning—being the best and beating others," and "Encouraging individual initiative," as well as (in a statement similar to one of Johnson & Johnson's statements) "Opportunity to achieve based on merit, not gender, race, or class."

We all readily connect Philip Morris's core-value statements to themes of American individualism and freedom. Note how the values of "individual initiative" and "reward for merit," which are part of the core values of both Johnson & Johnson and Philip Morris, take on a different coloring in the two cases. In the first case, they take on a humanistic coloring, and in the other, the coloring of "every man for himself." This coloring is the effect of our knowledge of the two sides to the "smoking Conversation" in which, we all know, individual freedom is pitted against social responsibility.

Note here, then, how values, beliefs, and objects play a role in the sorts of Conversations I am talking about. We know that in this Conversation some people will hold values and beliefs consistent with expressions about individualism, freedom, the "American way," and so forth, while others will express values and beliefs consistent with the rights of others, social responsibility, and protecting people from harm, even harm caused by their own desires. In turn, these two value and belief orientations can be historically tied to much wider dichotomies centering around beliefs about the responsibilities and the role of governments.

Furthermore, within this Conversation, an object like a cigarette or an institution like a tobacco company, or an act like the act of smoking itself, takes on meanings—symbolic values—within the Conversation, but dichotomous meanings. Smoking can be seen as an addiction, an expression of freedom, or a lack of caring about others. The point is that those familiar with the Conversation know, just as they can select the meaning of sentence 1 above out of 112 possibilities, the possible meanings of cigarettes, tobacco companies, and smoking.

The themes and values that enter into Conversations circulate in a multitude of texts and media. They are the products of historical disputes between and among different Discourses. Think, for example, of the historic debate between the Discourse of evolutionary biologists and the Discourse of fundamentalist creationists. This debate, over time, has constituted a Conversation that many people in society know something about. For that reason it is hard for a newspaper to discuss evolution in any terms without triggering people to think about this debate and to try to interpret what the newspaper is saying in terms of it.

Of course, people today often know these themes and values without knowing the historical events that helped create or sustain them in the past and pass them down to us today. For example, in the nineteenth century in Massachusetts, courts were asked to return escaped slaves to their Southern "owners" (von Frank 1998). These court battles, and the accompanying controversies in newspapers and public meetings, engaged two distinctive Discourses, among several others (for example, several Discourses connected to Black churches and to Massachusetts' significant population of free Black people, some of them professionals, such as ministers, doctors, and lawyers—note that it is hard to know what to call these people: they were of African descent, born in the U.S., but were not full citizens).

One Discourse, connected to people like Emerson and Thoreau, championed freedom, personal responsibility, and morality as constituting a "higher law" than the law of states, the federal government, or the courts. They argued and fought, not only to not return the slaves, but to disobey the court and the federal officials seeking to enforce its mandate. The other Discourse, heavily associated with nationally oriented political and business elites, championed the rule of law at the expense of either the slaves' freedom or one's own personal conscience.

These two Discourses were, by no means, just "statements" and "beliefs." There were, for example, distinctive ways, in mind, body, and social practice, to mark oneself, in nineteenth-century Massachusetts, as a "Transcendentalist" (i.e., a follower of Emerson and his colleagues) and to engage in social activities seen as part and parcel of this identity.

Many people today have no knowledge of the debates over escaped slaves in Massachusetts and nationally in the nineteenth century (though these debates, of course, helped lead to the Civil War). However, these debates sustained, transformed, and handed down themes and values that are quite recognizable as parts of ongoing Conversations in the mid twentieth century (e.g., in the Civil Rights Movement) and today.

Of course, I must hasten to add, again, that a number of other important Discourses played a significant role in the escaped-slave cases in Massachusetts. Blacks were part of some integrated Discourses, as well as their own distinctive Discourses, as well. Furthermore, all these Discourses interacted with each other, in complex relations of alliance and contestation, with some important overlaps between Discourses (e.g., between the Transcendentalists and John Brown's distinctive and violent Discourse in regard to slavery and abolition).

Because people are often unaware of historical clashes among Discourses, it is often easier to study Conversations, rather than Discourses directly, though it is always important and interesting to uncover the historical antecedents of today's Conversations. The point is, though, that the historical interactions of Discourses lead to certain debates ("Conversations"), for example debates over smoking or race, being known widely by people in a society or social group, even by people who are not themselves members of those Discourses or even aware of their histories.

Intertextuality

The term "social language" applies to specific varieties of language used to enact specific identities and carry out specific sorts of practices or activities. A single written or oral text can be in one social language or it can switch between two or more or even mix them up pretty thoroughly. The warning from the aspirin bottle switches back and forth between two different varieties of language.

Sometimes, however, a text spoken or written in one variety of language (one social language) will accomplish a sort of switching by incorporating ("borrowing") words from another text spoken or written in the same or a different variety of language. Such borrowing we will call "*intertextuality.*" One text can incorporate words from another one in a great variety of different ways. It can directly quote another text (as in "Shakespeare said 'Love is such sweet sorrow'"), or indirectly quote it (as in "Shakespeare said that love was such sweet sorrow"), or just allude to what hearers or readers in the know will realize are words taken from some other source (as in "My love for you is sweet sorrow, indeed").

Norman Fairclough has this to say about "intertextuality": "Intertextuality is basically the property texts have of being full of snatches of other texts, which may be explicitly demarcated or merged in, and which the text may assimilate, contradict, ironically echo, and so forth" (Fairclough 1992, p. 84).

For example, consider the text below, a part of the Oakland, California, School Board's official proposal to support "Ebonics" in its schools:

> Whereas, numerous validated scholarly studies demonstrate that African American students as part of their culture and history as African people possess and utilize a language described in various scholarly approaches as "Ebonics" (literally Black sounds) or pan African Communication behaviors or African Systems; and ... Whereas, the Federal Bilingual Education Act (20 USC 1402 et seq.) mandates that local educational agencies "build their capacities to establish, implement and sustain programs of instruction for children and youth of limited English proficiency." (http://linguistlist.org/topics/ebonics/ebonics-res1.html)

This text is an official policy document from a school board. As such it is written in a legalistic social language, clearly signaled by a style in which we get a series of sentences beginning with the word "whereas" followed by a comma (we only see two here, but the original text has many more). Each sentence following "whereas" is formal and complicated and contains a main verb in the present tense ("demonstrate," "mandates") followed by a "that" clause that contains another whole sentence's worth of information (see Table 4.1 opposite).

So we have a pretty distinctive social language here. However, this text is through and through intertextual in the ways in which it alludes to other texts. Consider the first "whereas" sentence. Here our text points to work by linguists ("scholarly studies demonstrate") without directly quoting that work. However, any linguist will readily recognize that the linguistic work being mentioned is, in fact, one distinctive and recognizable type of linguistic research. The terms "Ebonics," "Black sounds," "pan African Communication behaviors," and "African Systems" are all technical terms taken from and strongly associated with texts from one very specific type of linguistics, one carried out largely by

Table 4.1 Analysis of Oakland School Board's "Ebonics" proposal

Subject	Main verb + that	Subordinate clause
Numerous validated scholarly studies	demonstrate that	African American students as part of their culture and history as African people possess and utilize a language described in various scholarly approaches as "Ebonics" (literally Black sounds) or pan African Communication Behaviors or African Systems;
The Federal Bilingual Act	mandates that	local educational agencies "build their capacities to establish, implement and sustain programs of instruction for children and youth of limited English proficiency"

scholars of African or African-American descent with a strong Black Nationalist orientation, though after Oakland's decision, some of these terms spread into wider use (terms like "African-American Vernacular English" were originally more widely used in linguistics, see John Baugh's excellent work on linguistics and the Ebonics controversy in the Readings below).

Of course, it is meaningful and important that the Oakland policy document alludes to this type of linguistic research and not others. Furthermore, the document does not directly quote these linguists, but uses their words as part of the unquoted language of the document itself. This achieves a certain solidarity with this type of linguistic research and assumes without comment its authority over other forms of linguistic research. In fact, for readers uninformed about linguistics, the reference to "numerous validated scholarly studies" and the incorporation of words from this research without quotes will leave the impression that there are no other types of linguistic research relevant to the matter at hand. This is, by the way, typical in general of public policy documents. Research, when it is mentioned, tends to speak with one voice and a voice that supports the policy in the policy document.

On the other hand, the second "whereas" sentence quotes directly from the Federal Bilingual Education Act, a piece of federal legislation. One reason the policy document does this is that the whole document is, in part, an attempt to interpret the words of this piece of legislation in a certain way. The first "whereas" sentence about Ebonics is already an attempt to set the interpretation of the federal legislation in a certain framework. Ultimately, the policy document wants to argue that some African-American students are as entitled to federal aid as bilingual students are because these African-American students have limited proficiency not in English *per se*, but in the standard dialect of English used in schools (their native dialect is "Ebonics"). This argument, by the way, is fully senseful in that linguists do not make any rigorous distinction between different dialects (e.g., there are dialects of German that are not mutually interpretable) and different languages (e.g., there are dialects of German and Dutch that are mutually interpretable).

Thus, the Oakland text directly quotes a piece of federal legislation, setting it off between quotes. It allows the surrounding text (part of which is taken from a certain type of linguistics research which is given authority by being incorporated into the text more directly without direct quotation) to interpret it.

Social Languages, Conversations, Intertextuality, and Discourses as Tools of Inquiry

In this book I have treated the terms "social languages," "Conversations," "intertextuality," and "Discourses" realistically. That is, I have spoken about them as things that exist in the mind and in the world. And, indeed, this is, I believe, both true and the easiest way to grasp what they mean and how and why they are significant for discourse analysis.

But it is important to realize that, in the end, these terms are ultimately our ways as theoreticians and analysts of talking about and, thus, constructing and construing the world. And it is in this guise that I am primarily interested in them. They are "tools of inquiry." Social languages, Conversations, intertextuality, and Discourses are "thinking devices" that can guide us to ask certain sorts of questions. Faced with a piece of oral or written language, we can ask the following sorts of questions:

A. What social language(s) are involved? What sorts of grammatical patterns indicate this? Are different social languages mixed? How so?
B. What socially situated identities and activities do these social languages enact?
C. What Discourse or Discourses are involved? How is "stuff" other than language ("mind stuff" and "emotional stuff" and "world stuff" and "interactional stuff" and non-language symbol systems, etc.) relevant in indicating socially situated identities and activities?
D. In considering this language, what sorts of relationships among different Discourses are involved (institutionally, in society, or historically)? How are different Discourses aligned or in contention here?
E. What Conversations (public debates over issues or themes) are relevant to understanding this language and to what Conversations does it contribute (institutionally, in society, or historically), if any?
F. How does intertexuality work in the text, that is, in what ways does the text quote, allude to, or otherwise borrow words from other oral or written sources? What function does this serve in the text?

Readings
Bakhtin, M. M. (1986). *Speech genres and other late essays.* Austin: University of Texas Press. [A classic book on the ways in which conventions and creativity interact in language use. Bakhtin's notion of "speech genres" is an important notion related to

my notion of "social languages" and he has a great deal to say about intertextuality, though he does not use that term]

Baugh, J. (1999). *Out of the mouths of slaves: African-American language and educational malpractice*. Austin: University of Texas Press [An essential source on African-American dialects and the issues they raise in education]

Baugh, J. (2000). *Beyond Ebonics: Linguistic pride and racial prejudice*. New York: Oxford University Press. [The best discussion of the so-called "Ebonics Controversy" by one of the outstanding linguists writing on language, ethnicity, and culture today]

Billig, M. (1987). *Arguing and thinking: A rhetorical approach to social psychology*. Cambridge: Cambridge University Press. [A good discussion of what I have called "Conversations," though Billig does not use the term]

Collins, J. C. & Porras, J. I. (1994). *Built to last: Successful habits of visionary companies*. New York: Harper Business. [An influential business book that discusses companies' "vision statements," statements which almost always relate to Conversations]

Fairclough, N. (1992). *Discourse and social change*. Cambridge: Polity Press. [One of many works by the best-known scholar in critical discourse analysis—called "CDA" when Fairclough's work is being referred to]

Halliday, M. A. K. & Martin, James R. (1993). *Writing science: Literacy and discursive power*. Pittsburg, PA: University of Pittsburg Press. [An important discussion of how certain sorts of grammatical patterns characterize writing in science, with variation across different types of science and science writing]

Myers, G. (1990). *Writing biology: Texts in the social construction of scientific knowledge*. Madison: University of Wisconsin Press. [A fascinating and important book on how science is written and how such writing relates to social, cultural, institutional, and historical factors]

von Frank, A. J. (1998). *The trial of Anthony Burns: Freedom and slavery in Emerson's Boston*. Cambridge, MA: Harvard University Press. [An interesting book on the different historically important Conversations involved in slavery and returning runaway slaves]

CHAPTER FIVE

Form–Function Correlations, Situated Meanings, and Figured Worlds

Meaning

The primary tools of inquiry we will discuss in this chapter are "form–function correlations," "situated meanings," and "figured worlds." Form–function correlations deal with the general range of meanings that grammatical units (e.g., noun phrases, subjects of sentences, subordinate clauses) can have. Situated meanings deal with the highly specific meanings words and phrases take on in actual contexts of use. Figured worlds are (often unconscious) theories and stories that we humans use to understand and deal with the world. I will also discuss the nature of "critical discourse analysis" in this chapter.

Form–Function Correlations

Linguists make an important distinction between utterance-type meaning and utterance-token meaning. Any word, phrase, or structure has a general range of possible meanings, what we might call its meaning range. This is its utterance-type meaning. For example, the word "cat" has to do, broadly, with felines; the (syntactic) structure "subject of a sentence" has to do, broadly, with naming a "topic" in the sense of "what is being talked about."

However, words and phrases take on much more specific meanings in actual contexts of use. These are utterance-token meanings or what I will call "situated meanings." Thus, in a situation where we say something like "The world's big cats are all endangered," "cat" means things like lions and tigers; in a situation where we are discussing mythology and say something like "The cat was a sacred symbol to the ancient Egyptians," "cat" means real and pictured cats as symbols; and in a situation where we are discussing breakable decorative objects on our mantel and say something like "The cat broke," "cat" means a statue of a cat.

Subjects of sentences are always "topic-like" (this is their utterance-type meaning); in different situations of use, subjects take on a range of more specific meanings. In a debate, if I say, "The constitution only protects the rich," the subject of the sentence ("the constitution") is an entity about which a claim is being made; if a friend of yours has just arrived and I usher her in saying "Mary's here," the subject of the sentence ("Mary") is a center of interest or attention; and in a situation where I am commiserating with a friend and say something like "You really got cheated by that guy," the subject of the sentence ("you") is a center of empathy (signaled also by the fact that the normal subject of the active version of the sentence—"That guy really cheated you"— has been "demoted" from subject position through use of the "get-passive").

Discourse analysis can undertake one or both of two tasks: one related to utterance-type (general) meaning and one related to situated meaning (Levinson 1983). One task, then, is what we can call the utterance-type meaning task. This task involves the study of correlations between form and function in language at the level of utterance-type meanings (general meanings). "Form" here means things like morphemes, words, phrases, or other syntactic structures (e.g., the subject position of a sentence). "Function" means meaning or the communicative purpose a form carries out.

The other task is what we can call the utterance-token meaning or situated meaning task. This task involves the study of correlations between form and function in language at the level of utterance-token meanings. Essentially, this task involves discovering the situation-specific or situated meanings of forms used in specific contexts of use.

Failing to distinguish between these two tasks can be dangerous, since very different issues of validity for discourse analysis come up with each of these tasks, as we will see below. Let me start with an example of the utterance-type meaning task. Specific forms in a language are prototypically used as tools to carry out certain communicative functions (that is, to express certain meanings). For example, consider the sentence labeled (1) below (adapted from Gagnon 1987, p. 65):

1. Though the Whig and Tory parties were both narrowly confined to the privileged classes, they represented different factions and tendencies.

This sentence is made up of two clauses, an independent (or main) clause ("they represented different factions and tendencies") and a dependent clause ("Though the Whig and Tory parties were both narrowly confined to the privileged classes"). These are statements about form. An independent clause has as one of its functions (at the utterance-type level) that it expresses an assertion; that is, it expresses a claim that the speaker/writer is making. A dependent clause has as one of its functions that it expresses information that is not asserted, but, rather, assumed or taken-for-granted. These are statements about function (meaning).

Normally in English, dependent clauses follow independent clauses. Thus, the sentence (1) above might more normally appear as: "The Whig and Tory parties represented different factions, though they were both narrowly confined to the privileged classes." In (1) the dependent clause has been fronted (placed in front of the whole sentence). This is a statement about form. Such fronting has as one of its functions that the information in the clause is thematized, that is, the information is treated as a launching-off point or thematically important context from which to consider the claim in the following dependent clause. This is a statement about function.

To sum up, in respect to form–functioning mapping at the utterance-type level, we can say that sentence (1) renders its dependent clause ("Though the Whig and Tory parties were both narrowly confined to the privileged classes") a taken-for-granted, assumed, unargued for (i.e., unasserted), though important (thematized) context from which to consider the main claim in the independent clause ("they represented different factions and tendencies"). The dependent clause is, we might say, a concession. Other historians might prefer to make this concession the main asserted point and, thus, would use a different grammar, perhaps saying something like: "Though they represented different factions and tendencies, the Whig and Tory parties were both narrowly confined to the privileged classes."

At a fundamental level, all types of discourse analysis involve claims (however tacitly they may be acknowledged) about form–function matching at the utterance-type level. This is so because, if one is making claims about a piece of language, even at a much more situated and contextualized level (which we will see in a moment), but these claims violate what we know about how form and function are related to each other in language at the utterance-type level, then these claims are quite suspect, unless there is evidence the speaker or writer is trying to violate these sorts of basic grammatical relationships in the language (e.g., in poetry).

As I have already said, the meanings with which forms are correlated at the utterance-type level are rather general (meanings like "assertion," "taken-for-granted information," "contrast," etc.). In reality, they represent only the meaning potential or meaning range of a form or structure, as we have said. The more specific or situated meanings that a form carries in a given context of use must be figured out by an engagement with our next task, the utterance-token or situated-meaning task.

Form–function correlations give another "tool of inquiry" for discourse analysis. Form–function correlations define the potential any given form has for taking on much more specific meanings in contexts of actual use. These more specific meanings we will call "situated meanings." I assume any discourse analysis is aware of (and honors) the general form–function correlations that exist in the language being analyzed. In some cases, form–function analysis is all we may do, and such analyses can be informative and important. However, most often the real action of discourse analysis, where it really has its biggest bite, is at the level of analyzing situated meanings.

Situated Meaning

A second task that discourse analysis can undertake is what I called above the utterance-token or situated meaning task. For simplicity's sake, I will now just call this "the situated meaning task." When we actually utter or write a sentence it has a situated meaning. Situated meanings arise because particular language forms take on specific or situated meanings in specific different contexts of use.

Consider the word "coffee" as a very simple example of how situated meaning differs from utterance-type meaning. "Coffee" is an arbitrary form (other languages use different sounding words for coffee) that correlates with meanings having to do with the substance coffee (this is its meaning potential). At a more specific level, however, we have to use context to determine what the word means in any situated way. In one context, "coffee" may mean a brown liquid ("The coffee spilled, go get a mop"); in another one it may mean grains of a certain sort ("The coffee spilled, go get a broom"); in another it may mean containers ("The coffee spilled, stack it again"); and it can mean other things in other contexts, e.g., berries of a certain sort, a certain flavor, or a skin color. We can even use the word with a novel situated meaning, as in "You give me a coffee high" or "Big Coffee is as bad as Big Oil as corporate actors."

To see a further example of situated meanings at work, consider sentence (1) again ("Though the Whig and Tory parties were both narrowly confined to the privileged classes, they represented different factions"). We said above that an independent clause represents an assertion (a claim that something is true). But this general form–function correlation can mean different specific things in actual contexts of use, and can, indeed, even be mitigated or undercut altogether.

For example, in one context, say between two like-minded historians, the claim that the Whig and Tory parties represented different factions may just be taken as a reminder of a "fact" they both agree on. On the other hand, between two quite diverse historians, the same claim may be taken as a challenge (despite YOUR claim that shared class interests make no real difference in political parties, the Whig and Tory parties in seventeenth-century England were really different). And, of course, on stage as part of a drama, the claim about the Whig and Tory parties is not even a "real" assertion, but a "pretend" one.

Furthermore, the words "privileged," "contending," and "factions" will take on different specific meanings in different contexts. For example, in one context, "privileged" might mean "rich," while in another context it might mean "educated" or "cultured" or "politically connected" or "born into a family with high status" or some combination of the above or something else altogether.

To analyze Gagnon's sentence or his whole text, or any part of it, at the level of situated meanings—that is, in order to carry out the situated-meaning task— would require a close study of some of the relevant contexts within which that text is placed and which it, in turn, helps to create. This might mean inspecting the parts of Gagnon's text that precede or follow a part of the text we want to analyze. It might mean inspecting other texts related to Gagnon's. It might mean studying debates among different types of historians and debates about educational standards and policy (since Gagnon's text was meant to argue for a view about what history ought to be taught in schools). It might mean studying these debates historically across time and in terms of the actual situations Gagnon and his text were caught up in (e.g., debates about new school history standards in Massachusetts, a state where Gagnon once helped write a version of the standards). It might mean many other things, as well. Unfortunately, we do not have the space in this book to develop such an analysis here.

The issue of validity for analyses of situated meaning is quite different than the issue of validity for analyses of utterance-type meanings. We saw above that the issue of validity for analyses of utterance-type meanings basically comes down to choosing and defending a particular grammatical theory of how form and function relate in language at the level of utterance-type meanings, as well as, of course, offering correct grammatical and semantic descriptions of one's data. On the other hand, the issue of validity for analyses of situated meaning is much harder. In fact, it involves a very deep problem, the "frame problem." We will discuss the frame problem below.

The Frame Problem

The frame problem is this: Any aspect of context can affect the meaning of an (oral or written) utterance. Context, however, is indefinitely large, ranging from local matters like the positioning of bodies and eye gaze, through people's beliefs, to historical, institutional, and cultural settings. No matter how much of the context we have considered in offering an interpretation of an utterance, there is always the possibility of considering other and additional aspects of the context, and these new considerations may change how we interpret the utterance. Where do we cut off consideration of context? How can we be sure any interpretation is "right," if considering further aspects of the context might well change that interpretation?

Let me give an example of a case where changing how much of the context of an utterance we consider changes significantly the interpretation we give to that utterance. Take a claim like: "Many children die in Africa before they are five years old because they get infectious diseases like malaria." What is the appropriate amount of context within which to assess this claim? We could consider just medical facts, a narrow context. And in the context the claim seems unexceptional.

But widen the context and consider the wider context described below:

Malaria, an infectious disease, is one of the most severe public health problems worldwide. It is a leading cause of death and disease in many developing countries, where young children and pregnant women are the groups most affected. Worldwide, one death in three is from an infectious or communicable disease. However, almost all these deaths occur in the non-industrialized world. Health inequality affects not just how people live, but often dictates how and at what age they die. (See: http://www.cdc.gov/malaria/impact/index.htm and http://ucatlas.ucsc.edu/cause.php)

This context would seem to say that so many children in Africa die early not because of infectious diseases but because of poverty and economic underdevelopment. While this widening of the context does not necessarily render the claim "Many children die in Africa before they are five years old because they get infectious diseases like malaria" false, it, at least, suggests that a narrow construal of "because" here (limiting it to physical and medical causes) effaces the workings of poverty and economics.

The frame problem is both a problem and a tool. It is a problem because our discourse analytic interpretations (just like people's everyday interpretations of language) are always vulnerable to changing as we widen the context within which we interpret a piece of language. It is a tool because we can use it—widening the context—to see what information and values are being left unsaid or effaced in a piece of language.

The frame problem, of course, raises problems about validity for discourse analysis. We cannot really argue an analysis is valid unless we keep widening the context in which we consider a piece of language until the widening appears to make no difference to our interpretation. At that point, we can stop and make our claims (open, of course, to later falsification as in all empirical inquiry).

Critical Discourse Analysis

Some forms of discourse analysis add a third task to the two (the utterance-type meaning task and the situated meaning task) discussed so far. They study, as well, the ways in which either or both of language–form correlations at the utterance-type level (task 1) and situated meanings (task 2) are associated with **social practices** (task 3). While non-critical approaches can and do, indeed, study social practices, critical approaches and non-critical ones take a different approach to social practices and how to study them. Non-critical approaches tend to treat social practices solely in terms of patterns of social interaction (e.g., how people use language to "pull off" a job interview).

Thus, consider again the sentence from Gagnon we discussed above:

1. Though the Whig and Tory parties were both narrowly confined to the privileged classes, they represented different factions and tendencies

A non-critical form of discourse analysis could well point out the fact that using "Though the Whig and Tory parties were both narrowly confined to the privileged classes" as a dependent (and, thus, assumed and unasserted) clause sets up a social relationship with the reader in terms of which the reader should accept, as given and assumed, that distinctions of wealth in a society are less central to the development of democracy than political differences within elites in the society (which the main asserted clause is about).

Critical approaches, however, go further and treat social practices, not just in terms of social relationships, but, also, in terms of their implications for things like status, solidarity, the distribution of social goods, and power (e.g., how language in a job interview functions as a gate-keeping device allowing some sorts of people access and denying it to others). In fact, critical discourse analysis argues that language-in-use is always part and parcel of, and partially constitutive of, specific social practices and that social practices always have implications for inherently political things like status, solidarity, the distribution of social goods, and power.

So the issue becomes this: Is it enough to leave the analysis of the social at the level of how talk and texts function in social interactions or do we need to go further and consider, as well, how talk and text function *politically* in social interactions? Does the latter task render discourse analysis—and, thus perforce, critical discourse analysis—"unscientific" or "unacademic," a mere matter of "advocacy"?

Consider sentence (1) again. There are historians who think that class conflict—conflict between haves and have nots—drives history. They would say that the fact that the Whig and Tory parties were narrowly confined to the privileged classes is a key fact about the political situation of seventeenth-century England (though Gagnon places it in a subordinate clause). This fact, they will say, drove change because it led to the non-elites fighting for representation.

What Gagnon has done is put what these historians see as the key point in a subordinate clause and treated it as assumed and backgrounded information that, while important, does not challenge his main claim that the Whig and Tory parties represented different factions (and, thus, for Gagnon were in the forefront of the development of democracy in Western society). His formulation is a move not only in an academic argument with such historians but in political debates about what and how history ought to be taught in school.

This is an essential aspect to understanding not just what Gagnon is saying, but what he is trying to do. It moves us beyond social interactions between writer and reader and to value-laden positions that are "political." Claims, like Gagnon's, do not come out of nowhere. They are part of ongoing dialogue or debate and are understood within that dialogue or debate. Thus, a full discourse must discuss such matters and must, in that sense, be critical. When we discussed the "building tasks" in Chapter 2, I offered yet another, more general, reason why all language use is "political" and, thus, why discourse analysis ought to be critical. I defined what I meant by "politics" as contestation over "the distribution of social goods" and argued that all language use involves perspectives on the distribution of social goods.

Figured Worlds

Is the Pope a bachelor? Though the Pope is an unmarried man—and "bachelor" as a word is defined as "an unmarried man"—we are reluctant to call the Pope a bachelor. Why? The reason is that we do not use words just based on their definitions or what we called earlier their "general meanings." We use words based, as well, on stories, theories, or models in our minds about what is "normal" or "typical."

It is typical in our world that men marry women. A man who is somewhat past the typical age when people marry we call a "bachelor," assuming he is open to marriage but has either chosen to wait or has not found the "right" person. The Pope is both well past the normal age for marriage and has vowed never to marry. He just does not fit the typical story in our heads.

We use words based on such typical stories unless something in the context makes us think the situation is not typical. If the issue of gay marriage or the chauvinism of calling men "bachelors" and women "spinsters" comes up, then we have to think more overtly about matters and abandon, if only for the time, our typical picture. Indeed, things can change in society enough that what counts as a typical story changes or becomes contested. People may even stop using words like "bachelor" based on the typical story and form a new typical story—and, thus, start calling marriage-eligible women "bachelors" as well.

We use such typical pictures so that we can go on about the business of communicating, acting, and living without having to consciously think about everything—all the possible details and exceptions—all the time. This is good for getting things done, but sometimes bad in the ways in which such typical stories can marginalize people and things that are not taken as "normal" or "typical" in the story.

What counts as a typical story for people differs by their social and culture groups. For example, some parents confronted by a demanding two-year-old who angrily refuses to go to bed take the child's behavior as a sign of growth towards autonomy because they accept a typical story like this: Children are born dependent on their parents and then grow towards individual autonomy or independence. On their way to autonomy, they act out, demanding independence, when they may not yet be ready for it, but this is still a sign of development and growth. Other parents confronted by the same behavior take the behavior as a sign of the child's willfulness because they accept a typical story like this: Children are born selfish and need to be taught to think of others and collaborate with the family rather than demand their own way.

It is, perhaps, not surprising that this latter typical story is more common among working-class families where mutual support among family and friends is important. The former story is more common among middle- and upper-middle-class families with many more financial resources where people are expected to grow into adults who have the resources to go it more on their own.

Such typical stories are not "right" or "wrong." For example, children are, of course, born dependent on their parents. But are children primarily inherently selfish and in need of being taught how to cooperate with others or are they inherently reliant on caregivers and in need of learning to be independent? The different stories we discussed are probably both true in some sense, but one or the other can be stressed and form the main parenting style in the home. They are simplified theories of the world that are meant to help people go on about the business of life when one is not allowed the time to think through and research everything before acting. Even theories in science are simplified views of the world meant to help scientists cope, without having to deal with the full complexity of the world all at once.

These typical stories have been given many different names. They have been called "folk theories," "frames," "scenarios," "scripts," "mental models," "cultural models," "Discourse models," and "figured worlds" (and each of these terms has its own nuances). Such typical stories are stored in our heads (and we will see in a moment that they are not always only in our heads) in the form of images, metaphors, and narratives.

We will use the term "figured world" here for these typical stories. The term "figured world" has been defined as follows:

> A socially and culturally constructed realm of interpretation in which particular characters and actors are recognized, significance is assigned to certain acts, and particular outcomes are valued over others. Each is a simplified world populated by a set of agents who engage in a limited range of meaningful acts or changes of state as moved by a specific set of forces. (Holland *et al.*, 1998, p. 52)

A figured world is a picture of a simplified world that captures what is taken to be typical or normal. What is taken to be typical or normal, of course, varies by context and by people's social and cultural group (as we saw in the example of acting out two-year-olds above). For example, if I ask you to imagine a suburban bedroom you will populate the room with people and things in a quite different way than if I ask you to imagine a bedroom in a college dorm. You base what you take to be typical on your experiences, and since people's experiences vary in terms of their social and cultural groups, people vary in what they take to be typical. And, again, as society changes what people take as typical can and does change. Figured worlds are not static.

To give another example, consider the figured world (or typical story) that might arise in someone's mind if they think about an elementary school classroom: Typical participants include one teacher (a female) and a group of kids of roughly the same age and some support staff, including teachers who help kids with special problems (e.g., learning disabilities, reading problems, or who are learning English as a second language), sometimes by pulling them out of the classroom. The kids are sitting in desks in rows facing the teacher, who is doing most of the talking and sometimes asks the kids questions to which she knows the answers. There are activities like filling out sheets of paper with math problems on them. There are regular tests, some of them state standardized tests. There is an institution surrounding the teacher that includes a principal and other teachers as well as curriculum directors and mandates from officials. Parents are quasi "outsiders" to this institution. There are labels for individual kids, labels such as "SPED" (special education), "LD" (learning disabled), and "ESL" (English as a Second Language).

This figured world—with its typical participants, activities, forms of language, and object and environments—is, of course, realized in many actual classrooms. However, there are many exceptions, as well, but they do not normally come to mind when we think and talk about schools. In fact, every aspect of this figured world is heavily contested in one or more current school-reform efforts (e.g., age grading, lots of testing, skill sheets, too much teacher talk, children in rows, etc.). The taken-for-granted nature of the figured world, however, often stands in the way of change. Reforms just do not seem "normal" or "right" or "the way things should be." For example, today it is not uncommon that young children can teach adults things about digital technology, but the child teaching and the teacher learning violates our typical story. It also violates the values and structures of authority this typical story incorporates.

I have said that these typical stories—what we are calling figured worlds— are in our heads. But that is not strictly true. Often they are partly in our heads and partly out in the world in books and other media and in other people's heads, people we can talk to. The figured world in which children are born dependent and development is progress towards individual autonomy and independence as adults who can manage their own lives based on their own resources is a model that is found in lots of child-raising self-help books and in the talk and actions of many parents who are professionals (e.g., doctors, lawyers, professors, executives, and so forth) with whom we can interact if we live in the right neighborhood.

Figured worlds give us yet another tool for discourse analysis. For any communication, we want to ask what typical stories or figured worlds the words and phrases of the communication are assuming and inviting listeners to assume. What participants, activities, ways of interacting, forms of language, people, objects, environments, and institutions, as well as values, are in these figured worlds?

Form–Function Correlations, Situated Meanings, and Figured Worlds are Tools of Inquiry

In this chapter, I have once again treated the terms "form–function correlations," "situated meaning," and "figured worlds" realistically. That is, I have spoken about them as things that exist in the mind and in the world. And, indeed, this is, I believe, both true and the easiest way to grasp what they mean and how and why they are significant for discourse analysis.

But it is important to realize that, in the end, these terms are ultimately our ways as theoreticians and analysts of talking about and, thus, constructing and construing the world. And it is in this guise that I am primarily interested in them. They are "tools of inquiry." I will discuss figured worlds as tools of inquiry more thoroughly in the next chapter. Here I want to sketch out what I mean by "situated meaning" as a tool of inquiry.

At the outset of this chapter, I discussed form–function analysis, that is, general pairing of language forms with certain rather general functions they can carry out. This sort of analysis defines the potential any given form has for taking on much more specific meanings in contexts of actual use. These more specific meanings we have called "situated meanings." I assume any discourse analysis is aware of (and honors) the general form–function correlations that exist in the language being analyzed. In some cases, form–function analysis is all we may do and such analyses can be informative and important. However, most often the real action of discourse analysis, where it really has its biggest bite, is at the level of analyzing situated meanings.

"Situated meaning" is a "thinking device" that guides us to ask certain sorts of questions. Faced with a piece of oral or written language, we consider a certain key word or a family of key words, that is, words we hypothesize are important to understanding the language we wish to analyze. We consider, as well, all that we can learn about the context that this language is both used in and helps to create or construe in a certain way. We then ask the following sorts of questions:

A. What situated meaning or meanings for a given word or phrase is it reasonable to attribute to their "author," considering the point of view of the Discourse in which words were used (e.g., the Discourse of biology or the very different Discourse of fundamentalist creationism)?
B. What situated meaning or meanings for a given word or phrase is it reasonable to attribute to those who are listening to or reading these words or phrases, again considering the Discourse in which these words are used?
C. What situated meaning or meanings for a word or phrase is it reasonable to attribute to those who are listening to or reading these words or phrases, from the point of view of *other* Discourses than the one in which the words were uttered or written? These other Discourses might be ones that bring different values, norms, perspectives, and assumptions to the situation. For example, what sorts of situated meanings might a fundamentalist creationist give to a text in biology or a Native American to an American history text if they chose to interpret the text from the point of view of their own Discourse and not the one from which the text had originally been produced?
D. What situated meaning or meanings is it reasonable, from the point of view of the Discourse in which these words were used or of other Discourses, to assume are *potentially* attributable to these words by interpreters, whether or not we have evidence anyone actually activated that potential in the current case?

Our answers to these questions are always tentative. They are always open to revision as we learn more about the context. And, we can nearly always learn more about the material, social, cultural, and historical contexts in which the words were uttered or written. However, at some point, what we learn may well cease to change our answers to these sorts of questions in any very substantive way.

Our tentative answers are testable in a variety of different ways, including (but not exhausted by) asking actual and possible producers and receivers what they think (remembering that many, but not all, aspects of situated meanings and Discourse models are unconscious); looking at the verbal and non-verbal effects of the language in the present and future (e.g., how people react and respond); looking at how the past led up to these words and deeds; looking at similar and contrasting uses of language; and appealing to a wide and diverse array of linguistic and contextual factors, as well as different tools of inquiry, at different levels, that we hope converge on the same answer. These sorts of concerns lead us to issues about validity, issues which I will take up in Chapter 8 after I have introduced a variety of other tools of inquiry.

Readings
(Note: Readings relevant to cultural models and figured worlds are cited in the Readings section at the end of the next chapter, a chapter devoted to figured worlds.)

Duranti, A. (1992). *Linguistic anthropology*. Cambridge: Cambridge University Press. [The best introduction to linguistic anthropology]
Duranti, A. & Goodwin, C., Eds. (1992). *Rethinking context: Language as an interactive phenomenon*. Cambridge: Cambridge University Press. [A set of good papers on the role of context in interpretation]
Fairclough, N. (1989). *Language and power*. London: Longman. [Fairclough's approach to critical discourse analysis is just called "CDA" and is the best-known such approach]
Fairclough, N. (1992). *Discourse and social change*. Cambridge: Polity Press.
Fairclough, N. (1995). *Critical discourse analysis*. London: Longman.
Fairclough, N. (2003). *Analysing discourse: Textual analysis for social research*. London: Routledge.
Gagnon, P. (1987). *Democracy's untold story: What world history textbooks neglect*. Washington, DC: American Federation of Teachers. [I use this book for data, since it is a good example of an historian writing with a clear purpose to change public policy]
Gumperz, J. J. (1982). *Discourse strategies*. Cambridge: Cambridge University Press. [A classic on analyzing language in context]
Gumperz, J. J. & Levinson, S. C., Eds. (1996). *Rethinking linguistic relativity*. Cambridge: Cambridge University Press. [Good papers on language and culture]
Halliday, M. A. K. (1994). *An introduction to functional grammar*. Second Edition. London: Edward Arnold. [The best source for reflecting on form–function correlations in language]
Kress, G. (1985). *Linguistic processes in sociocultural practice*. Oxford: Oxford University Press. [A masterful book on language as practice from a social semiotic perspective]
Levinson, S. C. (1983). *Pragmatics*. Cambridge: Cambridge University Press. [A very good book on pragmatics—a close relative of discourse analysis—with a good discussion of form–function correlations and type-utterance and token-utterance meanings]
Rogers, R., Ed. (2004). *An introduction to critical discourse analysis in education*. Mahwah, NJ: Lawrence Erlbaum. [A good collection of papers on critical discourse analysis and its applications to education]

CHAPTER SIX

More on Figured Worlds

Figured Worlds

This chapter will focus exclusively on figured worlds, a concept we introduced in the last chapter. The term "figured world" is a name for something that people have called by many different names. Cultural model, discourse model, Discourse model, folk theory, as well as certain uses of schema, frame, and script, are a few of the names that have been used, each with somewhat different meanings. Figured worlds are simplified, often unconscious, and taken-for-granted theories or stories about how the world works that we use to get on efficiently with our daily lives. We learn them from experiences we have had, but, crucially, as these experiences are guided, shaped, and normed by the social and cultural groups to which we belong. From such experiences we infer what is "normal" or "typical" (e.g., what a "normal" man or child or policeman looks and acts like; what a "normal" marriage is like; what a "normal" classroom looks and acts like) and tend to act on these assumptions unless something clearly tells us that we are facing an exception.

Why use the term "figured worlds"? In the first edition of this book I used the term "cultural model." In the second edition I used the term "Discourse model." The term "figured world" has the advantage of stressing that what we are talking about here is ways in which people picture or construe aspects of the world in their heads, the ways they have of looking at aspects of the world. We humans store these figured worlds in our heads in terms of stories, ideas, and images. We build little worlds, models, simulations—whatever term we want to use—in our heads in terms of which we seek to understand and act in the real world. When I use the term "figured world" in this chapter, you can substitute, as well, terms like "model," "theory," "story," and "way of looking at some aspect of the world."

Figured worlds are an important tool of inquiry because they mediate between the "micro" (small) level of interaction and the "macro" (large) level of institutions. They mediate between the local interactional work we humans do in carrying out the seven building tasks discussed in Chapter 2 and Discourses as they operate to create the complex patterns of institutions and cultures across societies and history.

For example, when I was growing up, the Discourse of heterosexual romance (i.e., enacting and being recognized as an acceptable "date" and potential partner) and actual dating practices were mediated by a bevy of figured worlds, one of which held that women brought "beauty" as their prime asset to a relationship and men brought "intelligence" and potential career success as their prime asset. This model has changed a good bit, and, so, too, then, have actual dating practices.

The role of figured worlds was first made clear in a classic paper by the linguist Charles Fillmore (1975), who used the term "frame" instead of "figured world." Fillmore used a deceptively simple example: the word "bachelor." All of us think we know what the word "bachelor" means: like dictionaries, we all think it means "an unmarried man."

Fillmore, however, asked questions like: Is the Pope a bachelor? Is a thrice-divorced man a bachelor? Is a young man who has been in an irreversible coma since childhood a bachelor? What about a eunuch? A committed gay man? An elderly senile gentleman who has never been married? The answer to all these questions is either "no" or "I'm not sure" (as I have discovered by asking a variety of people). Why? After all, all these people are unmarried men.

The reason why the answer to these questions is "no," despite the fact that they all involve cases of clearly unmarried males, is that we actually use the word "bachelor" (and any other word) in relation to a largely taken-for-granted "theory," what, in the last chapter, I called a "figured world." One way to think about figured worlds is as images or storylines or descriptions of simplified worlds in which prototypical events unfold. They are our "first thoughts" or taken-for-granted assumptions about what is "typical" or "normal." We defined them in the last chapter as:

> A socially and culturally constructed realm of interpretation in which particular characters and actors are recognized, significance is assigned to certain acts, and particular outcomes are valued over others. Each is a simplified world populated by a set of agents who engage in a limited range of meaningful acts or changes of state as moved by a specific set of forces. (Holland *et al.*, 1998, p. 52)

We will see below that when figured worlds are brought to our attention, we can often acknowledge they are really simplifications about the world, simplifications which leave out many complexities. But, then, all theories, even theories in science, are simplifications useful for some purposes and not others. Unfortunately, the simplifications in figured worlds can do harm by implanting in thought and action unfair, dismissive, or derogatory assumptions about other people.

The most commonly used figured world for the word "bachelor" is (or used to be) something like the following by Fillmore (1975):

> Men marry women at a certain age; marriages last for life; and in such a world, a bachelor is a man who stays unmarried beyond the usual age, thereby becoming eminently marriageable. We know that this simplified world is not always true, but it is the one against which we use the word "bachelor," that is, make choices about what other words are excluded as applicable or not, and make assumptions about what the relevant context is in a given case of using the word. Thus, the Pope is not a bachelor because he just isn't in this simplified world, being someone who has vowed not to marry at any age. Nor are gay men, since they have chosen not to marry women.

Figured worlds often involve us in exclusions that are not at first obvious and which we are often unaware of making. In the case of "bachelor" we are actually excluding people like gay individuals and priests as "normal" men, and assuming that men come in two "normal" types: those who get married early and those who get married late. This assumption, of course, marginalizes people who do not want to get married or do not want to marry members of the opposite sex. It is part of the function of figured worlds, in fact, to set up what count as central, typical cases, and what count as marginal, non-typical cases.

There is, of course, another exclusion that is made via the figured world for "bachelor." If men become "eminently marriageable" when they stay unmarried beyond the usual age, then this can only be because we have assumed that after that age there is a shortage of "desirable" men and a surplus of women who want them, women who, thus, aren't "eminently marriageable," or, at least, not as "eminently marriageable" as the men. Hence, we get the most common figured world associated with "spinster."

Fillmore's example raises another important point that further shows up the connection between figured worlds and "politics." Thanks to feminism, lots of people have become consciously aware of the figured world behind the word "bachelor." Many have come to reject it, thereby either dropping the word or changing its meaning. For example, many people now use the word "bachelor" for unmarried women, thus giving the word new meanings and applying it against a new figured world. Other people use a word like "spinster" as a badge of honor and respect, once again creating new meanings and figured worlds.

The "bite" of Fillmore's example is this: if any word in English seems to have a clear "definition," it is a word like "bachelor." But this word is not used in terms of a definition, but rather against a set of social and Discourse assumptions that constitute a figured world. If this is true of a word like "bachelor," how much more likely is it to be true of words like "democracy," "justice," "intelligent," or "literate," for instance?

Simulations in the Mind

The "bachelor" example is, of course, too simple. There are lots of different sorts of figured worlds and lots of different ways to think and talk about them. Figured worlds are rooted in our actual experiences in the world, but, rather like movies, those experiences have been edited to capture what is taken to be essential or typical. In fact, figured worlds are linked to *simulations* we run in our minds, simulations that help us to think about things and to prepare ourselves for action in the world. Let me say how this works.

We have experiences in the world, including things we have experienced only in the media. Take as an example your experiences of weddings. These experiences are raw materials that our minds can work on—can seek to find order and pattern in—in order to think about and prepare actions in regard to future weddings and related events. Based on these experiences, we can build a *simulation* of a wedding in our mind. We can move around as a character in the simulation as ourselves, imaging our role in the wedding, or we can "play" other characters at the wedding (e.g., the minister), imaging what it is like to be that person.

Simulations are common in video games and in science today. Games like *SimCity*, *The Sims*, and *Spore* allow players to build simulations (virtual worlds) of aspects of cities, families, and worlds respectively. Scientists use computers to build simulations that model how things like weather patterns, chemicals inside cells, or traffic patterns work. The scientist can build a simulation of cars moving at various speeds and braking for other cars changing lanes on a crowded freeway, let the simulation run for a certain amount of time, and watch what happens to traffic flow under certain conditions. The scientist can then check to see if similar things happen in the real world when conditions are like those set up in the simulation. In turn, the scientist can change some of the variables (e.g., the speed of the cars, the number of cars, the number changing lanes at any one time, etc.) and see what then happens. Of course, there are many things—like warfare and natural disasters—that are much safer to study via simulations on a computer than they are to study in real life.

We humans can build such simulations in our minds. We can simulate a typical wedding, job interview, or confrontation with the boss, or we can imagine an untypical one, like a wedding between two men, a job interview in which the interviewer begs us to take the job, or a confrontation with the boss in which the boss admits he's wrong. In this respect, our heads are like a video game or a computer simulation, though, in fact, they are much more powerful and flexible than either games or computers. We build simulations both to help us understand what we are currently seeing, hearing, or reading and to prepare us for action in the world (e.g., the coming battle with the boss).

The simulations we build in our heads of things like weddings are not "neutral." Rather, the simulation is meant to take a *perspective* on weddings. It foregrounds certain aspects of weddings that we take as important or salient. It backgrounds other elements that we think are less important or less salient. It leaves some things out altogether. This is just like the scientist's simulation of traffic flow on the computer. Here, too, certain variables (e.g., number of cars) are foregrounded as central, others are included in the simulation, but backgrounded as less important (e.g., size of each car), and others still are left out altogether (e.g., color of the cars).

However, we do not build just one wedding simulation, store it away once-and-for-all in our minds, and apply it any time the word "wedding" comes up or any time we have to prepare for attending a wedding. No, what we do, rather, is build different simulations on the spot for different specific contexts we are in. In a given situation or conversation involving weddings, we build a simulation that fits that context and helps us to make sense of it. Our simulations are special-built to help us make sense of the specific situations we are in, conversations we are having, or texts we are reading. We imagine what might happen, based on what we have experienced in the past and what we have seen so far in the present, in order to understand what is going on, predict what might happen, and prepare for actions and decisions.

For example, in one case, we might build a simulation that foregrounds weddings as fun, blissful, and full of potential for a long and happy future (perhaps, we have just heard "I'm so happy" from the new bride). In another case, we might build a simulation that foregrounds weddings as complex, stressful, and full of potential for problematic futures (perhaps, we have just heard "I'm so scared" from the new bride). We have had experiences that allow us to build both types of simulations and, indeed, yet others.

As I said, one reason we build our simulations is to help us make sense of things. Sometimes this does not work all that well. For example, every time I see or hear about the sport of cricket, I build simulations based on my experiences of baseball. That is, I use my images and stories of baseball to try to make sense of cricket. I build different simulations on different occasions, since they never seem to work well to make really good sense of what I am seeing or hearing. If I ever got deeper and better experiences of cricket, I could make better simulations. Furthermore, I could then use those experiences, if I had enough of them, to build more direct simulations of cricket worlds, ones less influenced by baseball. I might even be able to use these to understand baseball in a new way by comparing it to some specific cricket simulations.

We also build our simulations to help us prepare for action in the world. We can act in the simulation and test out what consequences follow, before we act in the real world. We can role-play another person in the simulation and try to see what motivates their actions or might follow from them before we respond to them in the real world. In fact, it is this ability to think—really to imagine—before we act that is a large part of what makes us humans "smart."

Thanks to the fact that our experiences in the world are shared with others who are members of the same social and cultural groups as ourselves, our simulations of things like weddings—our expectations for what will happen and not happen at weddings—come to overlap with other people's simulations. They don't need to overlap perfectly, just enough for us to be able to communicate and act together.

Because we do share ways of looking at things with other members of our various social and cultural groups, we all have the capacity to form *prototypical simulations*. Prototypical simulations are what support figured worlds. Prototypical simulations are the sorts of simulations you will run in your head of something like weddings, marriages, committee meetings, romance, and families when you take the situation to be "typical." Of course, what is taken as "typical" differs across different social and cultural groups of people. Your figured world of weddings, for instance, is the sort of simulation you will run (imagine) when you imagine what you (and your social group) take to be "typical" weddings. This is your prototypical simulation of a wedding (in reality, you may have a related set of simulations that together capture what you take to be typical of weddings).

If I tell you to imagine a wedding and give you no more context than that, what you will run in your mind is your prototypical simulation and this is one that you share with other people who think about wedding in similar ways to you—people who have had lots of the same sorts of experiences of weddings that you have had. If I give you more context, say I tell you this is a wedding between two men, then you will realize your prototypical wedding simulation doesn't really work here, in this specific case—this isn't a "typical" case—and you may change your simulation (expectations) accordingly, though keeping as much of the prototypical simulation as you can. You may run a special-case simulation for a wedding between two men, keeping some aspects of the prototypical simulation (e.g., vows), dropping others (e.g., a wedding dress), and adding new elements that don't appear in the prototypical case (e.g., two best men, instead of a best man and a best woman). Of course, you might also stick with your prototypical simulation and refuse to see and call what the two males are doing a "wedding."

Thus, we can run (think of) prototypical simulations of things like weddings in our heads. And, we can adapt them, more or less radically, for specific circumstances. This contrast between prototypical simulations and more special-case simulations is important. Since we take the prototype simulations to capture what is "typical," we often use these prototypes to judge features of our more special-purpose simulations, the ones adjusted for special cases like men marrying men, as "non-normal" or "deviant" in some sense. This is a danger. We can often thereby translate "difference" into "deviance" by moving from "typical" (which we too often take to mean "normal," "acceptable," and "right") to "less typical" (which we then take to mean "non-normal," "not acceptable," and "not right").

Figured worlds are *linked* to simulations in our minds. Simulations are the way the mind handles figured worlds. We build worlds in our minds (much as video-game designers build worlds into their games). But these figured worlds are not just mental. They exist in books and other media, in knowledge we can gain from what other people say and do, and in what we can infer from various social practices around us. They exist, as well, in the metaphors we use. In many cases, individuals do not know all the elements of a figured world, but get parts of it from books, media, or other people as they need to know more. This is so because we humans are capable of gaining experiences vicariously from texts, media, and other people's stories.

For example, I can simulate in my mind a typical "military base," but I would have to trust to various media representations to fill it out more, should I need to, since I have not had near enough actual experiences of my own of such bases. Without such supplementation, I'm not sure I could tell the difference between a typical base and a non-typical one. I would need such supplementation to prepare for thought and action in regard to visiting such a base (let alone living on one). Many poor families feel this way in regard to schools and visits to teachers. Of course, sometimes we are aware that the simulations we can build are in need of such supplementation and sometimes we are not. Of course, there is a danger that we often supplement the aspects of figured worlds we can build on our own with texts, media, and talk that just reinforce what we already believe and value by engaging only with texts, media, and talk from sources we "trust" in the sense that they are "like us" socially, religiously, or culturally and don't challenge us.

All Meaning is Local

It is difficult to appreciate the importance and pervasiveness of figured worlds, or to understand how they work, if we stick only to examples from cultures close to our own. So let me give an example of figured worlds at work adapted from William Hanks's excellent book, *Language and Communicative Practices* (1996). This example will also let us see that figured worlds are at work in even the "simplest" cases of communication and in regard to even the simplest words.

When we watch language-in-action in a culture quite different from our own, even simple interactions can be inexplicable, thanks to the fact that we do not know many of the figured worlds at play. This means that even if we can figure out the situated meanings of some words, we cannot see any sense to why these situated meanings have arisen. So let's move, with Hanks, to Yucatan, Mexico.

In a small town in Yucatan, a Mayan Shaman named "Don Chabo" is sharing a meal with his daughter-in-law, Margot, and a visiting anthropologist. They are all in Margot's house. A young man, named "Yuum," approaches from the outside, and, standing at the window, asks: "Is Don Chabo seated?" Margot replies: "Go over there. He's drinking. Go over there inside." These are about as simple as sentences get.

And yet the meaning of these sentences is not so straightforward after all. For example, the people seated around the table are having a meal, so why does Margot say that Don Chabo is "drinking"? Furthermore, Margot's response implies that Don Chabo is "drinking," despite the fact that he was, at the moment, gazing off into space with a roll in his hand. Indeed, in Mayan, it would have been equally true here to say Don Chabo was "drinking" had he been altogether done with (eating) his meal.

Margot's response implies, as well, that Don Chabo was "seated." Yet, it turns out, it would have been equally true to say he was "seated" had he been standing or even off somewhere else, even taking a bath in his own home.

Or, to take one final example, Margot uses the Mayan word for "there" that means "maximally distant from the speaker," the same word people in Yucatan use for relatives who live outside Yucatan, in other states in the Mexican republic. She does this despite the fact that she is telling Yuum to go into her father-in-law's house, not 10 meters away from hers and within the same compound as her house.

How can it be that people can be "drinking" when they are eating or doing nothing at all? That they are "seated" when they are standing or taking a bath? That they are far distant from something 10 meters away?

Things work this way because Mayans (these Mayans, in any case), though they almost always take food with drink and vice versa, use the words "drink" and "eat" against a figured world of meals in terms of which their morning and evening meals are "drinking" and their larger main meal in the midafternoon is "eating." Furthermore, to these Mayans, as long as the social engagement of mealtime is still going on, regardless of whether the "meal" itself is finished or not, a person is still "drinking" or "eating."

Many Mayans live in walled compounds that contain several houses. Their figured worlds for house and home are, thus, rather different from (some of) ours. They use the word "seated" to mean that one is "at home" and available, regardless of where one is in the compound. Being "available" has, in addition, a special meaning for Shamans, since, of course, the whole business of Shamans brings to the fore a distinctive set of figured worlds. To ask whether a Shaman is "available" is to use this word against these figured worlds and is to ask, in part, whether he is available to engage in counseling.

Finally, Mayans have their own figured worlds, as all of us do, of how physical and social space work and are related. Margot is excluded from her father-in-law's house, unless she has a specific reason to be there, for social reasons having to do with Mayan Discourse figured worlds of social relation-ships and spaces within homes. Thus, she uses the word for "far distant" due to social, rather than physical, distance.

In this brief example, I have, in fact, given you very little of what you really need to know to fully understand these simple sentences (for example, why does Margot, rather than Don Chabo, respond?). To really understand them, even to understand just their "literal meaning," one needs to understand how social hierarchies, gender, meals, social engagements, Shamanism, and a great deal more, work day-to-day in local settings among (certain of the) Mayans.

Hanks devotes dozens of pages of dense, scholarly prose to explicating what these sentences mean, not at any deep symbolic or thematic level, just at the "literal" level. He points out that when a husband asks his wife, early in the morning, in English, "D'the paper come today, sweetheart?" and she answers "It's right on the table," the situation is no less strange, complex, and local, however invisible all this complexity (our own) may be to us.

The moral that Hanks draws from even so simple sentences as these is this: meaning, even literal meaning, is wedded to *local, "on site," social, and Discourse practices*. To put the matter another way: meaning is not general and abstract, not something that resides alone in dictionaries, or even in general symbolic representations inside people's heads. Rather, it is *situated* in specific social and Discourse practices, and is, in fact, continually transformed in those practices. Or to put the matter in the terms we introduced in the last chapter: meaning is a matter of situated meanings, customized in, to, and for context, used always against a rich store of Discourse knowledge (figured worlds and the adaptations we make to them when our prototypical cases do not work) that are themselves "activated" in, for, and by contexts.

This is, of course, as true of English as it is of Mayan, but, since we know our own local practices so thoroughly and unreflectively, the situated and local nature of meaning is largely invisible to us. It is easy for us to miss the specificity and localness of our own practices and think we have general, abstract, even universal meanings. We come to think, when we have confronted no other languages, that "sitting" is just sitting, "drinking" is just drinking, "over there" is just over there. In fact, the situated, social, and Discourse nature of meaning often becomes visible to us only when we confront language-at-work in languages and cultures far distant from our own.

Figured Worlds in Action: Middle-Class Parenting

I want to briefly discuss two now classic examples from the literature on figured worlds (in this research the term "cultural model" was used). Both examples demonstrate the connection between figured worlds and social class, though in different ways. Thus, too, these examples, and others that follow below from my own research, begin our discussion of the social, Discourse, and political issues that are implicated in the study of figured worlds.

The first example is a study of middle-class parents in Cambridge, Massachusetts, in the United States from the work of Harkness, Super, and Keefer (1992). When these parents talked about their children, two closely related and tightly integrated figured worlds were highly salient. One was tied to the notion of "stages of development" through which children pass (we might call it the "stage model"). The other was tied to the notion of the child's growing desire for "independence" as the central theme giving point and direction to these stages (we might call it the "independence model").

For example, consider how one mother talked about her son David:

> he's very definitely been in a stage, for the last three or four months, of wanting to help, everything I do, he wants to help ... And now, I would say in the last month, the intensity of wanting to do everything himself is ... we're really into that stage ... I suppose they're all together ... ya, I suppose they're two parts of the same thing. Independence, reaching out for independence. Anything he wants to do for himself, which is just about everything, that I move in and do for him, will result in a real tantrum. (pp. 165–166)

David's mother later gave as an example of his "wanting to do" things for himself: an episode where she had opened the car door for him when he was having a hard time getting out of the car: "He was very upset, so we had to go back and … close the door" (p. 166). She also attributed David's recent dislike of being dressed or diapered to his growing sense of independence: "he's getting to the point where it's insulting, and he doesn't want to be put on his back to have his diaper changed."

However, in the same interview, David's mother also mentioned another behavior pattern. To get David to sleep, she straps him into his car seat and pretends to be taking him for a drive. He almost immediately falls asleep, and then she returns home, leaving him in the car, with a blanket, to take a nap: "But he goes to sleep so peacefully, without any struggle, usually" (p. 167).

Though this latter pattern is a repeated daily routine, nonetheless, David's mother does not talk about this behavior as part of a "stage." Rather, she says, the behavior "just sort of evolved." This is somewhat remarkable. Being strapped into a car seat and taken for a ride that inevitably ends in a nap might be seen as inconsistent with David's need for "independence," just as having his diaper changed is, and thus equally cause for being "insulted."

Ironically, another pair of parents in the same study use their daughter's active resistance to being put in a car seat as an example of "this whole stage of development" and "the sort of independence thing she's into now," but in the same interview say "the thing that's interesting is that she allows you to clean her up, after changing her, a lot more easily than she used to. She used to hate to be cleaned up. She would twist and squirm."

So, here, too, parents appear to be inconsistent. They take the child's desire not to be manipulated into a car seat as a sign of a growing desire for "independence," but are not bothered by the fact that this desire doesn't seem to carry over to the similar event of having her diaper changed. And, oddly, this little girl exemplifies just the reverse pattern from David (who resents having his diaper changed, but willingly gets strapped into the car seat, even to take a nap).

Many parents, and many others in our culture, consider stages to be "real" things that are "inside" their children. Further, they interpret these stages as signposts on the way to becoming an "independent" (and a rather "de-socialized") person. But, it appears, parents label behaviors part of a stage only when these behaviors represent new behaviors of a sort that both could be seen as negative or difficult and that require from the parents new sorts of responses.

Behaviors that are not problematic in the parent–child relationship—e.g., David yielding to naps in his car seat or the little girl yielding peacefully to being diapered—are not labeled as stages. Furthermore, the parents interpret these potentially negative behaviors which get labeled as stages in terms of a socially valued notion of "independence," a notion that other social groups within our society may well view as socially disruptive or as "anti-social."

These "theories" of or "stories" about "stages" and "independence" are partially conscious and partially unconscious. They are figured worlds (ways to figure or construe the world) and need not be fully in any parent or child's head, consciously or unconsciously, because they are available in the culture in which these parents live—through the media, through written materials, and through interaction with others in the society.

These parents, situated within their own class-based Discourses, have a set of connected figured worlds about child development, stages, interaction between parents and children, and independence. Other social groups operate in terms of different figured worlds. For example, some working-class families operate in terms of figured worlds in which children are seen as inherently willful, independent, and selfish, and in need of socialization that leads not to more independence, but to collaboration with and caring about the needs of family and others.

It is striking that the figured worlds in terms of which the Cambridge families operate are quite similar to the "formal theories" found in child psychology and child-rearing books. This should not really be surprising, however, since these are just the sorts of people that read and write such books. What we have to ask, however, is how much of psychology reflects the figured worlds of upper-middle-class people because psychologists hold these models as part and parcel of their class and culture-bound experiences in the world, and not because they are "true" in any scientific sense?

In more recent work, Annette Lareau, in her book *Unequal Childhoods* (2003) has identified two different models of what it means to raise children. These models are what we would call figured worlds. Her work is a close ethnographic study of child rearing in different homes. One model she calls the "cultivation model." This model is applied mostly, though not exclusively, by middle- and upper-middle-class parents. The other model she calls the "natural growth model." This model is applied mostly, though not exclusively, by non-middle-class parents, parents in the working class or poor parents.

When parents hold the cultivation model they treat their child like a plant that must be constantly monitored and tended. They talk a good deal to their children, especially about topics that do not just involve the here and now. They use a good deal of "book language" and more adult vocabulary around their children, especially in the areas where their children have become "little experts" (e.g., on dinosaurs or trains), something these parents encourage.

Even though they are the ultimate authority in their homes, these parents negotiate with their children so that their children get lots of practice in developing arguments and explanations. They set up, monitor, and facilitate a great number of activities for their children, such as museum trips, travel, camps, special lessons (e.g., music), and special out-of-school activities (e.g., ballet). In the act, they heavily structure their children's free time (and, yes, sometimes over-stress the children). They encourage their children to look adults in the eye and to present themselves to others as a confident and knowledgeable person or at least one with a right to an opinion. They encourage their children to develop mastery with digital tools—using things like games as a gateway—and help their child to relate this mastery to literacy and knowledge development.

Cultivated children can be, in some cases, too empowered, perhaps even at times obnoxious. They can be over-stressed and in need of more free time to just be children or even childish. Their parents, at times, too, can be too empowered and obnoxious. However, regardless of what you think of such parents and their children, the evidence is overwhelming that the cultivated model is deeply connected to success in school and to some aspects of success in society, at least at the level of income and higher-status jobs.

When parents hold the natural growth model, they treat their children like a plant that, with rich enough soil and nutrients, can be left without a lot of extra tending to develop naturally. Such parents love their children and care for them deeply and well. But they do not feel the need to intervene constantly in their children's lives from the earliest years on. Often they cannot intervene as much as more well-off parents anyway because they are busy working and surviving. They talk less to their children and use less book-like and adult language with them. They tend to use more directives and commands with the children and not to negotiate with them much. They expect their children to be respectful and deferential to adults. They do not structure all their children's free time and expect them to learn to find things to do with their peers and by themselves. They do not attempt to direct their children's use of digital media (like games) towards other more school-based skills or engagement with computer software or higher-order literacy skills.

Children raised with the natural growth model are often hard-working, self-sustaining, and respectful. They are not always comfortable with putting themselves forward or presenting themselves as knowledgeable even when they are. They are not always comfortable with engaging in arguments, explanations, and opinions with adults, especially those they do not know. They have not built up lots of language, experience, and knowledge connected to the myriad of activities children raised on the cultivation model have.

Many children raised on the natural growth model have done just fine in school and have become significant successes in life. But, if we are thinking at a statistical level of group trends, they tend to do less well in school and in society, at least in regard to income and positions of power and status, which, of course, are not the only or even the most important markers of success. This is so, of course, in part, because schools themselves assume a cultivation model, but, by and large, leave it to parents to cultivate their children. And we must acknowledge, the two models we have discussed are really poles of a continuum and there are parenting styles in-between.

Lareau's work is a good example of how figured worlds and practices interact to have real effects in society. People "figure" or construe the world of child rearing in certain ways. The figured worlds they use come from experiences they have had, which is why Lareau's two models are class-based, passed on from family to family. Parents' figured worlds about child rearing guide their behavior, their practices in regard to their children.

These practices, in turn, produce different types of children. In turn, institutions in society, like schools, are set up to take certain sorts of children as the norm and to deal with other sorts of children as "deviant," "deficited," or "not ready." Such children, indeed, eventually come to seem "deviant" or "deficited" when the institution never offers them the "cultivation" the institution assumes all "normal" children have and need (so these kids get skill and drill and tracks in which they are closely supervised rather than trips to museums, one-on-one talk with adults, and immersion in passions of their own). Fairness would demand such institutions change either their assumptions or their practices.

Figured Worlds in Conflict

My second example demonstrates that each of us can have allegiance to competing and conflicting figured worlds. It also shows one way in which more powerful groups in society can influence less powerful groups. The example comes from Claudia Strauss"s (1992) studies of working-class men in Rhode Island (Strauss also uses the term "cultural model" instead of "figured world").

Consider for a moment a figured world common in the United States, a theory or story about "success" or "getting ahead," as discussed by Roy D"Andrade (1984):

> It seems to be the case that Americans think that if one has ability, and if, because of competition or one's own strong drive, one works hard at achieving high goals, one will reach an outstanding level of accomplishment. And when one reaches this level one will be recognized as a success, which brings prestige and self-satisfaction. (p. 95)

So pervasive is this figured world in U.S. culture that D"Andrade goes on to say: "Perhaps what is surprising is that anyone can resist the directive force of such a system—that there are incorrigibles" (p. 98). However, people from different social groups within American society relate to this figured world in quite different ways.

Claudia Strauss in her studies of working-class men in Rhode Island talking about their lives and work found that they accepted the above figured world of success. For example, one working man said:

> I believe if you put an effort into anything, you can get ahead. ... If I want to succeed, I"ll succeed. It has to be, come from within here. Nobody else is going to make you succeed but yourself ... And, if anybody disagrees with that, there's something wrong with them. (Strauss 1992, p. 202)

However, most of the men Strauss studied did not, in fact, act on the success model in terms of their career choices or in terms of how they carried out their daily lives. Unlike many white-collar professionals, these men did not choose to change jobs or regularly seek promotions. They did not regularly sacrifice their time with their families and their families' interests for their own career advancement or "self-development." These men recognized the success model as a set of values and, in fact, judged themselves by this model, concluded that they had not really been "successful," and thereby lowered their self-esteem.

The reason these men did not actually act on the success model was due to the influence of another figured world, a theory or story which did affect their actual behaviors. This was the figured world of "being a breadwinner." Unlike the individualism expressed in the success model, these workers, when they talked about their actual lives, assumed that the interests of the family came ahead of the interests of any individual in it, including themselves. For example, one worker said:

> [The worker is discussing the workers' fight against the company's proposal mandating Sunday work] But when that changed and it was negotiated through a contract that you would work, so you had to change or keep losing that eight hours pay. With three children, I couldn't afford it. So I had to go with the flow and work the Sundays. (Strauss 1992, p. 207)

This is in sharp contrast to the white-collar professionals studied in Bellah et al.'s classic book *Habits of the Heart* (1996), professionals who carried their individualism so far as to be unsure whether they had any substantive responsibility to their families if their families' interests stood in the way of their "developing themselves" as individuals. These Rhode Island workers accepted the breadwinner figured world not just as a set of values with which to judge themselves and others. They saw this model not as a matter of choice, but rather as an inescapable fact of life (e.g., "had to change," "had to go with the flow"). Thus, the values connected to this figured world (this way of figuring the world) were much more effective in shaping their routine daily behaviors. In fact, this very distinction—between mere "values" and "hard reality" ("the facts")—is itself a particularly pervasive figured world within Western society.

In contrast to these working-class men, many white-collar professionals work in environments where the daily behaviors of those around them conform to the success figured world more than daily behaviors on the factory floor conform to this way of construing the world. For these professionals, then, their daily observations and social practices reinforce explicit ideological learning in regard to the figured world for success. For them, in contrast to the working-class men Strauss studied, the success figured world, not the breadwinner one, is seen as "an inescapable fact of life," and, thus, for them, this way of construing the world determines not just their self-esteem, but many of their actual behaviors.

The working-class men Strauss studied are, in a sense, "colonized" by the success figured world (we are all, in fact, "colonized" by a good many figured worlds that have come to us without much reflection on our part about how well they fit our interests or serve us in the world). They use it, a way of looking at the world which actually fits the observations and behaviors of other groups in the society, to judge themselves and lower their self-esteem. But, as we have seen, since they fail to identify themselves as actors within that figured world, they cannot develop the very expertise that would allow and motivate them to practice it. In turn, they leave such expertise to the white-collar professionals, some of whom made the above worker work on Sunday against his own interests and wishes. On the other hand, many of these white-collar professionals fail to see that their very allegiance to the success figured world is connected to their failure to be substantive actors in their families or larger social and communal networks.

Different Sorts and Uses of Figured Worlds

What Strauss's study leads us to see is that we need to distinguish between figured worlds based on how they are put to use and on the effects they have on us. We can distinguish between, at least, the following sorts of figured worlds in regard to these issues:

A. *Espoused worlds*, that is, theories, stories, ways of looking at the world which we consciously espouse (say and often think we believe);
B. *Evaluative worlds*, that is, theories, stories, ways of looking at the world which we use, consciously or unconsciously, to judge ourselves or others;
C. *Worlds-in-(inter)action*, that is, theories, stories, or ways of looking at the world that consciously or unconsciously guide our actual actions and interactions in the world (regardless of what we say or think we believe).

Furthermore, figured worlds can be about "appropriate" attitudes, viewpoints, beliefs, and values; "appropriate" ways of acting, interacting, participating, and participant structures; "appropriate" social and institutional organizational structures; "appropriate" ways of talking, listening, writing, reading, and communicating; "appropriate" ways to feel or display emotion; "appropriate" ways in which real and fictional events, stories, and histories are organized and end, and so on and so forth.

Figured worlds are complexly, though flexibly, organized. There are smaller figured worlds inside bigger ones. Each figured world triggers or is associated with others, in different ways in different settings and differently for different socioculturally defined groups of people. And, we can talk about "master figured worlds," that is, sets of associated figured worlds, or single figured worlds, that help shape and organize large and important aspects of experience for particular groups of people, as well as the sorts of Conversations we discussed in Chapters 3 and 4.

It is not uncommon that figured worlds are signaled by or associated with metaphors. Very often people are unaware of the full significance of these metaphors, which usually have come to be taken for granted. Sometimes these metaphors are connected to "master models" in the sense that the tacit theories they imply are used widely to organize a number of significant domains for a given culture or social group.

Consider, in this respect, Naomi Quinn's (1987) studies on how people talk about marriage and divorce. Quinn finds that people organize a good deal of their thinking, acting, and interaction around marriage and divorce in terms of a small set of interlocked metaphors, e.g., "marriage is a form of effortful work like a job" or "marriage is an investment like investing money." For instance, consider the following remark by a woman, whom Quinn calls "Nan," talking about why she would not leave her marriage (Quinn 1987, p. 176):

> Why in the world would you want to stop and not get the use out of all the years you've already spent together?

Notice that Nan makes a series of metaphorical equations here. She equates marriage with *time spent* in it. The phrase "time spent" here, then, triggers the well-known metaphor in our culture: "time = money," so that time spent in marriage is being treated as an "investment" of time (like an investment of money). In terms of the investment metaphor, if we invest money/time, we are entitled to a "return." So, according to this model, it is silly not to wait long enough, having made an investment, to see it "pay off" and be able to "get the use out of" the time/money that has been invested (rather like a retirement fund!).

The whole idea of seeing things like effort and time as "investments" that will "pay off" is a master figured world (a master "theory" or way of seeing aspects of the world) that is used widely across a number of significant domains in our society. Here it is being used to talk about marriage, but the same model crops up in talk about careers, children, education, and so forth.

Another example of a figured world signaled by a set of metaphors is the way in which many people in our culture treat argumentation as a form of warfare: e.g., "she couldn't *defend* her argument," "I *defeated* his argument," "she *retreated from* her claims," "he wouldn't *give up* his claim," "she *marshaled* her evidence," etc. This can become a master figured world (a master way to figure aspects of the world), as well, when people begin to extend it to think about personal, institutional, and political relationships as battles or contests, as many, in fact, do.

Figured Worlds Can Be Partial and Inconsistent

It should be clear by now that figured worlds are deeply implicated in "politics." By "politics" I mean anything and anyplace (talk, texts, media, action, interaction, institutions) where "social goods" are at stake, things like power, status, or valued knowledge, positions, or possessions. Since figured worlds embed assumptions about what is "appropriate," "typical," and/or "normal," they are, through and through, political.

Figured worlds, though they are theories (explanations), need not be complete, fully formed, or consistent. Their partiality and inconsistency are sometimes the result of the fact that one figured world can incorporate different and conflicting values, or values connected to groups to which some people who use the figured world don't actually belong, or, at least, values that serve other people's interests better than their own. Sometimes it can be hard to tell whether a person is using two conflicting figured worlds (as in Claudia Strauss's work above) or one heterogeneous, conflicting one.

But ultimately, the partiality and inconsistency of figured worlds reflects the fact that we have all had a great many diverse and conflicting experiences; we all belong to different, sometimes conflicting groups; and we are all influenced by a wide array of groups, texts, institutions, and media that may, in reality, reflect our "best interests" more or less poorly.

To get at some of these matters, let us look at some remarks made by a middle-school Latina in the midst of an interview about her life, her attitudes towards family, school, and society, and her views on issues like racism and sexism. We will call this young women "Marcella" (not her real name). Below, I reprint Marcella's remarks. In Chapter 9 I will discuss "lines and stanzas," but, for now, just treat the numbered lines and the stanzas in the text below as a way to make Marcella's themes clearer.

Interviewer: Uh huh. Um, why do you think there are relatively few African-American and Hispanic doctors?

STANZA 1
1. Because like white people get more education. [I: mmhm]
2. Like Hispanic people don't, don't, some of the Hispanic don't like go to college and stuff like that. [I: mm hm]

STANZA 2
3. And you know, just, the white people just like, they like to, they want a future,
4. You know, they, some, some Hispanic and stuff they, they just,
5. I'm Hispanic but I'm saying
6. So [I: mm hm] um, they just like, like to hang around,
7. They don't want to go to school, you know,

STANZA 3
8. So white people don't, don't think like that.
9. They want to get an education
10. They want to have, their [?life]
11. And they really don't care what people say,

STANZA 4

12. Like if they make fun of em. [I: mm hm]
13. Like gringos and stuff like that.
14. They don't, they don't care,
15. They just do their work

STANZA 5

16. And then, they see after, they're like, they're married and they have their professions and stuff, made, then, let's see who's gonna like, be better,
17. Maybe the Hispanic boy that said that you gonna, that like you're a nerd or something? [I: mm hm]
18. Probably in the streets looking for sh, for money and stuff like that. [I: mm hm] [?sick]
19. And you have a house, you have your profession, you got money, [I: mm hm]

STANZA 6

20. I, it's like I think like white people are smarter.

Interviewer: You think white people are smarter?

21. Yeah.
22. Cos I think like, you guys get more education than we do. [I: mm hm]

Interviewer: Why, I'm not sure why you're saying white people are smarter?

23. Because they get more education, they're smarter. [I: mm hm]
24. I don't know, they,—

Interviewer: Going to school makes them smarter? Or you mean, you know they're smarter because they go to school more?

STANZA 7

25. They're just, they're just smarter.
26. They, they, both, they go to school
27. And they, they, it's like they make an effort to be smart.
28. They make a effort, not,
29. Some, some white people and some Hispanics try to be more than something else, they try to be more than somebody else,

STANZA 8

30. But not I've seen the white people they want, they just want to be, they just wanna be smart, you know,
31. For so, when you go to college or something you know, you know how many points you have so you can make your career
32. You study [?all that] and you, I think, don't care about anybody else,
33. You just care about you, your profession,

STANZA 9
34. And then, you have your kids and you teach them the same thing. [I: uh huh]
35. You know, like you pass already and all that. [I: uh huh]
36. You have example for your kids and stuff.

Interviewer: Uh huh. What do you mean you don't care about anybody else?

STANZA 10
37. You, just, you know, like, oh you are, you're a nerd, you're a nerd cos you always do your homework
38. and you gonna stop doing your homework so they won't call you nerd no more. [I: uh huh]
39. You know, they they they don't, they don't care,
40. They just keep on going.

Interviewer: What is it about white people do you think that makes them like that?

Stanza 11
41. They're just smart. [slight laugh] [I: Uh huh]
42. I think they were born smart.
43. There's something like, their moms or something they give em a little piece of smart or something. [slight laugh] [I: laughs]
44. [?So they"ll be smart]

One way to get at people's figured worlds is to ask: "What must I assume this person (consciously or unconsciously) believes in order to make deep sense of what he or she is saying?," or, to put the question another way: "What must I assume about how this person looks at (construes, 'figure') aspects of the world to make deep sense of what he or she is saying?"

Interestingly, when we ask these questions about Marcella's remarks, we see that she holds a figured world quite close, in some respects, to a formal theory in sociology, namely the theory of the reproduction of cultural capital. This theory says that certain sorts of homes, usually middle-class homes, socialize their children early in life through practices that "resonate" with the practices of schools. At the same time, schools honor these practices, as if they were "natural," universal, and "normal," while ignoring the practices and values of other sorts of homes.

Thus, these advantaged children not only "take to" school well, "buying into" its values and practices, they also come to school ahead of the game and look (and are often treated as if they are) "gifted" or "high ability." The cultural capital of the home translates into "value" in the school where it is "compounded" with "interest" and then passed on as an "inheritance" through the school-focused home-based socialization of the next generation. Thus, the cultural capital (that is, the values, attitudes, norms, beliefs, and practices, not just the economic "goods") of middle-class homes are "reproduced" (rewarded and sustained) by schools and renewed when the children, as adults, later socialize their own children at home.

In stanzas 8 and 9, Marcella comes close to her own version of the theory of the reproduction of cultural capital. But, it is clear from many different parts of her text that her figured world version of this theory is mixed with a tenet that "white people" are inherently smarter and more motivated than Hispanic people (see stanzas 1, 2, 3, 6, 7, 8, and 11—e.g., stanza 11: "I think they were born smart"). This is a tenet that is, in fact, inconsistent with the formal theory of the reproduction of cultural capital (which is meant to explain why certain sorts of people are treated by schools as if they were smarter than others, when they are not inherently so).

Marcella seems also to use a related figured world in terms of which motivation and effort follow from being inherently "smarter": e.g., in stanza 7, she says, "They're just, they're just smarter … And they, they, it's like they make an effort to be smart."

There is, then, a contradiction here with Marcella's figured world version of the reproduction of cultural capital. If home-based practices can account for the differential success of "white" people (see stanza 9), and if many of the attitudes, values, and practices that schools and certain middle-class homes reward are arbitrary (note Marcella's remarks in stanza 8: "you know how many points you have so you can make your career" and you "don't care about anybody else"), then we don't need to assume or appeal to the idea that "whites" are inherently smarter. Much as the working-class men in Claudia Strauss's studies were "colonized" by the way in which they used the "Success Model," so, too, the "bite" of the theory of the reproduction of cultural capital in terms of which Marcella might indict the schools for their "conspiracy" with certain homes and not others, is mitigated by her attributing success as an inherent inborn property of "whites."

At the same time, it is clear that authentic education has much to work with in Marcella's own social theorizing. She has already hit upon, based on her own experiences, some of the ways in which families, race, class, and schools function politically in society. On this basis, school could certainly help her build a more overt understanding and theorizing of history, society, politics, and institutions. That school has failed to do this for Marcella (and continues to as she now enters high school) is, of course, ironically part of the indictment inherent in the theory of the reproduction of cultural capital.

Figured Worlds as Tools of Inquiry

Figured worlds offer us another "tool of inquiry." They lead us to ask, when confronted with a piece of talk, writing, action, or interaction, questions like these:

A.   What figured worlds are relevant here? What must I, as an analyst, assume people feel, value, and believe, consciously or not, in order to talk (write), act, and/or interact this way?

B.   Are there differences here between the figured worlds that are affecting espoused beliefs and those that are affecting actual actions and practices? What sorts of figured worlds, if any, are being used here to make value judgments about oneself or others?

C.   How consistent are the relevant figured worlds here? Are there competing or conflicting figured worlds at play? Whose interests are the figured worlds representing?

D.   What other figured worlds are related to the ones most active here? Are there "master figured worlds" at work?

E.   What sorts of texts, media, experiences, interactions, and/or institutions could have given rise to these figured worlds?

F.   How are the relevant figured worlds here helping to reproduce, transform, or create social, cultural, institutional, and/or political relationships? What Discourses and Conversations are these figured worlds helping to reproduce, transform, or create?

We always assume, until absolutely proven otherwise, that *everyone* has "good reasons" and makes "deep sense" in terms of their own socioculturally specific ways of talking, listening (writing, reading), acting, interacting, valuing, believing, and feeling. Of course, we are all members of multiple Discourses and so the analytic task is often finding which of these, and with what blends, are operative in the communication.

The assumption of "good reasons" and "deep sense" is foundational to discourse analysis. It is not only a moral principle. It is based, as well, on the viewpoint, amply demonstrated in work in cognitive science, applied linguistics, and in a variety of different approaches to discourse analysis, that humans are, as creatures, *par excellence sense makers*. Within their Discourses, they move to sense, the way certain plants move to light.

We obviously do not gain our evidence for figured worlds by opening up people's heads. And we don't need to. Besides closely observing what they say and do, we look, as well, at the texts, media, social practices, social and institutional interactions, and diverse Discourses that influence them. As in the case of context and situated meanings in the last chapter, we can always gain more information. Thus, our conclusions are always tentative. However, here, too, we hope that eventually there comes a point where more information does not lead to substantive revision of our conclusions. This issue is related to the larger one of validity, an issue I take up in Chapter 8.

Readings
Barsalou, L. W. (1999a). Language comprehension: Archival memory or preparation for situated action. *Discourse Processes*, 28, 61–80. [This and the following article discuss how meanings arise from embodied experiences connected to goals and actions. These two papers are important for understanding my discussion in this chapter about simulations in the mind]

Barsalou, L. W. (1999b). Perceptual symbol systems. *Behavioral and Brain Sciences*, 22, 577–660.

Bellah, R. N., Madsen, R., Sullivan, W. M., Swindler, A. & Tipton, S. M. (1996). *Habits of the heart: Individualism and commitment in American life*. Updated Edition. Berkeley, CA: University of California Press.

Clark, A. (1989). *Microcognition: Philosophy, cognitive science, and parallel distributed processing*. Cambridge, MA: MIT Press. [Clark's books are the best ones on how humans think through their bodies, tools, and the environments they act in, not just inside their heads]

Clark, A. (1993). *Associative engines: Connectionism, concepts, and representational change*. Cambridge: Cambridge University Press.

Clark, A. (1997). *Being there: Putting brain, body, and world together again*. Cambridge, MA: MIT Press.

Clark, A. (2003). *Natural-born cyborgs: Why minds and technologies are made to merge*. Oxford: Oxford University Press.

D'Andrade, R. (1984). Cultural meaning systems, in R. A. Shweder & R. A. LeVine, Eds. *Culture theory: Essays on mind, self, and emotion*. Cambridge: Cambridge University Press, pp. 88–119. [A classic early source on "cultural models"]

D'Andrade, R. (1995). *The development of cognitive anthropology*. Cambridge: Cambridge University Press. [More on cultural models]

D'Andrade, R. & Strauss, C., Eds. (1992). *Human motives and cultural models*. Cambridge: Cambridge University Press. [Classic early collection of articles on cultural models]

Fillmore, C. (1975). An alternative to checklist theories of meaning, in C. Cogen, H. Thompson, G. Thurgood, K. Whistler, & J. Wright, Eds. *Proceedings of the First Annual Meeting of the Berkeley Linguistics Society*. Berkeley: University of California at Berkeley, pp. 123–131. [Early classic article on "frames" that helped lead to the cultural models literature]

Gee, J. P. (1992). *The social mind: Language, ideology, and social practice*. New York: Bergin & Garvey. [A book on so-called "connectionism" or "neural networks" and how this approach to the mind leads us to see the mind as social]

Gee, J. P. (2004). *Situated language and learning: A critique of traditional schooling*. London: Routledge. [A discussion of situated meanings and situated learning. This book contains a longer discussion of thinking as "simulations in the mind"]

Hanks, W. F. (1996). *Language and communicative practices*. Boulder, CO: Westview Press. [An excellent book on language, context, and culture]

Harkness, S., Super, C., & Keefer, C. H. (1992). Learning to be an American parent: How cultural models gain directive force, in R. D'Andrade & C. Strauss, Eds. *Human motives and cultural models*. Cambridge: Cambridge University Press, pp. 163–178. [Important paper on cultural models. This is where my discussion of different models of child rearing comes from]

Holland, D. & Quinn, N., Eds. (1987). *Cultural models in language and thought*. Cambridge: Cambridge University Press. [Important early collection of papers on cultural models]

Holland, D., Skinner, D., Lachicotte, W., & Cain, C. (1998). *Identity and agency in cultural worlds*. Cambridge, MA: Harvard University Press. [This is where the term "figured worlds" comes from, Holland's replacement for the term "cultural models"]

Lakoff, G. (1987). *Women, fire, and dangerous things: What categories reveal about the mind*. Chicago: University of Chicago Press. [This and the next book are influential discussions of how metaphors organize a good deal of language and thought]

Lakoff, G. & Johnson, M. (1980). *Metaphors we live by*. Chicago: University of Chicago Press.

Lareau, A. (2003). *Unequal childhoods: Class, race, and family life.* Berkeley: University of California Press.

Quinn, N. (1987). Convergent evidence for a cultural model of American marriage, in D. Holland & N. Quinn, Eds. *Cultural models in language and thought.* Cambridge: Cambridge University Press, pp. 173–192. [A classic paper on cultural models]

Strauss, C. (1992). What makes Tony run? Schemas as motives reconsidered, in R. D"Andrade & C. Strauss, Eds. *Human motives and cultural models.* Cambridge: Cambridge University Press, pp. 197–224. [A classic paper on cultural models—important material on how cultural models and socioeconomic class interact]

Strauss, C. & Quinn, N. (1997). *A cognitive theory of cultural meaning.* Cambridge: Cambridge University Press. [The best overall summary of the cultural models approach]

CHAPTER SEVEN
Context

Context and Reflexivity

In this chapter, I summarize where we have gotten so far and deal with the crucial notion of context. I show how our building tools and tools of inquiry relate to the role of context in language use. This will prepare us to discuss in the next chapter what constitutes an "ideal" discourse analysis (something we approach but never really reach) and what makes any analysis discourse "valid."

Context is an important notion for understanding language-in-use and for understanding the nature of discourse analysis (which is, after all, the study of language-in-use). When we speak or write we never say all that we mean. Spelling everything out in words explicitly would take far too long. Speakers and writers rely on listeners and readers to use the context in which things are said and written to fill in meanings that are left unsaid, but assumed to be inferable from context. Even a simple utterance like "The paper is on the table" requires that the hearer infer from context what paper and what table is meant.

We saw in Chapter 6, when we discussed Hanks's work on language in the Yucatan Peninsula, the crucial role shared cultural knowledge plays as part of the context in which we speak or write. Context includes more than shared knowledge, however. Context includes the physical setting in which a communication takes place and everything in it; the bodies, eye gaze, gestures, and movements of those present; what has previously been said and done by those involved in the communication; any shared knowledge those involved have, including shared cultural knowledge. However, when interpreting language (either as listeners/readers or discourse analysts) we really do not use all of the context. We use only the relevant parts of the context, the parts that are actually relevant to figuring out what the speaker or writer means to say.

Let me give an example of what I mean by relevant parts of the context, or parts of the context being relevant to interpreting what someone has said. Imagine an orange rubber duck is sitting near someone and the person says, "This duck really bothers me." The rubber duck is obviously a relevant part of the context and we use it to interpret the phrase "this duck" to mean "this orange rubber duck sitting next to the speaker."

If the speaker says, "I just got a gift," then maybe he means the duck and maybe he doesn't and we cannot really tell yet whether the rubber duck is a relevant part of the context. If the speaker says, "Let's go to a movie," then probably the rubber duck is not a relevant part of the context, not a part of the context that we need to use to fully interpret what the speaker means. The frame problem, which we discussed in Chapter 5, tells us that it can be hard to know sometimes how much of the context in which something has been said or written is relevant to interpreting what it means.

The example of the rubber duck is an example of the role of physical objects as context. What has been said or written before the current utterance or statement is also context, so is any shared knowledge and shared histories of interaction between speaker and listener. These, too, function like the rubber duck. What the speaker says and how the speaker says it makes them relevant or not or, if things are not totally clear, forces the listener to make a guess as to what is or is not relevant.

Context in writing is obviously somewhat different than context in speech because writer and reader are not face-to-face physically encountering each other. Gesture and eye gaze do not play a role as context in writing, for example. But the previous text before the current statement and shared knowledge and even shared histories (for example, in letters or text messaging), for example, are still parts of the context for writing.

When we think about how context works, we quickly face an important property of language, a property I will call "reflexivity." This is a rather "magical" property of language. We can see this property clearly by considering even so simple an exchange as: "How ya doin'?.," "Fine" between colleagues in an office corridor. Why do they use *these* words in *this context*? *Because* they take the context they are in to be but a brief and mundane encounter between fellow workers at work and these are "appropriate" words to use in such a situation. But why do they take the context to be *thus*? In part, *because* they are using just such words and related behaviors. Had the exchange opened with "What's YOUR problem, buddy?," the situation would have been construed quite differently.

Here we face, then, a chicken and egg question: Which comes first? The context or the language? This question reflects an important *reciprocity* between language and context: language simultaneously *reflects* context (what is out there in the world) and *constructs* (*construes*) it to be a certain way. While "reciprocity" would be a good term for this property of language, the more commonly used term is "reflexivity" (in the sense of language and context being like two mirrors facing each other and constantly and endlessly reflecting their own images back and forth between each other).

Language then always simultaneously reflects and constructs the context in which it is used. Usually, aspects of the context (for example, that I am talking to a friend) are really out there in the world, apart from my talk, and, at the same time, are produced (or reproduced) by my talk (for example, if I talk to my friend as a friend in a friendly way, then I make or mark the relationship between us as one of friendship). A person is a friend of mine even when I am not talking to that person, but he or she would soon cease to be a friend if I did not talk to and treat them as a friend in actual performances.

Context and the Building Tasks

Context and the building tasks we discussed in Chapter 2 have a good deal to do with each other. Speakers and writers use their language to signal to us what to build and how to build it. When we listeners and readers build appropriately (following the guides of the speaker or writer) we are actually building not just on the basis of what was said explicitly, but also on the basis of what the speaker or writer is signaling to us counts as the relevant parts of the context. We are construing the context in terms of which aspects of it are relevant for interpreting the words the speaker or writer has used.

   We build based on what is said and what is implied about how the context is relevant to interpretation. Below I list each building task in terms of how that task helps construct what are (or what we take to be) the relevant parts of the context in which something was said or written:

1. Significance: Given what the speaker has said or the writer has written, and how it has been said or written, what things and which people in this context are relevant and significant and in what ways are they significant? How is the speaker or writer trying to give significance to things?
2. Practices (Activities): Given what the speaker has said or the writer has written, and how it has been said or written, what practice (activity) or practices (activities) are relevant in this context and how are they being enacted?
3. Identities: Given what the speaker has said or the writer has written, and how it has been said or written, what identity or identities (for the speaker/ writer, the listener/ hearer, and in terms of how others are depicted) are relevant in this context?
4. Relationships: Given what the speaker has said or the writer has written, and how it has been said or written, what relationships are relevant in this context and how are they being enacted, recruited, and used?
5. Politics: Given what the speaker has said or the writer has written, and how it has been said or written, what social goods are relevant and at stake in this context and how are they being distributed or how is their distribution being viewed?
6. Connections: Given what the speaker has said or the writer has written, and how it has been said or written, what are the relevant connections and disconnections between things and people in this context and how are these connections or disconnections being made or implied?
7. Sign Systems and Knowledge: Given what the speaker has said or the writer has written, and how it has been said or written, what are the relevant sign systems (e.g., languages or social languages) and forms of knowledge (ways of knowing) that are relevant in this context and how are they used and privileged or disprivileged?

   Any piece of language, oral or written, is composed of a set of grammatical *cues* or *clues* that help listeners or readers (in negotiation and collaboration with others in an interaction) to *build* the things our seven building tasks build. We build based on what is explicitly said and what we infer from context. The speaker or writer cues us or clues us into what are the relevant parts of the context for full interpretation of what is said or written.

Thus, in an utterance like "The paper is on the table," the definite article ("the") on "paper" and "table" is a cue that the listener already knows (from previous talk or shared background knowledge) or can see which paper and table is meant. The listener uses these parts of the context to make the right paper and table relevant and significant in this context for this communication.

Or to take another example, imagine that John asks Mary, "Do you think Susan is a racist?" and Mary answers, "Well, she's a Southerner, isn't she?" The way Mary has formulated her answer cues the listener into taking the past racial problems of the South in the United States as a relevant part of the context. It also cues the listener into the fact that Mary is operating with a figured world that assumes all Southerners are racists and that she is taking this figured world to be a relevant part of the context (taking it to be shared knowledge, when, in fact, the listener might not believe it).

We see here that building with language is a *mutual* process. The speaker or writer builds the seven things our building tasks are concerned with through explicitly saying things and through cues as to how the listener or reader ought to construe what is relevant in the context. In turn, the listener or reader (if he or she is being cooperative) builds accordingly, using the speaker or writer's words, in order to build up a view of the world the speaker or writer is operating with. Together, they build significance, enact practices and identities, and relation-ships, make connections, engage in politics (the distribution of social goods), and privilege or disprivilege various system systems (e.g., languages) and ways of knowing the world. According to the reflexive property of language and context, these things may be already "out there" in the world, but they do not operate until we make them do so. They are not relevant until we make them so, through performing the active process of building, interpreting, and construing how the world works and is relevant here and now for this communication.

Situated Meanings and Figured Worlds Revisited

Situated meanings and figured worlds, which we introduced as tools of inquiry in Chapter 5, are also integrally related to how language and context work. Situated meanings are the specific meanings words and phrases take on in specific contexts of use. While figured worlds are (partly) theories or stories people have in their heads, we must use what is said in context, how it is said, and what are the relevant bits of context to figure out what figured worlds a speaker or writer is using in a given context. People have many different, sometimes inconsistent, figured worlds in their heads. So we must figure out in given contexts which ones are operating at that time and place.

A situated meaning is assembled "on the spot" as we communicate in a given context, based on our construal of that context. In Chapter 5, I used the example: "The coffee spilled, go get a mop"; "The coffee spilled, go get a broom." In the first case, triggered by the word "mop" in the context, you assemble a situated meaning something like "dark liquid we drink" for "coffee"; in the second case, triggered by the word "broom," you assemble either a situated meaning something like "grains that we make our coffee from" or like "beans from which we grind coffee." Visible brown liquid on the ground can accomplish the same thing as the word "mop" and the speaker can say "The coffee spilled, clean it up" relying on the liquid in the context telling us to get a mop. Of course, in a real context, there are many more signals as to how to go about assembling situated meanings for words and phrases.

Situated meanings don't simply reside ready-made in individual minds; very often they are *negotiated* between people in and through communicative social interaction. For example, imagine someone in a relationship saying "I think good relationships shouldn't take work." A good part of the conversation following such a remark might very well involve mutually negotiating what "work" is going to mean for the people concerned, in this specific context, as well as in the larger context of their ongoing relationship. Furthermore, as conversations (and, indeed, relationships) develop, participants continually revise their situated meanings.

Figured worlds relate to situated meanings in this way: Figured worlds are theories or stories that often help guide us in the process of constructing situated meanings. When someone says, "Relationships take work," we can only figure out what specific situated meanings they are giving "relationships" and "work" if we know or can guess what their figured worlds for relationships and work are. What theory or story about relationships and work are they using here? As a listener, I may come to see that I "figure" (construe, story, theorize), based on my experiences in the world, relationships and work differently than you do. In turn, this may lead to dispute or negotiation over what, in this context, we ought to mean by "relationships" and "work."

Some figured worlds are shared widely across many Discourses, some are not. My own figured world of how avid bird watchers go about bird watching in nature has been built out of my experiences with birders, though from the periphery of the Discourse (I am not a "real" birder), and it is probably not shared in any great degree with non-birders. And, by the way, if you don't think bird watchers constitute a Discourse, read Mark Cocker's book *Birders: Tales of the Tribe* (2001) and you will quickly realize that birders enact and recognize distinctive social identities and activities.

On the other hand, my figured world of how politics and money work in the United States (i.e., that money often speaks louder than votes) is shared with many other people in the United States, regardless of whether we are members of all the same Discourses or not, though, of course, not with all of the other people in the United States. Even here it may be the case that members of some Discourses (e.g., academics, professionals, or working-class people) may share the details of my figured world more or less closely thanks to our shared Discourses.

Figured worlds "explain," relative to the standards of some group, why words have the various situated meanings they do and fuel their ability to grow more. Figured worlds, too, are usually not completely stored in any one person's head. Rather, they are distributed across the different sorts of "expertise" and viewpoints found in the group much like a plot to a story (or pieces of a puzzle) that different people have different bits of and which they can potentially share in order to mutually develop the "big picture."

In Chapter 6 I pointed out that figured worlds are connected to prototypical simulations we can run in our heads. Because we humans share ways of looking at things with other members of our various social and cultural groups, we all have the capacity to form *prototypical simulations*. Prototypical simulations are the sorts of simulations you will run in your head (of things like weddings, parenting, voting, and so forth) when you take the situation to be "typical." Of course, what is taken as "typical" differs across different social and cultural groups of people. Your figured world of weddings, for instance, is connected to the sort of simulation or simulations you will run (imagine) when you imagine what you (and your social group) take to be "typical" weddings.

However, figured worlds, while connected to the prototypical simulations we can run in our heads, are, as we have said, not just in our heads. An upper-middle-class parent may have specific figured worlds in her head about child rearing (e.g., a piece of one may be that early experiences in childhood are crucially connected to the child's later gaining admission to a prestigious college). The parent, however, shares these figured worlds with her social group, from whom she picked them up, and can learn more about them from that group.

Figured worlds link to each other in complex ways to create bigger and bigger storylines. Such linked networks of figured worlds help organize the thinking and social practices of sociocultural groups. For example, we saw in Chapter 6 that some people use a figured world (really a connected set of them) for raising young children that runs something like this: Children are born dependent on their parents and then they go through various stages during which they often engage in disruptive behaviors in pursuit of their growing desire for independence. This figured world, too, is not solely in people's heads—it is often supplemented from sources like self-help guides for raising children, guides that tend to reflect the theories and values of middle-class people.

This figured world, which integrates models for children, child rearing, stages, development, and independence, as well as others, helps parents explain their children's behavior in terms of values the group holds (e.g., independence). It is continually revised and developed (consciously and unconsciously) in interaction with others in the group, as well as through exposure to various books and other media. Other social groups view children differently: for example, as beings who start out as too unsocialized and whose disruptive behaviors are not so much signs of their growing desire for independence as they are signals of their need for greater socialization within the family, i.e., for less independence (less "selfishness").

An Example

Let me give you an example of how situated meanings and figured worlds interact. Consider the sentence below:

> yet I believe [Milton] Friedman is right that thoroughgoing restrictions on economic freedom would turn out to be inconsistent with **democracy**. (http://www. becker-posner-blog.com/archives/2006/11/on_milton_fried.html)

The word "democracy" in a general dictionary means "forms of government where people vote for representatives." So how could "thoroughgoing restrictions on economic freedom" be inconsistent with democracy? Surely people in some countries could vote to enact such restrictions and this would seem to be an example of democracy in action.

A reader can only know what specific situated meaning the word "democracy" has here if the reader knows the figured worlds with which the author is operating. This writer assumes that free and unregulated markets (i.e., where people in a society are free to buy and sell things as they please) are both what makes wealth in a society and what keeps each individual free from coercion by others (who cannot then just take his or her possessions or life). People would not choose, on this view, to enter and take part in a voting society that could vote away economic freedom in this sense, since then others could take away their wealth and possessions. Since a democracy is based on the "consent of the governed" to abide by the outcome of votes, it assumes people have agreed, in some sense, to enter and take part in the democracy. Thus, with strong "economic freedom" (free markets) a democracy would not really have the "consent of the governed."

This figured world is an assumed part of the context on the part of the writer. The mention of Milton Friedman (the Nobel Prize-winning economist) who strongly advocated this worldview keys us into that fact. Once we bring this figured world into play, we can situate a specific meaning for the word "democracy" here (something like: "a society that votes for representation but cannot vote to take away economic freedom in any way that would greatly restrict the operation of free markets").

If you do not know the figured world sketched above, then you do not know it is both part of the context of the sentence and a relevant part of it. You cannot situate a meaning for the word "democracy," and its general-dictionary-like meaning will only make the sentence seem contradictory. Knowing this figured world also helps you engage in the building tasks. For example, it tells you the author is speaking out of an identity as a "neo-liberal" (a believer in free markets). Together with the rest of what the writer says, a reader can also see that the writer is advocating (this is a practice or activity) his figured world as the correct way to make the world work.

The author's figured world was part of an academic theory (in economics) that Milton Friedman held. Since it is not fully spelled out in the article from which I took the quote, it functions there more like a figured world than a formal theory. However, even in Friedman's work—and certainly in the ways in which he advocated U.S. policies in South America, for instance (where the U.S. used coercion to install regimes favoring Friedman's views)—it is arguable that his "theory" often functioned more as a figured world (i.e., a taken-for-granted and oversimplified view of how the world works or should work) than a theory for which there was strong impartial evidence. In the end, in any case, formal theories (which are also simplified ways of understanding a complex reality) are types of figured worlds, though we hope that they are less taken for granted and more impartially vetted than most everyday figured worlds.

Social Languages and Discourses Revisited

I turn now to our other two tools of inquiry: social language and Discourses. These are integrally connected to our building tasks, since they are both ways of enacting (performing) identities and practices (activities): two of our building tasks. Thus, when we speak or write we use social languages and Discourses to signal (build, enact) different identities and practices. When we listen or read we use the social languages and Discourses we see or assume to be at play to guide us in construing what identities and practices are being enacted.

What is important to discourse analysis are not languages at the level of English and Navaho. All languages, whether English or Navaho, are, as we argued in Chapter 4, composed of many different *social languages*. Physicists engaged in experiments don't speak and write like street-gang members engaged in initiating a new member, and neither of these speak or write like "new capitalist" entrepreneurs engaged in "empowering front-line workers." Each social language uses somewhat different and characteristic grammatical resources to carry out our seven building tasks.

All of us control many different social languages and switch among them in different contexts. In that sense, no one is a monolingual. But, also, all of us also fail to have mastery of some social languages even though these social languages use the grammatical resources of our "native language." Thus, too, in that sense, we are not (any of us) "native speakers" of the full gamut of social languages which compose "our" language.

It is important, as well, to note that very often social languages are not "pure," but, rather, people mix ("hybridize") them in complex ways for specific purposes. It is sometimes quite hard to know whether it is best to say that someone is switching from one social language to another ("code switching") or actually mixing two of them to assemble, for a given context, a transformed (even novel) social language (which may, of course, eventually come to be seen as a "pure" and different social language in its own right, when people forget that it arose as a mixture). It is, of course, more important, in a discourse analysis, to recognize this matter than to settle it. People can even mix or switch between different social languages that are drawn from different languages at the level of things like English and Navaho.

It is social languages which contain the clues or cues that guide the seven building tasks above. Different social languages contain different sorts of cues or clues, that is, they use grammar in different ways as a resource for the seven building tasks. For example, consider again the young woman above who said to her parents, "Well, when I thought about it, I don't know, it seemed to me that Gregory should be the most offensive," and to her boyfriend, "What an ass that guy was, you know, her boyfriend," when she was talking about the same character in the same story. These utterances are in two different social languages.

In the first case, when the young woman is speaking to her parents, the following sort of *pattern* of grammatical features is indicative of a particular social language: a preliminary clause about having been reflective ("when I thought about it"); mitigators ("I don't know," "seemed to me"); complex subordinating syntax (*when*-clause, *it-seems-that* construction); repeated references to self ("I," "me") as careful claimer/knower; Latinate vocabulary ("offensive"); complex modality ("should be"). This social language contains clues and cues for deference, respect, school-based learning, reflection, attention to knowledge and claims, and so forth.

In the second case, when the young woman is speaking to her boyfriend, the following sort of pattern of grammatical features is indicative of another sort of social language: Exclamation ("What an ass ..."); informal vocabulary ("ass," "guy"); right dislocation ("her boyfriend"); attention to hearer ("you know"); directly making claims with no mitigators or attention to self as claimer. This social language contains clues or cues for solidarity, informality, participatory communication, attention to shared values, and a focus on the social world and not the self.

Such patterns are part and parcel of the collocational patterns (patterns created by the way we combine traditional grammatical units) we discussed in Chapter 4. Interpreters (listeners or readers) who are members of the Discourses whose social languages these are recognize (however unconsciously) the patterns in the same rapid and intuitive way they recognize the situated meanings of words.

Discourses are ways of enacting socially significant identities and associated practices in society through language (social languages) and ways of acting, interacting, valuing, knowing, believing and using things, tools, and technologies at appropriate times and places. For someone to "pull off" being recognized as a nuclear physicist, a viable politician, or a street-gang member requires more than language and it requires that language integrates smoothly with ways of being and doing in the world.

Often in discourse analysis what we are trying to do is to use language to uncover the workings of Discourse in society. Society is basically composed of Discourses and it is their interactions with each other that determine a good deal of history and the workings of society for good or ill.

An Example

Let me give an example of how social languages and Discourses work together. The data below is a project where university academics and middle-school teachers worked together to discuss and build a curriculum around school children doing history (especially oral history, collecting oral stories) in their own communities. The group had just had a long and contentious meeting in which there was conflict between the university historian on the project and some of the teachers. The conflict had involved the claim that the historian had failed to consult with the teachers sufficiently in plans she had made for the project.

The meeting is over at the point the data below starts and only a few people are left. Two teachers, Karen and Jane, and Joe, an administrator from a school involved in the project, and Sara, the university historian, are still present. They are now engaging in "small talk"—no longer talking about the project—before themselves leaving.

Karen, Jane, and Joe were all born in the town where the project took place, a town we will call Middleview (all names have been changed). So were their parents. Middleview is a largely working-class town that was suffering at the time with the loss of many industrial jobs. Sara was born and educated elsewhere and was a professor at a local prestigious private university. She was not born in Middleview and did not plan to stay there for her whole career.

There had been much tension in project meetings between how teachers talk and think about issues and how university professors do. That is, there had been tensions between the teachers' Discourse as teachers in Middleview and the professors' Discourse as university academics.

Here is the data (The symbols "/" and "//" will be explained in the next chapter—you can ignore them for now):

Karen:

1. My mother used to talk about in the 40s /
2. You'd hang around at Union Station /
3. And anybody would just pick you up /
4. Because everybody was going down to dance at Bright City /
5. Whether you knew them or not //

Joe:

6.   Lakeside Ballroom //

Jane:

7.   Yeah definitely //

Joe:

8.   My father used to work there //

Jane:

9.   And also, once you finally get into the war situation /
10. Because you have Fort Derby /
11. Everybody would get a ride in to come to Bright City /
12. To the amusement park //
13. So it was this influx of two, three cars' worth of guys /
14. That were now available to meet the girls that suddenly were there //

Sara:

15. Well actually street, street cars had just come in in this /
16. And as I recall um from a student who wrote a paper on this /
17. Bright City and Park was built by the street car company /
18. In order to have it a sort of target destination for people to go to /
19. And to symbiotically make money off of this //

Jane:

20. Because once you got there /
21. You could take a boat ride /
22. And go up and down a lake /
23. And there were lots of other ways to get the money from people //

Here the Middleview teachers and the administrator are no longer speaking as (no longer using a social language associated with) teachers or adminis-trators—no longer speaking as school people—but now they are speaking as (using a social language associated with) "everyday people" and long-term residents and citizens of Middleview. They are engaged in the practice of using "small talk" to bond over their shared backgrounds, identities, and values. They are speaking out of their "life world Discourses" (their identity as "everyday people" not specialists of any sort, not, for example, as educators). They are also speaking out of their Discourse as long-term Middleview residents and citizens.

Here are some things you do not know about the ways of thinking and valuing typical of Middleview Discourse, but things that will make the talk above more meaningful. Long-term residents of Middleview are the products of nineteenth- and early twentieth-century immigration from Europe. They value their shared history as part of Middleview and see places where all the citizens of Middleview used to congregate as central to the identity of the town. They are concerned today, faced with new immigration from South America, Asia, and the West Indies, as well as economic problems, that there are no such central congregating places anymore, in part because people tend to stay in their own neighborhoods and the central district has deteriorated.

The Middleview school people are interacting within their shared Middleview Discourse as a way of bonding, using the social language of "small talk" about shared stories of the past they have heard from their relatives. Their Discourse is, of course, more than just ways of talking, but also ways of acting, interacting, thinking, valuing, and knowing about and using the geography of their town.

Sara, the university professor, cannot enter the Middleview Discourse. She is not a long-term resident of Middleview and does not view the town the way they do. She has no relevant stories to share. At the same time, she wants to engage in their bonding through small talk, especially since there has just been conflict in terms of their professional Discourses. Sara, however, mixes "everyday language" and her professional language as an academic (two different social languages). She also mixes two different Discourses, her life world Discourse as an "everyday person" and her historian Discourse.

Examples of "academic language" mixed into "everyday" talk are: "in order to," "target destination," and "symbiotically." An example of mixing academic Discourse into an "everyday person" life world Discourse is the move of using a student paper as evidence. This is something academic historians do. However, the Middleview Discourse people are using shared stories from their parents and grandparents as evidence, not research papers—the fact that they can use such evidence is part of what lets others recognize them as members of the Middleview Discourse. So Sara has set up a possible conflict again. On the other hand, she has no other way to participate in the bonding here.

However, Jane incorporates Sara's comment nicely. She engages in the typical Middleview talk that has been going on as a form of bonding, but closes on "money" as a way to tie back to and incorporate Sara's point.

It is an irony, perhaps, that Sara was seeking to get the teachers to engage in and value oral history with their students. Here the long-term Middleview residents are sharing oral history stories to mark their identity as fellow members of the Middleview Discourse, but Sara seeks to have written evidence (a research paper) "trump" oral stories as evidence. This, by the way, is also a good example of Building Task 7, privileging one form of knowing over another.

The data above is an intricate play between ways of being (identities, Discourses) and ways with words (styles of language, social language) within the common practice (activity) of "small talk" after an official meeting. The tensions in this small talk may go some way to explaining tensions in the formal meetings, which overlaid professional Discourse differences (teachers, university academics) over the tensions between "real" Middleview citizens and newcomers (like Sara or, for that matter, the new "brown" immigrants).

Intertextuality and Conversations

In society Discourses ("kinds of people," people enacting different identities) "talk" to each other, not just individuals. When a Los Angeles policeman is talking as a policeman to a street-gang member as a street-gang member it is not just two people interacting, but the Discourse of L.A. policemen and the Discourse of gang members (and there are different gang Discourses based on ethnic groups and neighborhoods). This "dialogue" has been going on a long time. It started before the current encounter and will last beyond it. Furthermore, the current encounter is deeply influenced by past interactions between these two Discourses. So, too, with the long-running interactions between biologists and creationists, liberals and conservatives, and cattle ranchers and environmentalists in the American West, to take just a few examples of conflicting Discourses. Sometimes, Discourses interact in complicity with each other, not in conflict. For example, there is, in the United States, a good deal of complicity (though sometimes some tension too) between a far-right conservative Discourse and certain fundamentalist Christian Discourses.

Intertextuality and Conversations (big "C" Conversations), two of our tools of inquiry, are centrally about the interaction of Discourses in society. Intertextuality is about mixing together or juxtaposing different social languages, often connected to different Discourses, in various ways. Two styles of language come to interact (with complicity or tension) with each other in the same "text" (stretch of speech or writing).

Conversations are public debates, arguments, motifs, issues, or themes that large numbers of people in a society or social group know about. When I use "Conversations," with a capital "C," I am speaking metaphorically as if the various sides in debates around issues like abortion or smoking were engaged in one big grand conversation (or debate or argument, whatever we want to call it). Of course, this big Conversation is composed of a myriad of interactional events taking place among specific people at specific times and places. The key point is that people know what the different "sides" or "poles" are in such Conversations, even if they only agree with one side.

The interactions of Discourses in society give rise to intertextuality and Conversations when the traces of their interactions show up in our talk and writing. Indeed, intertextuality is often a textual reflex or trace of

Conversations among Discourses in a society. Conversations that are widely known in a society or social group are often assumed to be known (and taken as part of the potentially relevant part of the context) by anyone who is engaged as a listener or reader in that society or social group.

An Example

In a delightful paper entitled "The Ontological Status of Burritos" (2008, unpublished paper), Richard Ruiz, a sociolinguist and anthropological linguist at the University of Arizona, has this to say (I have bolded terms I will discuss below):

> In fact, many Mexicans in my circle would say that "taco" is **metaphorical** (actually **metonymic**—the Mexicans I know tend to be precise in their use of **classical root-words**), an icon that stands for much more than a piece of food. *Vamos a echarnos un taco*, literally "let's go throw a taco on ourselves," means something like "let's do lunch" or, more liturgically, "let us break bread **together**." Here, no one is really talking about bread. It is a way of indicating an interest in establishing or reinforcing a friendship beyond whatever formal roles the participants may be playing. In this, "taco" may be **socio-linguistically** unique; you don't hear people inviting someone to throw an enchilada or tamale (sic) on each other, thankfully. (If they did, I imagine it would be taken as an invitation to some sort of **kinky** Mexican duel—but that would be different.)

Ruiz incorporates into his text a number of terms that make reference to different Discourses. The terms "metaphorical," "metonymic," "classical root-words," and "sociolinguistically" come from the Discourse of linguistics. "*Vamos a echarnos un taco*," of course, mixes Spanish with English. "Let's do lunch" comes from "business talk." "Let us break bread together" comes from religious Discourse. Finally, "kinky" references "sex talk" of a sort that occurs in a number of different Discourses concerned with sex.

So within Ruiz's text—written primarily in a conversational, though literary form—snatches of language associated with different Discourses are intermixed with his basic conversational style in the essay. Each such intertextual reference has a purpose. The links to linguistics are there because eventually Ruiz uses his knowledge as a linguist to give both his personal (cultural) and professional opinion about a court case where the issue at stake was whether a burrito is a sandwich. The link to Spanish is there because one of the issues in the essay is the role of different language and cultures in American society. The links to business, religion, and sex are there to serve as "translations" of culturally specific practices and terms (e.g., "taco" as Ruiz's friends used the terms, "*Vamos a echarnos un taco*") for readers unfamiliar with these practices and terms.

From this passage alone, the role of Conversations in this text may not be apparent. But consider the following passage from Ruiz's essay:

> It is not new that judges and courts decide questions for which their background may be deemed inadequate. Some of these decisions are much more important

than resolving the ontological status of burritos. In 1896, a court decided that a law requiring Black and white people to use separate public facilities was constitutional; the plaintiff was Homer Plessy, a man who was one-eighth Black. In 1927, in a test case challenging the Plessy decision in the area of school segregation, a court decided that a Chinese girl was legally black (actually "negro," the term of the day). In 1954, a court in Texas declared that Mexican Americans were Caucasians. (I now know the cause of the brief bout of cold shivers resulting from the chemical reorganization I went through when I became white as a young boy.) In retrospect, many of us would now agree that the judges had no special qualification to decide these questions, and that they were just wrong to boot.

Ruiz is using a court case about whether burritos are sandwiches (a sandwich chain in a mall wanted to keep a burrito restaurant out of the mall since they had a legal agreement with the mall that no other sandwich restaurants could set up shop in the mall) to make a much larger point about judges making decisions on issues about which they are culturally incompetent or culturally blind.

In the U.S. there has been a longstanding Conversation, which has gone on for a long time in many places over many specific issues, as to whether justice should be "blind" or whether judges should use their distinctive cultural knowledge or seek out such knowledge if they do not have it. This Conversation (debate) intersects today in the United States with the Conversations (debates) about the growing role of Spanish and Mexican culture in the United States. Though Ruiz wrote his essay before Sonia Sotomayor (the first Hispanic judge appointed to the U. S. Supreme Court) was nominated to the Supreme Court, her nomination energized both these Conversations (were one historical instance of these long-running Conversations). These Conversations are a relevant part of the context of Ruiz's essay, though he does not mention them explicitly, but assumes them.

It should be clear from this example how intertextuality (different styles of language associated with different Discourses mixing in a text or being juxtaposed in a text) and Conversations (public debates whose sides or poles are widely known) are ways in which the interactions of Discourses show up in our talk and writing.

Readings

Cocker, M (2001). *Birders: Tales of a tribe.* New York: Atlantic Monthly Press.

Duranti, A. (1997). *Linguistic anthropology.* Cambridge: Cambridge University Press. [An introduction to linguistic anthropology that uses a good deal of discourse analysis and contains good discussions of the role of context]

Duranti, A. & Goodwin, C., Eds. (1992). *Rethinking context: Language as an interactive phenomenon.* Cambridge: Cambridge University Press. [Important articles that reflect the current view of language and context as reflexively related and context as socially negotiated through interaction]

Gumperz, J. J. (1982). *Discourse strategies.* Cambridge: Cambridge University Press.

[A book about how listeners use "contextualization cues" to build interpretations, by a leading twentieth-century anthropologist linguist]

Gumperz, J. J., Ed. (1982). *Language and social identity.* Cambridge: Cambridge University Press. [An important and still timely collection on language and identity as constructed in and through social interaction]

Hymes, D. (1974). *Foundations of sociolinguistics.* Philadelphia: University of Pennsylvania Press. [A classic and foundational book on language as a cultural competence]

Van Dijk, T. A. (2009). *Society and discourse: How social contexts influence text and talk.* Cambridge: Cambridge University Press. [A good discussion of the role of context in interpretation]

CHAPTER EIGHT
Discourse Analysis

Transcription

In this chapter I first discuss the nature of transcriptions of data for our discourse analyses, a topic about which I will say more in Chapter 9. Next I turn to what an "ideal" discourse analysis would look like and argue that any real discourse analysis is always just a partial realization of this ideal. Finally, I discuss what constitutes validity for a discourse analysis. We start in this section with transcription.

With ever more sophisticated recording and computer equipment, it is possible to get incredibly detailed records of speech that include small pauses, slight hesitations, subtle changes in sound, pitch, rate, and loudness, as well as close synchronizations of overlaps between speakers. It is tempting to believe that such detailed records represent some pure, objective, and unanalyzed "reality." In fact, they do no such thing. Speech always has far more detail in it than any recording or transcription system could ever capture (or that the human ear can hear).

A discourse analysis is based on the details of speech (and gaze and gesture and action) or writing that are arguably deemed *relevant* in the context *and* that are relevant to the arguments the analysis is attempting to make. A discourse analysis is not based on *all* the physical features present, not even on all those that might, in some conceivable context, be meaningful, or might be meaningful in analyses with different purposes. Such judgments of relevance (what goes into a transcript and what does not) are ultimately theoretical judgments, that is, they are based on the analyst's theories of how language, contexts, and interactions work in general and in the specific context being analyzed. In this sense, a transcript is a theoretical entity. It does not stand outside an analysis, but, rather, is part of it.

Any speech data can be transcribed in more or less detailed ways such that we get a continuum of possible transcripts ranging from very detailed (what linguists call "narrow") transcripts to much less detailed (what linguists call "broad") ones. While it is certainly wise to begin one's analysis by transcribing for more detail than may in the end be relevant, ultimately it is the purposes of the analyst that determine how narrow or broad the transcript must be. The validity of an analysis is not a matter of how detailed one's transcript is. It is a matter of how the transcript works together with all the other elements of the analysis to create a "trustworthy" analysis.

There is not space here to go into the linguistic details of transcripts. Instead, I will simply give one example of how "minor" details can take on "major" importance in interaction, and, thus, must, in those instances, be included in transcripts. Consider the interaction below between an Anglo-American female researcher ("R") and a fourth-grade African-American girl ("S" for student) with whom the researcher is discussing light as part of a school science education project. This student comes from a very poor home and her schooling has been continuously disrupted by having to move in order to find housing. The researcher is about to start an interaction with the student in which the student will be asked to reason about light by manipulating and thinking about a light box and how a light beam focused by the box interacts with different plastic shapes, including a prism (which causes the light to break into a rainbow of colors).

The following transcript uses notational devices to name features of speech which we have not yet discussed, but which we will discuss in the next chapter (Chapter 9). For now, it is enough to know that each line of the transcript represents a "tone unit," that is, a set of words said with one uniform intonational contour (that is, they are said as if they "go together"— see Chapter 9). A double slash ("//") indicates that the tone unit is said with a "final contour," that is, a rising or falling pitch of the voice that sounds "final," as if a piece of information is "closed off" and "finished" (the fall or rise in pitch is realized over the underlined words and any words that follow them). A tone unit that has no double slash is said on a "non-final contour," a shorter rising or falling contour that sounds as if there is more information to come.

I have organized the text below into "stanzas," a language unit that we will discuss in Chapter 9. Stanzas are "clumps" of tone units that deal with a unitary topic or perspective, and which appear (from various linguistic details) to have been planned together. In this case, the stanzas are interactively produced. Words that are underlined carry the major stress in their tone unit (as we will see in Chapter 9, stress in English is marked by bumping or gliding the pitch of the voice up or down or increasing loudness or both). Capitalized words are emphatic (said with extra stress). Two periods ("..") indicates a hearable pause. Two dots following a vowel ("die:d") indicate that the vowel is elongated (drawn out). "Low pitch" means that the preceding unit was said on overall low pitch. This transcript is certainly nowhere as narrow as it could be, though it includes some degree of linguistic detail.

STANZA 1
1. R: Where does the <u>light</u> come from
2. R: when it's <u>outside</u>? //
3. S: <u>Sun</u> (low pitch) //
4. R: From the <u>sun</u> (low pitch) // .. hum

STANZA 2
5. S: Cause the <u>sun</u> comes up
6. S: <u>REALLY early</u> //
7. R: um .. And that's <u>when</u> we get light (low pitch) //

STANZA 3
8. S: And that's how the, the the me .. my .. <u>me and my class</u>
9. S: is talkin' about <u>dinosau:rs</u>
10. S: and how they <u>die:d</u> //

11. S: And we <u>found out</u> ..
12. S: some things . about how they <u>die:d</u> //
13. R: Oh <u>really</u> //

Start of STANZA 4
14. R: Does that have to do with <u>LIGHT</u>? //

(interaction continues)

After a long interaction of which the above data is but a part, the researcher felt that the child often went off topic and was difficult to understand. However, it can be argued, from the above data, that the researcher "co-constructed" (contributed to) these topic changes and lack of understanding.

Children in school are used to a distinctive school activity in which an adult asks them a question (to which the adult already knows the answer, but to which the answer is not supposed to be obvious), the child answers, and the adult responds in some way that can be taken as evaluating whether the child's answer was "acceptable" or not.

There is also a common and related practice in schools in which the teacher asks one or more obvious and rather "everyday" questions in order to elicit items that will subsequently be treated in much more abstract ways than they typically are in "everyday" (life world) interaction. A science teacher might ask "What is this?" of a ruler. Receiving the answer "a ruler," she might ask "What do we do with rulers?" Having elicited an answer like "measure things," the teacher may very well go on to treat measuring devices and measurement in quite abstract ways.

In the interaction above, the researcher appears to want to elicit some everyday information about light in order to subsequently get the child to treat light in terms of abstract notions like "light sources," "directions," "reflection," and "refraction," that is, much more abstractly than specific things like the sun. There is ample evidence from what we otherwise know about the student being discussed here that she is, in all likelihood, unfamiliar with and unpracticed in this sort of (on the face of it rather odd) school-based practice.

In the above interaction, the researcher starts with a question to which the student responds with the word "sun" said on a low pitch and with a final falling contour. This way of answering indicates (in many dialects of English) that the respondent takes the answer to be obvious (this already constitutes a problem with the question-answer-evaluation activity).

The researcher's response is said in exactly the same way as the child's (low pitch, final falling contour)—and in just the position that a student is liable to expect an evaluation—indicating that she, too, takes the answer to be obvious. The student might well be mystified, then, as to why the question was asked.

In 5 and 6 the student adds tone units that are said on a higher pitch than the previous ones. Furthermore, line 6 contains an emphatic "really." This way of saying 5 and 6 indicates that the student takes this information to be new or significant information. She may well have added this information in a search for some response that would render the initial question something other than an request for obvious information and in a search for some more energetic response from the researcher, one that would let the student know she was "on the right tract" in the interaction.

However, the student once again gets a response from the researcher (low pitch, falling final contour) that indicates the researcher takes the student's contribution, again, to be obvious. The student, then, in 8, launches off on yet another contribution that is, once again, said in a way that indicates she is trying to state new or significant information that will draw a response of interest from the researcher.

The student also here uses a technique that is common to some African-American children (Gee 2007). She states background information first (in stanza 3) before getting to her main topic (light), though her "found out / some things" clearly implies, in this context, that these things will eventually have to do with light (which they, indeed, do—she has studied how a meteor blocked out sunlight and helped destroy the dinosaurs). The researcher, listening for a more foregrounded connection to light, stops the student and, with emphasis on "light," clearly indicates that she is skeptical that the student's contribution is going to be about light, a skepticism that is, from the student's perspective, not only unmerited, but actually surprising and a bit insulting (as subsequent interaction shows).

Here the "devil" is, indeed, in the details: aspects of the school-based "known question-answer-evaluation" activity, different assumptions about how information is introduced and connected, as well as details of pitch and emphasis (as well as a good many other such details), all work together to lead to misunderstanding. This misunderstanding is quite consequential when the adult authority figure attributes the misunderstanding to the student and not to the details of language and diversity (most certainly including the researcher's own language and diversity).

One may wonder why the researcher asked the questions she did and responded as she did. To make a long story short, the research project was based on the idea that giving children too much explicit information or overtly challenging responses would restrict their creativity and "sense making," especially with minority students who may not interpret such overt instruction and challenging the same way the instructor does. Ironically, a situation set up to elicit the "best" from the child by leaving her as "free" as possible, led to her being constructed as not making sense, when, in fact, she was making sense at several levels in a deeply paradoxical setting created by the researchers.

Note, then, too, how the details of the transcript are rendered relevant in the analysis and how the transcript is as detailed as it needs to be, no more, no less (other details in the transcript could well have been brought into the analysis). Of course, it is always open to a critic to claim that details we have left out *are* relevant. But some details will always have to be left out (e.g., Should we mark just how much vowels are adapted to final consonants? Just how much pitch declines across a tone unit?) and, thus, such a criticism cannot mean that we must attempt to put in all the details. The burden simply falls on the critic to show that details we have left out are relevant by adding them in and changing the analysis (thus, discourse analysts must always be willing to share their data).

An "Ideal" Discourse Analysis

Before discussing, in the next section, what constitutes validity for a discourse analysis, let me summarize the components of an "ideal" discourse analysis. Actual analyses, of course, usually develop in detail only a small part of the full picture. However, any discourse analysis needs, at least, to give some consideration, if only as background, to the whole picture.

Essentially a discourse analysis involves asking questions about how language, at a given time and place, is used to engage in the seven building tasks we have discussed earlier. The tools of inquiry we have introduced are meant to constitute six areas where the analyst can ask such questions. These tools are: situated meanings, social languages, figured worlds, intertextuality, Discourses, and Conversations.

We have seven building tasks and six tools of inquiry. A discourse analysis uses each of the tools of inquiry to ask questions about each building task. This means we have six questions to ask about seven things, a total of 42 questions (each of which is a "big question" that can lead to other sub-questions):

1. Building Task 1: Significance: How are situated meanings, social languages, figured worlds, intertextuality, Discourses, and Conversations being used to build relevance or significance for things and people in context?
2. Building Task 2: Practices (Activities): How are situated meanings, social languages, figured worlds, intertextuality, Discourses, and Conversations being used to enact a practice (activity) or practices (activities) in context?
3. Building Task 3: Identities: How are situated meanings, social languages, figured worlds, intertextuality, Discourses, and Conversations being used to enact and depict identities (socially significant kinds of people)?
4. Building Task 4: Relationships: How are situated meanings, social languages, figured worlds, intertextuality, Discourses, and Conversations being used to build and sustain (or change or destroy) social relationships?
5. Building Task 5: Politics: How are situated meanings, social languages, figured worlds, intertextuality, Discourses, and Conversations being used to create, distribute, or withhold social goods or to construe particular distributions of social goods as "good" or "acceptable" or not?
6. Building Task 6: Connections: How are situated meanings, social languages, figured worlds, intertextuality, Discourses, and Conversations being used to make things and people connected or relevant to each other or irrelevant to or disconnected from each other?

7. Building Task 7: Sign Systems and Knowledge: How are situated meanings, social languages, figured worlds, intertextuality, Discourses, and Conversations being used to privilege or disprivilege different sign systems (language, social languages, other sorts of symbol systems) and ways of knowing?

In earlier chapters I have suggested various sub-questions one can ask about each of our tools of inquiry. So we have 42 large questions we can ask about any piece of data and sub-questions within each of these. Asking and answering these 42 questions about any one piece of data would lead to a very long analysis indeed. But that is what would constitute a "full" or "ideal" discourse analysis. For the most part, any real discourse analysis deals only with some of the questions. Nonetheless, analysts should be aware that the remaining questions still serve as an unfinished background to the analysis and it is fair game for any critic to raise one or more of them in questioning the validity of our analyses, which may mean we have to do more work.

Validity

I have held off until now discussing the question of what constitutes validity for a discourse analysis. This question could not be answered until enough of the "tools of inquiry" used in a discourse analysis had been laid out. However, now we are ready to deal with the issue of validity, an issue that has continually vexed so-called "qualitative research."

Validity is not constituted by arguing that a discourse analysis "reflects reality" in any simple way. This is so for at least two reasons. First, humans *interpret* the world, they do not have access to it "just as it is." They must use some language or some other symbol system with which to interpret it and thereby render it meaningful in certain ways. A discourse analysis is itself an interpretation, an interpretation of the interpretive work people have done in specific contexts. It is, in that sense, an interpretation of an interpretation.

These two considerations do not mean that discourse analyses are "subjective," that they are just the analyst's "opinion." I take validity to be something that different analyses can have more or less of, that is, some analyses are more or less valid than others. Furthermore, validity is never "once and for all." All analyses are open to further discussion and dispute, and their status can go up or down with time as work goes on in the field.

The 42 questions we have discussed above—the six questions based on our six tools of inquiry that we can ask about each of the seven building tasks—play a crucial role in my definition of validity for discourse analysis to be given below. A discourse analysis—as any empirical inquiry—is built around making arguments for a specific claim (or claims) or hypothesis (or hypotheses). The claim or hypothesis is the point of the analysis.

An example of such a claim would be something like: Conflict in meetings between teachers and university academics in my data (or research project) was caused by unacknowledged tensions between their different Discourses. Since Discourses involve situating meanings in certain ways, figured worlds of certain kinds, social languages of certain sorts, engagement with certain societal Conversations (debates with other Discourses), and, perhaps, various distinctive uses of intertextuality (i.e., all our other tools of inquiry), this claim or hypothesis will potentially involve all our tools of inquiry. The data we collect will show us some or all of the seven building tasks at work. We support the claim or hypothesis by showing how our tools of inquiry display these building tasks at work in ways that support our claim or hypothesis.

Each tool of inquiry is linked to all the others both in what people do with language in specific contexts and in our analyses. Just as Discourses involve all the other tools, so, too, for figured worlds, or any of the other six tools. Any claim or hypothesis about figured worlds, for example, will potentially involve us in looking at Discourses, situated meanings, social language, Conversations, and intertextuality.

Validity for any discourse analysis is constituted (made) by four elements. These are:

1. *Convergence*: A discourse analysis is more, rather than less valid (i.e., "trustworthy"), the more the answers to the 42 questions *converge* in the way they support the analysis or, to put the matter the other way round, the more the analysis offers *compatible* and *convincing* answers to many or all of them.

2. *Agreement*: Answers to the 42 questions above are more convincing the more "native speakers" of the social languages in the data and "members" of the Discourses implicated in the data agree that the analysis reflects how such social languages actually can function in such settings. The native speakers do not need to know why or how their social languages so function, just that they can. Answers to the 42 questions are more convincing the more other discourse analysts (who accept our basic theoretical assumptions and tools), or other sorts of researchers (e.g., ethnographic researchers), tend to support our conclusions.

3. *Coverage*: The analysis is more valid the more it can be applied to related sorts of data. This includes being able to make sense of what has come before and after the situation being analyzed and being able to predict the sorts of things that might happen in related sorts of situations.

4. *Linguistic Details*: The analysis is more valid the more it is tightly tied to details of linguistic structure. All human languages have evolved, biologically and culturally, to serve an array of different communicative functions. For this reason, the grammar of any social language is composed of specific forms that are "designed" to carry out specific functions, though any form can usually carry out more than one function. Part of what makes a discourse analysis valid, then, is that the analyst is able to argue that the communicative functions being uncovered in the

analysis are linked to grammatical devices that manifestly can and do serve these functions, according to the judgments of "native speakers" of the social languages involved and the analyses of linguists (see Chapter 5 on form–function correlations).

Why does this constitute validity? Because it is *highly improbable* that a good many answers to 42 different questions, the perspectives of different "inside" and "outside" observers, additional data sets, and the judgments of "native speakers" and/or linguists *will* converge unless there is good reason to trust the analysis. This, of course, does not mean the analysis is true or correct in every respect. Empirical science is social and accumulative in that investigators build on each other's work in ways that, in the long run, we hope, improves it. It does mean, however, that a "valid" analysis explains things that any future investigation of the same data, or related data, will have to take seriously into account.

Validity is social, not individual. A given piece of discourse work will have a major point or theme, or a small set of them. These are the work's hypotheses. Authors will normally argue for the validity of their analyses by arguing that some aspects of convergence, agreement, coverage, and linguistic details are met in their analysis. But no piece of work can, or should, ask all possible questions, seek all possible sources of agreement, cover all the data conceivably related to the data under analysis, or seek to deal with every possibly relevant linguistic detail.

A discourse analysis argues that certain data supports a given theme or point (hypothesis). In many cases, for the individual piece of work, convergence and linguistic details are the most immediately important aspect of validity—that is, showing that answers to a number of questions like our 42 questions above and linguistic details converge to support the analysis. It is important, as well, that these questions come from a consideration of different building tasks, and not just one, and that a number of different linguistic details support the conclusions drawn. It is important, too, that the researcher openly acknowledges if any answers to these questions or any linguistic details support opposing conclusions. Various aspects of agreement and coverage are also important in different ways in different sorts of studies (sometimes through citations to, and discussion of, the literature).

The individual piece of work is, then, of course juxtaposed with earlier and later work in the field. This juxtaposition allows further aspects of convergence, agreement, coverage, and linguistics to be socially judged and adjudicated. Validity is as much, or more, in those social judgments and adjudications as it is in an individual piece of work.

Starting to do Discourse Analyses

In the next chapter I will deal with some aspects of how language is planned and produced and with some ways that a discourse analyst can start to organize his or her thinking about a piece of language. In Chapters 10–12 I turn to examples of discourse analysis. It is here that my warning in the Introduction to this book must be most heeded: the method I have developed in this book is not intended as a set of "rules" to be followed "step-by-step." In turn, the examples in Chapters 10–12 are not meant as "recipes" or "how to" manuals. Rather, they are meant merely to show some of the tools we have discussed in this book put to use, not in and for themselves, but to speak to particular themes, points, and issues. These examples, then, are meant as "thinking devices" to encourage others to engage in their own discourse-related reflections. Many other examples could have been used, and other examples would have used the tools in somewhat different ways.

What I would suggest for "beginners" who are pursuing their first discourse analyses is this: Pick a piece of data (a big or small interaction, narrative or other extended piece of language, an interview, or a written text, for example) that both interests you and that you believe will speak to or illuminate an important issue or question. If the data is speech, transcribe it as closely as you can, but with an eye to the features you think will be most important for the issue or question in which you are interested. Start with a reasonable amount of your data (you don't need to use it all) and use more of it as the need arises (if it does).

Pick some key words and phrases in the data, or related families of them, and ask what *situated meanings* these words and phrases seem to have in your data, given what you know about the overall context in which the data occurred. Think about what figured worlds these situated meanings appear to implicate. Think about the social languages and Discourses that appear to be relevant, in whatever ways, to your data. If it is easier to think about what Conversations (see Chapter 4) are relevant to your data, then do that.

As you think about social languages, Discourses, and Conversations, you are thinking about what and how social activities and socially situated identities are being enacted and/or recognized in your data (recognized by participants and/or yourself as analyst). As you think about all these things, look closely at your data, ask yourself what linguistic details appear to be important for how situated meanings, figured worlds, social activities, socially situated identities, social languages, and Discourses are being "designed," enacted, or recognized in your data.

After some initial reflections on these matters, or as a way to engage in these reflections, ask yourself the 42 questions (six tool of inquiry questions about each of our seven building tasks), taking notes and reflecting on your answers to these questions, guided by the theme or question with which you started, but paying attention to any others that seem to emerge. Pay particular attention to where answers to several different questions seem to converge on the same point or theme (whether or not these are related to the original theme, interest, or question that started you off). Some of the 42 may not be relevant or may not yield illuminating answers for the data you have picked. That is fine.

As you think about the points or themes that emerge from asking the 42 questions, either relate them to the theme or question with which you started or revise that theme or question. Then, organize your analysis so that the material you have developed (the answers to the questions you have asked about the building tasks and the reflections you have made on them) speaks to, argues for, and illuminates the final main point(s), theme(s), or issue(s) you have chosen to address in your work.

Be sure you appeal to a variety of linguistic details in your analysis and try to address different building tasks (and their related questions) to begin to achieve some degree of validity in regard to convergence. You can, if appropriate, try to extend your analysis to other parts of your data or new sources of related data (or to data in the literature) to begin to achieve some degree of validity in regard to coverage. You can use interviews with participants (keeping in mind that they are not always conscious of what they mean and do), citations from related literature, and collaboration with others to begin to achieve some degree of validity in regard to agreement.

Readings

Duranti, A. (1997). *Linguistic anthropology*. Cambridge: Cambridge University Press. [Contains a good and up-to-date discussion of transcription conventions and issues]

Edwards, J. A. & Lampert, M. D., Eds. (1993). *Talking data: Transcription and coding in discourse research*. Hillsdale, NJ: Erlbaum. [Good discussion of transcription conventions]

Gee, J. P. (2007). *Social linguistics and literacies: Ideology in Discourses*. Third Edition. London: Falmer. [Contains discussions of the language of African-American children and citations to the literature]

Hutchby, I. & Wooffitt, R. (2008). *Conversation analysis*. Malden, MA: Polity Press. [A good introduction to the "CA" ("Conversational Analysis") approach to discourse analysis, an approach based in sociology]

Jefferson, G. (2004). Glossary of transcript symbols with an introduction, in G. H. Lerner, Ed. *Conversation analysis: Studies from the first generation*. Amsterdam and Philadelphia: John Benjamins, pp. 13–31. [Jefferson has developed the best-known set of conventions for transcription used in "Conversational Analysis" ("CD") approaches to discourse analysis]

Ochs, E. (1979). Transcription as theory, in E. Ochs & B. Schieffelin, Eds. *Developmental pragmatics*. New York: Academic Press, pp. 43–71. [Classic paper on the fact that decisions about what and how to transcribe are theoretical decisions]

Schiffrin, D., Tannen, D. & Hamilton, H. E., Eds. (2001). *The handbook of discourse analysis*. Malden, MA: Blackwell [A good handbook with many articles representing different approaches to and areas in discourse analysis]

CHAPTER NINE
Processing and Organizing Language

Speech is Produced in Small Spurts

This chapter deals with a few aspects of how speech is produced and what this has to do with the sorts of meanings we speakers hope to convey and we hearers (always actively and creatively) try to "recover." We will deal here with a few technical details about the structure of sentences and of discourse. However, these details are not important in and of themselves. What is important is that the discourse analyst looks for patterns and links within and across utterances in order to form hypotheses about how meaning is being constructed and organized. What grammatical terminology we choose to use is less important than the patterns we find and the hypotheses we form and test.

Notions like "situated meanings," "figured worlds," and "Discourses" will take a back seat here. In this chapter we are primarily concerned with some initial ways into a text. We are concerned with ways in which the analyst can start to organize his or her thinking about a piece of language. Of course these initial insights must quickly lead to thinking about situated meanings, figured worlds, and Discourses. In turn, ideas about these will influence and, at times, change how the analyst thinks about the linguistic patterns in a text. Discourse analysis is a reciprocal and cyclical process in which we shuttle back and forth between the structure (form, design) of a piece of language and the situated meanings it is attempting to build about the world, identities, and relationships in a specific context.

Thanks to the way the human brain and vocal system are built, speech, in all languages, is produced in small spurts. Unless we pay close attention, we don't usually hear these little spurts, because the ear puts them together and gives us the illusion of speech being an unbroken and continuous stream. In English, these spurts are often, though not always, one "clause" long.

In a rough and ready way we can define a "clause" here as any verb and the elements that "cluster" with it. So in a sentence like "Mary left the party because she was tired," we have two clauses, "Mary left the party" and "because she was tired." The sentence "Mary left the party" contains only one clause. In a sentence like "Mary intended to leave the party," we also have two clauses: "Mary intended" and "to leave the party" (where "Mary" is understood as the subject of "to leave"). Here the second clause ("to leave the party") is embedded in the first clause ("Mary intended") as the direct object of the verb "intend." These two clauses are so tightly bound together that they would most often be said as a single spurt.

In the example below, taken from a story told by a seven-year-old child, each spurt is one clause long, except 1b and 1e where the child has detached parts of clauses to be spurts on their own (of course, children's speech units tend to be shorter than adults):

1a.   there was a hook
1b.   on the top of the stairway

1c. an' my father was pickin me up
1d. an' I got stuck on the hook
1e. up there
1f. an' I hadn't had breakfast
1g. he wouldn't take me down
1h. until I finished all my breakfast
1i. cause I didn't like oatmeal either

To understand how these spurts work in English (they work differently in different languages), we need to discuss a set of closely interrelated linguistic concepts: function words, content words, information, stress, intonation, lines, and stanzas. We will start with the distinction between function words and content words.

Function Words and Content Words

Content words (sometimes also called "lexical words") belong to the major parts of speech: nouns, verbs, and adjectives. These categories are said to be "open categories" in the sense that they each have a large number of members, and languages readily add new members to these categories through borrowing from other languages or the invention of new words.

Function words (also sometimes called "grammatical words") belong to smaller categories, categories which are said to be "closed categories" in the sense that each category has relatively few members, and languages are resistant to borrowing or inventing anew such words (though they sometimes do). Such categories as determiners (e.g., "the," "a/n," "this/that," "these/those"—these are also sometimes called "articles"), pronouns (e.g., "he/him," "she/her," "it," "himself," "herself"), prepositions (e.g., "in," "on," "to," "of"), and quantifiers (e.g., "some," "many," "all," "none") are function word categories.

Function words show how the content words in a phrase, clause, or sentence relate to each other, or how pieces of information fit into the overall ongoing communication. For example, the definite determiner "the" signals that the information following it is already "known" to the speaker and hearer. Pronouns signal that their referents have been previously mentioned, or are readily identifiable in the context of communication or on the basis of the speaker and hearer's mutual knowledge. Prepositions link nouns and noun phrases to other words (e.g., in "lots of luck" *of* links *luck* to *lots*; in "ideas in my mind" *in* links *my mind* to *ideas*; and in "look at the girl" *at* links *the girl* to the verb *look*). I have not yet mentioned adverbs. Adverbs are messy and complicated. Very often they function in a way that is midway between a function word and a content word.

Since function words show how content words relate to each other, they can help us make guesses about what categories (e.g., nouns or verbs) of content words accompany them and what these words mean. To see this consider the first stanza of Lewis Carroll's poem "Jabberwocky":

Twas bryllyg, and the slythy toves
Did gyre and gymble in the wabe:
All mimsy were the borogoves;
And the mome raths outgrabe.

I have underlined the function words. I have also underlined the plural affix ("es" and "s") since it functions just like a function word, though it is not a separate word. In this poem, Carroll uses real English function words, but nonsense content words (how do we know they are content words? By how they are placed in relation to the function words). Despite the fact that half the "words" in this text are nonsense, any speaker of English can use the function words to unravel the grammar of the sentences and to make good guesses about what content word categories (noun, verb, adjective) the nonsense content words belong to. The speaker of English can even make some good guesses about what the nonsense words might mean or what they might refer to. Thus, we readily interpret the stanza as a description of an outdoor scene with creatures of various sorts frolicking or moving about.

Information

Since function words carry less of the real content of the communication (their job being to signal the grammar of the sentence), we can say that they tend to be *informationally less salient* than content words. While they are certainly helpful, they are often dispensable, as anyone who has written a telegram knows.

Thus, let us make a distinction between two types of information in a sentence. First, information that is relatively new and relatively unpredictable I will call "informationally salient." The actual specific meaning of any content word in a sentence is unpredictable without knowing exactly what the content word means. In the Carroll poem, we vaguely know that "toves" are probably active little animate creatures, but we have no idea what exactly they are. Thus, content words are usually informationally more salient than function words.

Second, information that is given, assumed already known, or predictable, I will call "informationally less salient." Very often even if you have not heard a function word you could pretty well predict where it should have been and what word exactly it would have been. For example, if you heard "Boy has lots ideas," you could predict that "the" is missing in front of "boy," and "of" between "lots" and "ideas." If, however, you heard "That man has lots of," you could not predict what content word should come after "of." Thus, function words are usually informationally less salient than content words.

In general, then, the content word–function word distinction is a distinction between two types of information. However, beyond this gross dichotomy, the distinction between information that is more or less salient is one that can only be drawn in the actual context of communication. We turn to this matter now.

Stress and Intonation

Information saliency in English is marked by *stress*. In turn, the different stress patterns in a spurt of speech set up its *intonational contour*. To see what these terms mean, consider the little dialogue below:

1. Speaker A: Have you read any good books lately?
   Speaker B: Well, I read a shocking book recently.
                [Goes on to describe the book]

How speaker B crafts her response is partially set up by the remark made by speaker A, which here represents part of the context in which B's response occurs. Let's think a moment about how the sentence uttered by B might have been said. English speakers mark the information saliency of a word by how much *stress* they give the word.

Stress is a *psychological concept, not a physical one.* English speakers can (unconsciously) use and hear several different degrees of stress in a speech spurt, but this is not physically marked in any uniform and consistent way. Stress is physically marked by a combination of increased loudness, increased length, and by changing the pitch of one's voice (raising or lowering the pitch, or gliding up or down in pitch) on a word's primary ("accented") syllable. Any one or two of these can be used to trade off for the others in a quite complicated way.

In any case, English speakers unconsciously use and recognize stress, and it can be brought to conscious awareness with a little practice (some people are better than others at bringing stress differences to consciousness awareness, though we can all unconsciously use and recognize it). A word with more stress than another word sounds more salient (it often sounds louder, though it may not really be louder, but just be longer or have a pitch change on it, both of which will make English speakers think it sounds louder).

So let's return to speaker B's response and assume it was said as one spurt of speech. Its first word, "well," can be said with little stress, on a relatively low pitch and/or with little loudness, since it carries no content, but simply links speaker B's turn to speaker A's. This is not to say that words like "well" are not important in other ways; such words, in fact, have interesting discourse functions in helping to link and package information across sentences. Since "well" is the first word of speaker B's spurt of speech, and starts her turn, it will be said on a pitch that is taken to be close to the "basic pitch" at which speaker B will be speaking (perhaps, kicked up a bit from B's basic pitch and, too, from where speaker A left off, to mark B's turn as beginning).

"I" is completely predictable in the context of the question speaker A has asked, and it is a function word. Thus, it is not very salient informationally and will receive little stress, just enough loudness to get it said and with a pitch close to the basic pitch speaker B has chosen (for this spurt or related run of spurts as she keeps speaking). The content word "read" is predictable because it has already occurred in speaker A's preceding question. So, too, for the word "book" later in B's remark. Both of these words will have a fairly low degree of stress. They will have more than the function words "well," "I," and "a," since as content words they do carry content, but certainly much less than the word "shocking," which carries new and non-redundant information. The indefinite article "a," of course, is informationally very unsalient and will get little stress. The speaker will mark what stress words like "read" and "book" have by bumping the pitch of her voice a bit up or down from the "basic pitch" she has established or is establishing and/ or by increasing loudness a bit relative to words like "I" and "a."

On the other hand, the word "shocking" is the most unpredictable, informationally salient, new information in the sentence. The speaker will mark this saliency by giving this word the most stress in the sentence. Such a word or phrase, which carries the greatest degree of stress in a sentence (or a given spurt of speech), is marked not just by bumping the pitch of the voice up or down a bit in pitch and/or by increasing loudness, but by a real *pitch movement* (called a "glide").

The speaker begins to glide the pitch of her voice up or down (or even up-then-down or down-then-up) on the word "shocking," allowing the pitch movement to continue to glide up or down (whichever she has chosen) on the words that follow it, here "book" and "recently." Of course, what sort of pitch movement the speaker chooses, that is, whether up, down, up-then-down, or down-then-up, has a meaning (for example, the speaker's pitch glide rises in certain sorts of questions and falls in certain sorts of statements). We are not now concerned, however, with these meaning differences.

The pitch glide which begins on the word "shocking" marks "shocking" as the *focus* of the *intonation unit*. An "intonation unit" is all the words that precede a pitch glide and the words following it over which the glide continues to move (fall or rise). The next intonation unit begins when the glide is finished. The speaker often hesitates a bit between intonation units (usually we pay no attention to these hesitations) and then steps the pitch up or down a bit from the basic pitch of the last intonation unit on the first word of the next unit (regardless of whether it is a content word or not) to "key" the hearer that a new intonation unit is beginning.

In B's response to A, the content word "recently" is fairly redundant (not too salient) because, while it has not been mentioned in A's question, it is certainly implied by A's use of the word "lately." Thus, it receives about as much stress, or, perhaps a little more, than the content words "read" and "book." The speaker may increase her loudness a bit on "recently" and/or bump the pitch of her voice up or down a bit on its main syllable (i.e., "cent") as her pitch continues basically to glide up or down over "recently" as part of (and the ending of) the pitch glide started on the word "shocking."

Below, I give a visual representation of how speaker B might have said her utterance:

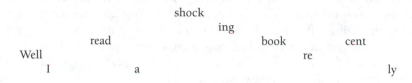

There are, of course, other ways to have said this utterance, ways which carry other nuances of meaning.

There is one last important feature of English intonation to cover here. In English, if the intonation focus (the pitch glide) is placed on the last content word of a phrase (say on "flower" in the phrase "the pretty red flower"), then the salient, new information is taken to be either just this word *or* the material in the phrase as a whole (thus, either just "flower" or the whole phrase "the pretty red flower"). Of course, the context will usually determine which is the case. If the intonation focus (pitch glide) is placed on a word other than the last word in the phrase, then that word is unequivocally taken to be the salient, new information (e.g., if the intonation focus is on "red" in "the pretty red flower," then the salient, new information is taken to be just "red"). In our example above, "shocking" is not the last word in its phrase (it is an adjective in a noun phrase "a shocking book") and, thus, is unequivocally the new, salient information.

An interesting situation arises when the intonation focus (pitch glide) is placed in the last (content) word in a sentence. Then, we cannot tell whether the salient, new information the speaker is trying to indicate is just that word or also other words that precede it and go with it in the phrase or phrases to which it belongs. So in an utterance like "This summer, Mary finished fifteen assigned books," if the speaker starts her glide on "books," the new salient information she intends to mark may be just "books" (answering a question like "Mary finished fifteen assigned whats?"), or "assigned books" ("Mary finished fifteen whats?"), or "fifteen assigned books" ("What has Mary finished?"), since "books" is part of the noun phrase "fifteen assigned books." The new salient information could even be "finished fifteen assigned books," since these words constitute together a verb phrase ending with, and containing, the word "book" ("What has Mary done?"). In fact, since "books" is the last word of the sentence, everything in the sentence could be taken to be new and salient ("What happened?"). Of course, in actual contexts it becomes clearer what is and what is not new and salient information.

Ultimately, the context in which an utterance is uttered, together with the assumptions that the speaker makes about the hearer's knowledge, usually determines the degrees of informational saliency for each word and phrase in a sentence. Speakers, however, can also choose to downplay or play up the information saliency or importance of a word or phrase and ignore aspects of the context or what they assume the hearer to know and not know already. This is part of how speakers actively create or manipulate contexts, rather than just simply respond to them. Of course, if speakers take this too far, they can end up saying things that sound odd and "out of context."

In a given context, even a function word's information might become important, and then the function word would have a greater degree of stress. For example, consider the context below:

2. A: Did Mary shoot her husband?
   B: No, she shot YOUR husband!

In this context, the information carried by "your" is unpredictable, new, and salient. Thus, it gets stressed (in fact, it gets extra stress because it is contrastive—*yours* not *hers*—and surprising). In fact, in 2B, given its context (2A), it will be the focus of the intonation unit. When speakers want to contrast or emphasize something, they can use extra stress (marked by more dramatic pitch changes and/or loudness)—this is sometimes called "emphatic stress."

Lines

Each small spurt out of which speech is composed usually has one salient piece of new information in it that serves as the focus of the intonation contour on the spurt (e.g., "shocking" in 1 and "your" in 2 above). There is often a pause, slight hesitation, or slight break in tempo after each spurt.

Speaking metaphorically, we can think of the mind as functioning like the eye (Chafe 1980, 1994). To take an example, consider a large piece of information that I want to communicate to you, such as what happened on my summer vacation. This information is stored in my head (in my long-term memory). When I want to speak about my summer vacation, my "mind's eye" (the active attention of my consciousness) can only focus on one small piece of the overall information about my summer vacation at a time.

Analogously, when my eye looks at a large scene, a landscape or a painting, for example, it can only focus or fixate on one fairly small piece of visual information at a time. The eye rapidly moves over the whole scene, stopping and starting here and there, one small focus or fixation at a time (watch someone's eye as they look over a picture, a page of print, or at a scene in the world). The "mind's eye" also focuses on one fairly small piece of information at a time, encodes it into language, and puts it out of the mouth as a small spurt of speech. Each small chunk in speech represents one such focus of the mind's eye, and usually contains only one main piece of salient information.

Such chunks (what I have heretofore been referring to as "spurts") have sometimes been called "idea units" when people want to stress their informational function and "tone units" when people want to stress their intonational properties. I will refer to them here, for reasons that will become apparent later, as "lines."

To see lines operating, consider the example below, taken from the opening of a story told by a seven-year-old African-American girl (we saw some of these lines at the outset of this chapter). Each line is numbered separately. Within each one, the word or phrase with the most stress and carrying the major pitch movement (i.e., the focus of the intonation contour), and which, thus, carries the new and most salient information, is underlined (in cases where more than one word is underlined, the last word in the phrase was where the pitch glide occurred and I am judging from context how much of the phrase is salient information):

3a. last yesterday
3b. when my <u>father</u>
3c. in the <u>morning</u>
3d. an' he …
3e. there was a <u>hook</u>
3f. on <u>the top of the stairway</u>
3g. an' my father was <u>pickin' me up</u>
       ("pick up" is verb + particle pair, a single lexical unit whose parts can be separated; the pitch glide starts on "pick")
3h. an' I got <u>stuck</u> on the hook
3i. <u>up there</u>
3j. an' I <u>hadn't had breakfast</u>
3k. he <u>wouldn't take me down</u>
       ("take down" is also a verb + particle pair)
3l. until I finished <u>all my breakfast</u>
3m. cause I <u>didn't like oatmeal</u> either

Notice that each underlined word or phrase (minus its function words, which are necessary glue to hold the phrase together) contains new information. The first line (3a above) tells us when the events of the story happened (in this child's language "last yesterday" means "in the recent past"). The second line (3b) introduces the father, a major character in the story to follow. The third line (3c) tells us when the first event of the story (getting stuck on a hook) took place. The fourth line (3d) is a speech dysfluency showing us the child planning what to say (all speech has such dysfluencies). The fifth line (3e) introduces the hook; the sixth line (3f) tells us where the hook is. The seventh line (3g) introduces the action that leads to getting stuck. Thanks to having been mentioned previously in 3b, the father is now old information and thus "my father" in 3g has little stress. Therefore, "my father," now being old information, can be part of the line "my father was pickin' me up," which contains only one piece of new information (the action of picking up). The eighth line (3h) gives the result of the previous one, that is, the result that the narrator gets stuck.

The rest of the lines work in the same way, that is, one salient piece of information at a time. Adults, of course, can have somewhat longer lines (thanks to their increased ability to encode the focuses of their consciousness into language), but not all that much longer.

Notice, too, that once the child gets going and enough information has been built up (and thus, some of it has become old information), then each line tends to be one clause long. After line 3f all the lines are a single clause, except for 3i. And as the child continues beyond the point I have cited, more and more of her lines are a single clause. Most, but not all, lines in all speech are one clause long, though styles of speaking differ in interesting ways in this regard, with some styles having more single-clause lines than others.

When readers read written texts, they have to "say" the sentences of the text in their "minds." To do this, they must choose how to break them down into lines (which, thanks to the luxury of saying-in-the-mind, rather than having to actually produce and say them anew, can be somewhat longer than they would be in actual speech). Such choices are part of "imposing" a meaning (interpretation) on a text and different choices lead to different interpretations. Writers can, to a greater or lesser degree, try to guide this process, but they cannot completely determine it.

For example, consider the two sentences below, which I have taken at random from the beginning of a journal article. I have put slashes between where I, on my first "silent reading," placed line boundaries:

> My topic is the social organization of remembering / in conversation. My particular concern is to examine / how people deal with experience of the past / as both individually and collectively relevant. (David Middleton, The social organization of conversational remembering: Experience as individual and collective concerns, *Mind, Culture, and Activity*, 4.2, 71–85, 1997, p. 71)

I find myself treating "in conversation" as a separate line in the first sentence—perhaps, because remembering can be socially organized in many ways, of which conversation is but one, though the one in which Middleton is interested. The way in which I have parsed the second sentence above into lines treats Middleton's main topic, announced in his first sentence ("the social organization of remembering in conversation," and referred back to by "my particular concern [in this topic] is to examine"), as having two parts: "how people deal with experience of the past" (one line) and "as both individually and collectively relevant" (another line). That is, he is going to deal a) with memory and b) with memory as both an individual and collective phenomenon. Note that this bi-partite division is announced, as well, in the title of Middleton's article, where the colon separates the two themes. Lines reflect the information structure of a text, whether that text is oral or written.

Stanzas

The information embraced within a single line of speech is, of course, most often too small to handle all that the speaker wants to say. It is necessary usually to let several focuses of consciousness (which lines represent) scan a body of information larger than a single focus. This is to say that the speaker has larger chunks than single focuses of consciousness in mind, and that several such focuses may constitute a single unitary larger block of information.

Consider again the beginning of the young girl's story in the last section. These focuses of consciousness (lines) constituted the opening or setting of her story, the background material one needs to know in order to situate and contextualize the main action of the story that follows. That is, these lines constitute a larger unitary block of information (the setting) within the story as a whole. However, within this block of information, there are smaller sub-blocks: the little girl devotes several lines to one topic (namely, getting stuck) and several other lines to another topic (namely, having breakfast). I will call such sets of lines devoted to a single topic, event, image, perspective, or theme a *stanza*.

Below, I lay out the opening of the little girl's story in terms of its lines and stanzas:

SETTING OF STORY:
STANZA 1 (getting stuck):
4a. last yesterday
4b. when my father
4c. in the morning
4d. an' he ...
4e. there was a hook
4f. on the top of the stairway
4g. an' my father was pickin' me up
4h. an' I got stuck on the hook
4i. up there

STANZA 2 (having breakfast):
4j. an' I hadn't had breakfast
4k. he wouldn't take me down
4l. until I finished all my breakfast
4m. cause I didn't like oatmeal either

Each stanza is a group of lines about one important event, happening, or state of affairs at one time and place, or it focuses on a specific character, theme, image, topic, or perspective. When time, place, character, event, or perspective changes, we get a new stanza. I use this term ("stanza") because these units are somewhat like stanzas in poetry.

Connected speech is like a set of boxes within boxes. The focuses of consciousness (lines), most of which are single clauses, are grouped together as one larger, unitary body of information, like the setting for a story. This larger body of information is itself composed of stanzas each one of which takes a single perspective on an event, state of affairs, or character. Presumably this distribution of information has something to do with how the information is stored in the speaker's head, though speakers can actively make decisions about how to group or regroup information as they plan their speech.

Macrostructure

Larger pieces of information, like a story about my summer vacation, an argument for higher taxes, or a description of a plan for redistributing wealth, have their own characteristic, higher-level organizations. That is, such large bodies of information have characteristic parts much like the body has parts (the face, trunk, hands, legs, etc.). These parts are the largest parts out of which the body or the information is composed. They each have their own smaller parts (ultimately body parts are composed of skin, bones, and muscles, and the parts out of which a body of information is composed are ultimately composed themselves of stanzas and lines). The setting of the child's story we have been discussing is a piece of the larger organization of her story. It is a "body part" of her story.

Below, I reprint this child's story as whole. Each larger "body part" of the story is numbered with a Roman numeral and labeled in bold capitals (SETTING, CATALYST, CRISIS, EVALUATION, RESOLUTION, and CODA). These larger "body parts" of the story as a whole can be called its "macrostructure," as opposed to its lines and stanzas which constitute its "microstructure."

In order to see the patterning in the little girl's story all the more clearly, I do something a bit different below in the way I represent lines and stanzas. I remove from the girl's story the various sorts of speech hesitations and dysfluencies that are part and parcel of all speech (and that tell us something about how planning is going on in the speaker's head). I also place the little girl's lines back into clauses when they are not full clauses (save for "last yesterday" which is a temporal adverb with scope over most of the story). What I have produced here, then, are what I will call *idealized lines*.

Idealized lines are useful when we are interested in discovering meaningful patterns in people's speech and in getting at their basic themes and how they are organized. Using them does not mean that we have totally ignored the more superficial patterns of the actual speech. In fact, we can use hesitations, pauses, dysfluencies, and non-clause lines as indicators of how planning is working, where stanza boundaries exist, and how the speaker views her information at a micro-level. In actual analyses we always shuttle back and forth between the actual lines and idealized lines.

A SEVEN-YEAR-OLD CHILD'S STORY

I. SETTING
STANZA 1
1. Last yesterday in the morning
2. there was a hook on the top of the stairway
3. an' my father was pickin' me up
4. an' I got stuck on the hook up there

STANZA 2
5. an' I hadn't had breakfast
6. he wouldn't take me down
7. until I finished all my breakfast
8. cause I didn't like oatmeal either

II. CATALYST
STANZA 3
9. an' then my puppy came
10. he was asleep
11. he tried to get up
12. an' he ripped my pants
13. an' he dropped the oatmeal all over him

STANZA 4
14. an' my father came
15. an' he said "did you eat all the oatmeal?"
16. he said "where's the bowl?"
17. I said "I think the dog took it"
18. "Well I think I'll have t'make another bowl"

III. CRISIS
STANZA 5
19. an' so I didn't leave till seven
20. an' I took the bus
21. an' my puppy he always be following me
22. my father said "he—you can't go"

STANZA 6
23. an' he followed me all the way to the bus stop
24. an' I hadda go all the way back
25. by that time it was seven thirty
26. an' then he kept followin' me back and forth
27. an' I hadda keep comin' back

IV. EVALUATION
STANZA 7
28. an' he always be followin' me
29. when I go anywhere
30. he wants to go to the store

31. an' only he could not go to places where we could go
32. like to the stores he could go
33. but he have to be chained up

V. RESOLUTION
STANZA 8
34. an' we took him to the emergency
35. an' see what was wrong with him
36. an' he got a shot
37. an' then he was crying

STANZA 9
38. an' last yesterday, an' now they put him asleep
39. an' he's still in the hospital
40. an' the doctor said he got a shot because
41. he was nervous about my home that I had

VI. CODA
STANZA 10
42. an' he could still stay but
43. he thought he wasn't gonna be able to let him go

This girl's story has a higher-order structure made up of a SETTING, which sets the scene in terms of time, space, and characters; a CATALYST, which sets a problem; a CRISIS, which builds the problem to the point of requiring a resolution; an EVALUATION, which is material that makes clear why the story is interesting and tellable; a RESOLUTION, which solves the problem set by the story; and a CODA, which closes the story. Each part of the story (except the Evaluation and Coda) is composed of two stanzas.

In some ways this is the structure of all stories, regardless of what culture or age group is telling them. However, there are also aspects of story structure that are specific to one cultural group and not another. For example, devoting a block of information to an Evaluation prior to a story's Resolution is more common among some African-American (young) children than it is with some other groups of children. Adults tend to spread such Evaluation material throughout the story or to place it at the beginning, though African-American adults engage in a good deal of "performance" features, which are a type of Evaluation, and tend to use Evaluation material to "key" a hearer into the point of the story, rather than to hit them over the head with the point bluntly indicated. Of course, such cultural information is never true in any very exclusive way: there are many varieties of African-American culture, as there are of any culture (and some African-Americans are in no variety of African culture, but in some other variety of culture or cultures). And other groups do similar or overlapping sorts of things.

Another aspect of this story that is more specific to African-American culture, though also in a non-exclusive way, is the large amount of parallelism found in the way language is patterned within the stanzas. Note, to take one example of many, how stanza 3 says "an' then my puppy came" and then gives four things about the puppy, and then stanza 4 says "an' my father came" and then says four things (all of them speech) about the humans involved. This parallel treatment of the father and the puppy forces the hearer to see the story as, in part, about the conflict between the puppy as a young and exuberant creature and the adult world (home and father) as a place of order and discipline. As a seven-year-old child, the teller of the story is herself caught in the conflict between her own urges to go free and her duty to go to school and ultimately enter the adult world.

Notice that the part of the story labeled Evaluation makes clear that the essential problem with the puppy is that he wants to freely *go* places where he cannot go, just as, we may assume, a child often wants to go where she is not allowed to go and must go where she doesn't want to go. In line 21, the child says "my puppy he always be following me," and repeats this in the Evaluation. This "naked *be*" is a form in African-American Vernacular English that means an action is habitual (regularly happens). Here it indicates that the puppy's urge to follow and go with the girl is not just a once or sometime thing, but a regular and recurrent event that follows from the nature of the puppy. It is a problem that must be resolved.

The resolution of the conflict between the puppy and the adult world takes place at a hospital where a doctor (an adult) gives the puppy a shot and puts him to "sleep." Thus, the adult world dictates that in the conflict between home and puppy, the adult norms must win. The child is working through her own very real conflicts as to why she can't have her puppy and, at a deeper level, why she must be socialized into the adult world of order, duty, and discipline (by the way, the hook in the first stanza is just a dramatic device—the child is simply trying to say that her parents require discipline in the home; she is not, by any means, accusing anyone of mistreatment. The girl may also mean in stanza 2 that the father would not get her down until she agreed to go finish her breakfast). This, in fact, is the basic function of narrative: narrative is the way we make deep sense of problems that bother us.

Linguists and psychologists have proposed many other approaches to the higher-order structure of stories and other connected sorts of language (exposition, argument, description). But they all agree that such connected blocks of information are stored in the mind in terms of various "body parts" and that, in telling or writing such information, we often organize the information in terms of these parts, though of course we can actively rearrange the information as we produce it and we often discover structure in information as we produce it.

Macro-lines

So far I have used a young child's story as my source of examples of lines and stanzas. Lines and stanzas are often quite easy to find in children's language.

With adults, complex syntactic structures within and across sentences sometimes make it harder to find the boundaries of lines and stanzas. Adults sometimes use the syntactic resources of their language to get lines and stanzas to integrate tightly with each other, to meld rather smoothly together. Indeed, in such language the beginning of the stanza is often constructed to link back to the last stanza, and the end of the stanza to link forward to the next, with the "heart" of the stanza in the middle.

And, of course, adults often have much more complex language than children. It is often said that, in speech, there are no such things as "sentences," that the sentence as a linguistic unit is a creature of writing only. I do not believe this is true. What is true is that sentences in speech are much more loosely constructed, much less tightly packaged or integrated, than in writing. Nonetheless, people often use the syntactic resources of English to tie together two or more lines into something akin to a sentence. I will call these "sentences" of speech *macro-lines*, referring to what we have so far called "lines" (i.e., intonational units, idea units, tone groups) as "micro-lines" when I need to distinguish the two. So by "macro-line" I mean "what counts as a sentence in speech."

Let me give an example of what I mean by "macro-lines." The example is part of a much longer stretch of speech from a woman in her twenties suffering from schizophrenia. As part of a battery of tests, this woman (who is, like many schizophrenics, poor and not well educated) was placed in a small room with a doctor in a white coat and told to talk freely for a set amount of time, the doctor giving her no responses or "feedback cues" the whole time.

This "language sample" was used to judge whether she showed any communication disorders connected with her mental state. Not surprisingly (given the limitations of collecting data in this way) the doctors (with little sophistication in linguistics) concluded the woman's text was "disturbed" and not fully coherent. In fact, I have argued elsewhere that the text is wonderfully coherent and a typical, if striking, example of human narrative sense making.

Below, I reprint just the first two stanzas of this young woman's long series of narratives. Below, each unit on a numbered line (e.g., 1a and 1b) is a micro-line. I include unfinished (cut-off) micro-lines as separate micro-lines. I underline the focus of each micro-line. Each unit that has a single number (e.g., "1" or "2") is a macro-line (thus, 1a and 1b together constitute a macro-line):

STANZA 1 (Play in thunderstorms)
1a. Well when I was <u>little</u>
1b. the <u>most exciting</u> thing that we used to do is

2a. There used to be <u>thunderstorms</u>
2b. on the <u>beach</u> that we lived on

3. And we walked down to <u>meet</u> the thunderstorms

4a. And we'd turn around and <u>run home</u>
4b. <u>running away</u> from the
4c. running away from the <u>thunderstorms</u>

STANZA 2 (Play in waves from storms)
5a. That was most <u>exciting</u>
5b. one of the most <u>exciting</u> times we ever had
5c. was doing <u>things</u> like that

6. Besides having like—

7a. When there was hurricanes or <u>storms</u> on the ocean
7b. The <u>waves</u>
7c. they would get really <u>big</u>

8. And we'd go down and <u>play</u> in the waves when they got big

Consider stanza 1 (the grammatical details to follow in the next few paragraphs are not important in and of themselves—the point is simply to ask oneself how various intonation units or micro-lines are related to each other). 1a is a *when*-clause that is syntactically subordinated to 1b as its main clause. So 1a and 1b together constitute a sentence. 2a and 2b are clearly part of one sentence, since 2b is an argument of the verb ("to be") in 2a. 3 is a two-clause sentence ("we walked down" and "to meet the thunderstorms") that has been said as a single intonation unit (micro-line). 4b is an incomplete micro-line that is said completely in 4c. 4c is a participial clause (an *-ing* clause) that is subordinated to 4a as its main clause.

Now turn to stanza 2. 5a is an incomplete micro-line. 5b is the subject of the predicate in 5c, the two together making up a single sentence (5b contains the phrase "one of the most exciting times" and the relative clause "we ever had"). 6 is a false start that does not get continued. 7a is a *when*-clause that is subordinated to 7b/c as its main clause. In 7b, the speaker has made "the waves," the subject of the sentence "The waves would get really big," a separate micro-line and then repeated this subject as a pronoun in the full sentence in the next micro-line ("they would get really big"). This pattern, common in speech, is called "left dislocation." 8 is a single sentence with two clauses in it ("we'd go down and play in the waves" and "when they got big"). The speaker could have chosen to say this sentence as two micro-lines (intonation units), rather than one.

In many oral texts, it is possible, then, to identify "sentences" (macro-lines) by asking how various micro-lines (intonation units) are syntactically connected to each, though the connection may be rather loose. In any case, the whole point of macro-lines is get the analyst to think about how syntax is used to stitch intonation units (micro-lines) together.

Let me give one more example of macro-lines. My example comes from the first formal meeting of a project sponsored by an educational research institute. The meeting was attended by a researcher from the institute, several undergraduate and graduate students, research assistants, six elementary school teachers, a university professor, and two curriculum consultants. The purpose of the meeting was to start a joint institute–university–schools project on teaching history in elementary schools in the town in which the meeting was being held. The text below comes from the opening remarks of the researcher from the institute who was leading the meeting and the project (for a full analysis, see Gee 1993):

1a.   I'm sort of taking up a <u>part</u> of
1b.   coordinating this <u>project</u>
1c.   bringing the two schools <u>together</u>
1d.   and trying to <u>organize</u>
1e.   well what we're going to <u>do</u> in these meetings

2a.   what it <u>means</u>
2b.   for teachers and researchers and historian and curriculum <u>people</u>
2c.   to come on and try to organize a <u>team</u>
2d.   and students interested in <u>history</u> and other things
2e.   to try to organize a team to get a <u>piece</u> of curriculum
2f.   essentially up and running and working in the <u>schools</u>

   1b is, of course, the object of the preposition in 1a. 1c and 1d are coordinate clauses (two clauses connected by "and") that are subordinated to the main clause in 1a/b. 1e represents the complement of the verb "organize" in 1d (note that thanks to "well" it is only quite loosely integrated with 1d).
   All of 2 is a recast of 1e. Since all of 2 can also be seen as appositive to the sentence in 1, 1 and 2 could just as easily be seen as one macro-line and all labeled "1." 2b is part of the material that goes with the verb "means." 2c is a predicate (verb phrase) whose subject is in 2b. 2d is also loosely understandable as a clause conjoined to "a team" ("to organize a team and students interested in …"), and, thus, along with "team," it is a direct object to the verb "organize" in 2c. 2e recasts and adds to 2c. Finally, 2f is a complement to the verb "to get" in 2e (the syntax here is: "to get (verb) the curriculum (object) up and running and working (complement)").
   This is a perfect example of how loosely integrated sentences often are in speech. Nonetheless, the syntactic resources of the language are used to link micro-lines together and thereby to indicate some clues as to how the hearer can integrate and link up information across intonation units (micro-lines).
   In many respects the speaker often discovers or modifies some of these links as she is speaking. For various reasons, having to do with personality and social and institutional relationships, it turns out the speaker of the text above did not want to be the person responsible in the future for running meetings or even the rest of this first meeting. Thus, having said that she is

trying to organize "well what we're going to do in these meetings," she, then, recasts this throughout all of 2 as trying to organize not meetings, but "what it means" for all the participants to "try to organize" (themselves as) a team to get certain work done. Of course, "what it means" does not really fit semantically with the verb "organize" in 1d, despite the fact that it is recasting, and, thus, loosely taking on the role of the direct object of this verb in 1e.

This is a good example of how syntax, meaning, and organization are an emergent phenomenon "on line" as we speak and interact with each other in real time. There is a good deal more in the details of this text (e.g., "taking up a part of coordinating this project," rather than just "coordinating this project," or "try to organize a team," rather than "organize a team") through which we could uncover the workings of individual, social, and institutional factors, or which we could relate to what we may know or suspect about such factors from other sources of evidence.

How Meaning is "Carved Up"

Lines, macro-lines, stanzas, and macrostructure are important because they represent how speakers marry structure and meaning. They show us how speakers carve up or organize their meanings. At the same time, the way in which we analysts break up a text in terms of these units represents our hypothesis about how meaning is shaped in the text. It depicts our analysis of the patterning of meaning in the text.

We ask ourselves where we think lines, macro-lines, stanzas, and macrostructural units exist in the text, based on intonational, syntactic, and discourse features in the language we are analyzing, and what we know about the speaker's possible meanings, from whatever other sources (e.g., the larger context, other texts, interviews, ethnographic information, etc.). We make these structural decisions based partly on our emerging ideas about the overall themes and meaning of the text. We, then, use the structures (e.g., lines and stanzas) that are emerging in our analysis to look more deeply into the text and make new guesses about themes and meaning. We may come to think that some of the units we have demarcated are wrong, based on a deeper inspection of the intonation, syntax, and discourse features of the text, as well as on the basis of the deeper meanings we are coming to believe and argue that the text has.

In the end, a line and stanza representation of a text, like the one given above for the seven-year-old's story about her puppy, simultaneously serves two functions. First, it represents what we believe are the patterns in terms of which the speaker has shaped her meanings "on line" as she spoke. Second, it represents a picture of our analysis, that is, of the meanings we are attributing to the text. As analysts, we must tie back to this representation all the situated meanings and figured worlds we are attributing to the text and its context.

Readings

Bolinger, D. (1989). *Intonation and its uses: Melody in grammar and discourse*. Stanford, CA: Stanford University Press. [A classic book on intonation by a man who was a master of the field]

Brazil, D., Coulthard, M., & Johns, C. (1980). *Discourse intonation and language teaching*. London: Longman. [An older book, but, nonetheless, still the best introduction to intonation and its uses in discourse]

Chafe, W. L. (1979). The flow of thought and the flow of language, in T. Givon, Ed. *Syntax and semantics 12: Discourse and syntax*. New York: Academic Press, pp. 159–181. [Chafe's work is seminal on how language-in-use relates to the organization of language in the mind]

Chafe, W. L. (1980). The deployment of consciousness in the production of a narrative, in W. L. Chafe, Ed. *The pear stories: Cognitive, cultural, and linguistic aspects of narrative production*. Norwood, NJ: Ablex, pp. 9–50.

Chafe, W. L. (1994). *Discourse, consciousness, and time: The flow and displacement of conscious experience in speaking and writing*. Chicago: University of Chicago Press. [One of the best books ever written on discourse. Good discussion of idea units and the organization of language-in-use]

Finegan, E. (2007). *Language: Its structure and use*. Fifth Edition. Boston: Thomson Wadsworth. [Good introduction to linguistics]

Gee, J. P. (1985). The narrativization of experience in the oral style. *Journal of Education*, 167, 9–35. [Reprinted in C. Mitchell & K. Weiler, Eds. (1992) *Rewriting literacy: Culture and the discourse of the other*. New York: Bergin & Garvey, pp. 77–101]. [Explicates my approach to lines and stanzas in analyzing African-American children's language]

Gee, J. P. (1986). Units in the production of discourse. *Discourse Processes*, 9, 391–422. [Explicates the notion of lines and stanzas]

Gee, J. P. (1991). A linguistic approach to narrative. *Journal of Narrative and Life History*, 1, 15–39. [Explicates my approach to narrative]

Gee, J. P. (1993). Critical literacy/socially perceptive literacy: A study of language in action. *Australian Journal of Language and Literacy*, 16, 333–355.

Gee, J. P. (2007). *Social linguistics and literacies: Ideology in Discourses*. Third Edition. London: Falmer. [Updates material in my articles cited above]

Halliday, M. A. K. (1989). *Spoken and written language*. Oxford: Oxford University Press. [Classic book on the nature of and contrasts between speech and writing]

Halliday, M. A. K. & Greaves, W. (2008). *Intonation in the grammar of English*. London: Equinox Publishing. [Best technical book on intonation and its uses in discourse available]

Huddleston, R. & Pullum, G. K. (2002). *The Cambridge grammar of the English language*. Cambridge: Cambridge University Press. [An excellent descriptive grammar. The most comprehensive account of English grammar available today]

Hymes, D. (1981). *In vain I tried to tell you: Essays in Native American ethnopoetics*. Philadelphia: University of Pennsylvania Press. [Important work on the organization of lines and stanzas in Native American languages]

Hymes, D. (1996). *Ethnography, linguistics, narrative inequality: Toward an understanding of voice*. London: Taylor & Francis. [Collection of some of Hymes's work on lines, stanzas, and narrative]

Labov, W. (1972). The logic of nonstandard English, in *Language in the inner city*. Philadelphia: University of Pennsylvania Press, pp. 201–240. [Classic work on African-American Vernacular English and is relation to Standard English]

Labov, W. (1972). The transformation of experience in narrative syntax, in *Language in the inner city*. Philadelphia: University of Pennsylvania Press, pp. 354–396. [Labov's approach to the analysis of oral narratives is now standard]

Labov, W. & Waletzky, J. (1967). Narrative analysis: Oral versions of personal experiences, in J. Helm, Ed. *Essays on the verbal and visual arts: Proceedings of the 1966 Annual Spring Meeting of the American Ethnological Society*. Seattle, WA: University of Washington Press, pp. 12–44 [Classic article explicating a much used approach to linguistic narrative analysis]

Quirk, R., Greenbaum, S., Leech, G., & Svartvik, J. (1985). *A comprehensive grammar of the English language*. London: Longman. [An outstanding technical functional grammar based on actual English usage]

CHAPTER TEN
Sample of Discourse Analysis 1

Interview Data as an Example

This chapter and the two following will deal with data in an attempt to exemplify some of the tools of inquiry discussed in this book. As I pointed out in Chapter 8, actual discourse analyses will rarely, if ever, fully realize the ideal model sketched there. Real analyses, differently in different cases, concentrate more on some of the building tasks we have discussed than on others; they use some tools of inquiry more thoroughly than they do others. Since discourse analysis, like all science, is a social enterprise, we hope and trust the gaps in our own work will be filled in by others.

In this chapter, I do not attempt any full discourse analysis. Furthermore, I do not want to suggest that there is any "lock step" method to be followed in doing a discourse analysis. Thus, I use data here simply to give some examples relevant to a number of points raised in earlier chapters.

The data I use here comes from extended interviews with middle-school teenagers conducted by my research team. Our interviews take a specific form. In the first part, we ask teenagers questions about their lives, homes, communities, interests, and schools. We call this the "life part" of the interview. In the second part, the teens are asked to offer more "academic-like" explanations and opinions about societal issues such as racism and sexism. We call this the "society part" of the interview. In addition, we "shadow" the teenagers in their lives in school, at home, in their communities, and with their peer groups, as well as collect data about those schools, homes, and communities.

Each teenager is interviewed by a different research assistant on our project who is familiar with the teenager and his or her environment. The teens all view the interviewer as a "school-based" (indeed, college-based) person. And, in fact, we are interested in whether and how each teenager will accommodate to this identity. We have also interviewed, in a similar way, some of the teenagers' teachers and some university academics to see how they talk about similar issues.

I will concentrate here on two sets of our interviews. One set is interviews with teenagers from what I will call "working-class families." They all live in a post-industrial urban area in Massachusetts (U.S.) where, in fact, traditional working-class jobs are fast disappearing. The other set is interviews with teenagers from what I will call "upper-middle-class" families. These teens attend elite public schools in Massachusetts' suburban communities and all have parents one or both of whom are doctors, lawyers, or university professors.

I do not focus on two contrasting groups because I think any simple binary distinction exists here. There are clearly multiple and complex continua at play. Nonetheless, this particular contrast is an important starting place in today's "new capitalist," high-tech, global world. Across much of the developed world, young people from traditional working-class communities face a future with a severe shortage of good working-class jobs, thanks to the decline of unions and the outsourcing of jobs to low-cost centers across the world. They often attend troubled schools with limited resources, schools that engage in what from the point of view of current school-reform efforts are less efficacious ways of teaching. On the other hand, many students in wealthy suburbs and ex-urban "edge cities" live in communities and attend schools that, unlike those available to less well-off urban students, often give them "cultural capital" for an information-driven global world.

It has been argued that our new global capitalism is fast turning these two groups into separate "cultures" composed of people who share little or no "co-citizenship." The wealthier group is coming progressively to feel more affiliation with similar elites across the world and less responsibility for the less well off in their own country. And, of course, such affiliations are both the product and cause of shared figured worlds, social languages, and Discourses. The same phenomenon is happening across much of the globe.

Our "social-class" labels ("working class" and "upper middle class") have no more import than what the last paragraph has tried to convey. In fact, discourse analysts often look at two contrasting groups not to set up a binary contrast, but in order to get ideas about what the poles of a continuum may look like. We can get ideas that can then inform the collection of new data out of which emerges a much more nuanced and complex picture.

Co-constructing Socioculturally Situated Identities

In Chapter 8 we talked about how our seven building tasks are the seven components of any context we want to study via discourse analysis. I want to start with a consideration of Building Task 3 (Identities). I will look at how socially significant identities are mutually constructed in language and what this has to do with situated meanings, social languages, figured worlds, and Discourses. Here is what we had to say about Building Task 3 (Identities) as a component of contexts in Chapter 8:

> Building Task 3: Identities: How are situated meanings, social languages, figured worlds, intertextuality, Discourses, and Conversations being used to enact and depict identities (socially significant kinds of people)?

Socially situated identities are mutually co-constructed in interviews, just as much as they are in everyday conversations. For example, consider the following brief extracts from our interviews. The first one is from a college academic (an anthropologist) who teaches at a prestigious college in the town where our working-class teens live. The other is from a middle-school teacher who has had a number of our working-class teenagers in her classes. In these extracts, each numbered line is what I referred to in Chapter 9 as a "macro-line." If one macro-line is interrupted by another one, I use a notation like "2a" and "2b" to connect the two separated parts of the discontinuous macro-line.

A. **College Professor** (Female)

Interviewer: How do you see racism happening, in society, let's put it that way.

1. Um, well, I could answer on, on a variety of different levels. [I: uh huh]
2a. Um, at the most macro level, um, I think that there's um, um,
3. I don't want to say this in a way that sounds like a conspiracy, [I: mm hm]
2b. But I think um, that um, basically that the lives of people of color are are, are irrelevant to the society anymore. [I: mm hm]
4. Um, they're not needed for the economy because we have the third world to run away into for cheap labor, [I: uh huh]

B. **Middle-School Teacher** (Female)

Interviewer: I'm just curious whether 8th graders will tie that [consideration of social issues in their social studies class, JPG] into their, or maybe you in like leading the class would you ever tie that into like present power relations or just individual experiences of racism in their lives or something like that.
...

1. uh I talk about housing,
2. We talk about the [????] we talk about a lot of the low income things,
3. I said "Hey wait a minute,"
4. I said, "Do you think the city's gonna take care of an area that you don't take care of yourself?" [I: uh huh]
5. I said, "How [many of] you [have] been up Danbury Street?"
6. They raise their hands,
7. I say "How about Washington Ave.,"
8. That's where those gigantic houses are,
9. I said, "How many pieces of furniture are sitting in the front yard?" [I: mm hm] "Well, none."
10. I said "How much trash is lying around? None."
11. I said, "How many houses are spray painted? How many of them have kicked in, you know have broken down cars"

Throughout her interview, the professor treats actors, events, activities, practices, and Discourses in terms of economic and nation-state-level politics. She treats "racial problems" as transcending her city and as a global affair, despite the fact that she could well point to specific instances in her city. However, this "global voice" is co-constructed with the interviewer who very often couches both her main questions (which concern the same basic topics in each interview) and her follow-up questions in much more "theoretical," "abstract," and "global" terms than she does those to the middle-school teacher.

Though the middle-school teacher is interviewed by the same interviewer, the interviewer and teacher co-construct a very different, much more local sort of socially situated identity and voice for the teacher. In fact, researchers and teachers alike usually assume that school teachers, unlike college academics, have only a "local voice." Rarely are teachers invited to speak in more global and national ways about racial, literacy, or schooling issues.

Even these short extracts can lead us to some hypotheses about different figured worlds being used by the middle-school teacher and the university academic. The professor seems to apply a widespread academic figured world in terms of which actual behavior ("the appearances") follow from larger, deeper, more general, underlying, and hidden causes. The teacher seems to apply a widespread figured world in terms of which people's problems flow from their own behaviors as individuals, not from larger institutional, political, and social relationships among groups.

Any close inspection of the college professor's language and the middle-school teacher's would show that they are using different linguistic resources to enact two different social languages. The college professor uses more academic-like lexical items (e.g., "variety," "levels," "macro," "conspiracy," "people of color," "irrelevant," "the economy," "the third world," "cheap labor") and more complex syntax (e.g., "At the most macro level … I think that there's …" or "They're not needed for the economy because we have the third world to run away into for cheap labor"), as well as a clear argumentative structure, to speak in a global and abstract way that distances her from individuals and local realities.

The middle-school teacher uses less academic-like lexical items (e.g., "the low income things," "gigantic houses," "trash," "broken down cars") and somewhat less complex syntax (e.g., there are no instances of syntactic subordination between clauses in the above extract, save for the relative clause in macro-line 4), together with enacting dialogues in which she plays both the teacher and student parts. She speaks in a way that is dramatic, personal, and directly situated in her local experience.

We can see here, then, the ways in which the middle-school teacher and the college professor each use a distinctive social language and a distinctive set of figured worlds to situate the meanings of their words within two different and distinctive Discourses. The middle-school teacher speaks out of "teacher Discourse," inflected, of course, with the concrete realities of her school and community. The college academic, on the other hand, speaks out of a recognizable academic Discourse, again, of course, inflected by her own discipline and institution (note, by the way, how I have here myself constructed a more global identity for the academic by talking about "disciplines" and "institutions" and a more local one for the teacher by talking about "school" and "community").

Building Socially Situated Identities and Building Different Worlds

Let me start this section by stating a hypothesis we have drawn from our interviews with middle-school teenagers, and then looking at some of the data that we believe support this hypothesis. In looking at our data, we have tentatively reached the following conclusion: The working-class teens in our interviews use language to fashion their identities in a way that is closely attached to a world of "everyday" social and dialogic interaction (what Habermas calls "the life world"). The upper-middle-class teens in our interviews use language to construct their identities in a way that detaches itself from "everyday" social interaction and orients more towards their personal biographical trajectories through an "achievement space" defined by the (deeply aligned) norms of their families, schools, and powerful institutions in our society. In addition, the upper-middle-class teens often seem to use the abstract language of rational argumentation to "cloak" (or "defer") their quite personal interests and fears, while the working-class teens much more commonly use a personalized narrative language to encode their values, interests, and themes (a difference, perhaps, not unlike that between the college professor and the middle-school teacher).

One way, among many, to begin to get at how the working-class and upper-middle-class teenagers build different socially situated identities in language is to look at when they refer to themselves by speaking in the first person as "I." Let us call such statements "I-Statements" (e.g., "I think that the lives of people of color are irrelevant to the society" in the extract from the college professor above). We can categorize different I-Statements in terms of the type of predicate that accompanies "I," that is, in terms of what sort of thing the teenager says about him or herself. We will consider the following kinds of I-Statements:

a) "Cognitive statements" when the teenager talks about thinking and knowing (e.g., "I think ...," "I know ...," "I guess ...");
b) "Affective statements" when the teenager talks about desiring and liking (e.g., "I want ...," "I like ...");
c) "State and Action statements" when the teenager talks about his or her states or actions ("I am mature," "I hit him back," "I paid the bill");
d) "Ability and Constraint statements" when the teenager talks about being able or having to do things ("I can't say anything to them," "I have to do my paper route"); and
e) A category of what I will call "Achievement statements" about activities, desires, or efforts that relate to "mainstream" achievement, accomplishment, or distinction ("I challenge myself," "I want to go to MIT or Harvard").

These categories are, obviously, not randomly chosen. We have picked categories that, given our overall consideration of all the interviews, we believed might be important and interesting. Table 10.1 below shows, for seven of our teenagers, the distribution of different types of I-Statements in terms of the percentage of each type out of the total number of I-Statements the interviewee used in his or her whole interview (thus, e.g., Table 10.1 says that 32 per cent of all Sandra's I-Statements were "Affective statements," such as "I don't like them"). For the time being ignore the fact there are two sets of numbers for Brian—we will explicate why this is so in a later section (see Table 10.1).

Now is a good time to make a point about numbers in discourse analysis. The numbers in Table 10.1 are not meant to be "significant" in themselves. In

Table 10.1 Distribution of I-Predicates in interviews

	Working class			Upper middle class			
	Sandra	Jeremy	Maria	Brian	Emily	Ted	Karin
Category A							
AFFECTIVE	32	21	28	7/5	8	12	13
ABILITY-CONSTRAINT	7	7	7	5/6	1	4	2
STATE-ACTION	39	49	40	44/36	24	18	7
Sub-total (A)	78	77	75	57/48	33	28	22
Category B							
COGNITIVE	22	23	23	28/34	54	50	65
ACHIEVE	0	.5	2	15/18	13	22	13
Sub-total (B)	22	23	25	43/52	67	72	78

fact, discourse analysis, as I have construed it in this book, is not primarily about counting things. We use such numbers simply to guide us in terms of hypotheses that we can investigate through close scrutiny of the actual details and content of the teenagers' talk.

In Table 10.1, I have sub-totaled the scores for "Affective," "Ability-Constraint," and "State-Action" I-Statements, on the one hand, and the scores for "Cognitive" and "Achievement" I-Statements, on the other. I will call the first combination "Category A" and the second "Category B." When we make such combinations, we find something interesting and suggestive. The working-class teens are high in Category A and low in Category B, while the upper-middle-class teens are low in A and high in B. Why should this be so? It is, I would argue, our first indication that the working-class teens fashion themselves in language as immersed in a social, affective, dialogic world of interaction, and our upper-middle-class teens in a world of information, knowledge, argumentation, and achievements built out of these.

What the teens actually say in each category is more important than how many times they say certain sorts of things. In our studies we have found that working-class and upper-middle-class teenagers talk about quite different things when they speak in the first person, even when they are using the same I-Statement category (e.g., "Cognitive" or "Affective"). For example, consider a few typical examples of Cognitive I-Statements and Affective I-Statements from the "life part" of Sandra's and Maria's (working-class) and Emily's and Karin's (upper-middle-class) interviews:

COGNITIVE I-STATEMENTS

Sandra (Working Class):
I think it is good [her relationship with her boyfriend];
I think I should move out [of the house];
I didn't think it was funny [something she had done that made others laugh].

Maria (Working Class)
I guess they broke the rules;
I think I'm so much like a grown up;
I don't think they'd let me.

Emily (Upper Middle Class):
I think it's okay for now [living in her current town];
I think I have more of a chance of getting into college;
I think she's the coolest person in the whole world [a trip leader she admired].

Karin (Upper Middle Class)
I think they [her parents] want me to be successful;
I think of that as successful;
I don't really know anyone who doesn't understand me.

AFFECT/DESIRE

Sandra (Working Class)
Like I wanted to say, "Kinda kinda not. How could you kinda kinda not?";
I don't want to sit next to her, I don't want her huggin me or something;
(They [her friends] give me the answer) I want to hear.

Maria (Working Class)
I like hanging around with my aunt;
I like hanging around with big people;
I want to get out of my house.

Emily (Upper Middle Class)
Now I want to go to Europe;
I want to go to MIT [Massachusetts Institute of Technology, JPG];
I like backpacking and outdoor stuff.

Karin (Upper Middle Class)
I don't really care what other people think of me;
I feel pretty accomplished;
I'd like to be comfortable with my work [what she will do in the future].

The working-class teens' cognitive statements (here and throughout our data) almost always assume a background of dialogue and interaction. For example, Sandra makes clear elsewhere in her interview that other people don't like her boyfriend and that there is a debate about who should move out of the house. Or, to take another example, when Maria says, "I think I'm so much like a grown up," she has made it completely clear that this is a response to an ongoing struggle with her parents who will not give her the independence she wants.

The upper-middle-class teens' cognitive statements are explanatory claims within an explicit or assumed argumentative structure, rather than directly dialogic and interactional. We can point out, as well, that the upper-middle-class teens are very often focused on direct or implied assessment and evaluation of self and others. For example, when Emily says, "I think it's okay for now [living in her current town]," nothing in her interview suggests that this is in reaction to anything anyone else has said or thought. It is simply her assessment of her own autobiographical trajectory towards her own goals for success. When Karin says, "I think they want me to be successful," nothing in her interview suggests that this is in response to any doubts or debates about the matter. Karin, in fact, repeatedly says how supported and well understood she is by her parents.

If we consider the teenagers' Affective I-Statements (examples above) and I-Statements about their actions (not given above), we see that the upper-middle-class teens very often talk about relationships and activities in ways that seem to have a direct or indirect reference outside of themselves to achievement, success, and/or distinction in the adult world and in their futures. The working-class teens, on the other hand, seem to talk about activities and relationships in and of themselves and without such a side-long glance at their implications for the future. For example, considering two of our upper-middle-class teens, Emily's interview makes it clear that going to Europe and backpacking (see her Affective I-Statements above), and other similar activities mentioned throughout her interview, are like items on a résumé that will help towards getting into a prestigious college like MIT; Karin's remarks, here and throughout her interview, are heavily focused on what her present desires, feelings, and activities portend for the future in terms of achievement and success.

To see this point about activities further, consider a representative sample of Maria's (working-class) and Karin's (upper-middle-class) I-Statements that refer to actions (some of Karin's actions are actually classified in the category of Achievement I-Statements). I list actions involving speech separately below:

Karin (Upper Middle Class)
Action

I went a lot over the summer (to Boston)	I go sometimes to Faneuil Hall
I go to the Community center	On weekends I hang around with friends
I've met people with different racial ethnicity	I go to school

I play a lot of sports

I go to gymnastics two nights a week
I did well at that

I do soccer and gymnastics and
  tennis
I do tennis in Holiston
I always make sure that I do it
  [homework]

Speech

I'd say an event that changed my life
  (was) ...
I'd say over half of the people
but I've heard many ...

I usually let them know

I heard (about Rodney King)
I'm not saying that they didn't
  choose that

Maria (Working Class)
Actions

I look at her
I see (teenagers) walking places
when I do something right
I'll do the dishes
I go up to this one kid
I would help her cook

I see something pretty
after I come from New York
I wash the dishes
I watch (the videos)
I did my project on AIDS
I go crying to her

Speech

I talk to her a lot
I always tell her
I ask on Monday
I ask and they'll say no
I was like "I'm going to kill myself"
I'm like "why did I do that"

I'm like "I don't want to"
I ask once a week
I'm going to ask
I'll just go "fine"
I was like "what am I doing?"
I don't talk to her as much

It is clear that Karin's actions and activities are often tied to institutions and personal achievements, Maria's are not. In fact, the closest Maria comes to activities that appear to refer outside themselves to institutions or achievements is her remark that "I did my project on AIDS." Interestingly, she introduces this as a way to talk about her relationship with and attitude toward her younger sister, whom she considers much less mature than herself ("Last year I did my project on AIDS ... we had condoms on our board and my sister used to be like all yelling and she was all laughing").

When Karin talks about speech events, her verbs of saying are, in many cases, "cognitive," that is, estimates or claims (e.g., "I'd say over half of the people ...," "I ... let them know"—most of Karin's few speech events are in the society section of her interview and part of the arguments she is making to a fictionalized audience). Maria devotes far more of her interview to depicting herself as a speaker and her speech events are much more interactional and dialogical (even when speaking to herself she is responding to what has happened in an interaction).

One other indication that the working-class teens are more focused on the world of interaction than the upper-middle-class teens is the fact that they narrativize far more than the upper-middle-class teenagers. The percentage of lines in each teenager's transcript involved in a narrative is given in Table 10.2 below ("line" here means "micro-lines" in the "lines and stanzas" sense, basically "clauses" or "tone units," see Chapter 8 above).

Let me conclude this section by briefly summarizing the differences I have pointed to, thus far. The upper-middle-class teenagers are focused on knowledge claims, assessment, evaluation, their movement through achievement space, and the relationship between the present and the future. The working-class teens are focused on social, physical, and dialogic interactions.

It is important to see, as well, that these teenagers not only build different socially situated identities in language, they also build different worlds. They make the material world and the world of institutions mean different things. We see some indication above of what would emerge yet more strongly if we had the space to consider the interviews in full: the upper-middle-class teenagers' interviews express, directly and indirectly, an alignment (and trust) among family, school, community, adult, and teen in terms of norms, values, and goals. The working-class teens express, directly and indirectly, much less alignment (indeed, in many cases active disalignment) among family, school, community, adult, and teen in terms of norms, values, and goals. More importantly, the world for the upper-middle-class teens (as they construct it in these interviews) is a space where families, schools, and institutions create trajectories of achievement leading from their homes through prestigious schools to successful lives (in terms of things like status and careers). The world for the working-class teens (as they construct it in these interviews) is a space where schools and other institutions impinge much less directly on the world of the family, peer group, and "everyday" social interaction.

Social Languages

Speaking in the first person ("I") is only one of many ways in which people build identities in and through language. But, no matter how they do so, building different identities in language always implicates different social languages, since it is in and through different social languages, as they are

Table 10.2 Percentage of lines in each transcript involved in a narrative

Sandra	Jeremy	Maria	Brian	Emily	Ted	Karin
57%	35%	36%	19%	17%	12%	8%

embedded in different Discourses, that we enact, perform, and recognize different socially situated identities.

In fact, we have already pointed out that the working-class teenagers engage in narrative much more than do the upper-middle-class teenagers. And this is part of the difference between the distinctive social languages the teenagers are using in these interviews. Of course, in reality, each teen uses different social languages at different points of the interview. Nonetheless, we can see the narrative difference as connecting to a type of social language that is dominant in the working-class interviews as against the upper-middle-class interviews. The opposite side of this narrative difference is the fact that our upper-middle-class teens engage in a great deal more of what we might call "viewpoint and argument giving" ("argument" here is used in the sense of a set of grounded claims, not in the sense of a dispute). Such viewpoint and argument give recruits a quite different and distinctive form of language.

Since our interviews had a second part (what we called above the "society part") that was based on more abstract, academic-like questions, we might have expected that all of our interviewees would, especially in this part of the interview, have engaged in a lot of fairly impersonal or abstract viewpoint and argument giving. This is, in fact, true for the upper-middle-class teens, but not for the working-class teens. In fact, our expectation that "viewpoint and argument giving" will be accomplished through fairly impersonal and abstract language turns out simply to be a prejudice stemming from our own academic Discourses. The working-class teens often discuss social and personal events and feelings in the society part of the interview, just as they do in the life part. At the same time, the upper-middle-class teens by no means restrict their more impersonal "viewpoint and argument giving" to the society part of the interview, but engage in such talk in the life part, as well. I will argue below that the upper-middle-class teens' "viewpoint and argument giving" actually does often reflect personal motifs or themes, but in a fairly "impersonal" language.

Thus, we find that the upper-middle-class teenagers devote far more of their interviews, in both parts, to stating their viewpoints and constructing arguments for them in relatively distanced and impersonal ways. For example, consider two of our upper-middle-class teens: Brian devotes 39% of the lines in his interview to stating viewpoints and constructing arguments, and Karin devotes 44% of hers to these tasks. Such talk, though it does occur in our interviews with the working-class teenagers, is vanishingly rare in these interviews.

However, a deeper look at the interviews seems to show, I believe, that when the upper-middle-class teens are engaged in "viewpoint/argument" talk, they are often rhetorically clothing their own very personal interests and concerns in a more distanced language than the working-class teenagers typically use. At the very least, they are probably very much aware of the connections between their "distanced arguments" and their personal interests, values, and favored themes or motifs. For example, consider first Jeremy (working class) and Brian (upper middle class) on racism, and then a piece of talk from Karin (upper middle class). To save space, here and below I run transcript lines together and print texts continuously:

Jeremy

Interviewer: ... Is there racism [in society]?

... like colored people I don't, I don't like. I don't like Spanish people most of 'em, but I like, I like some of 'em. Because like if you, it seems with them, like they get all the welfare and stuff. Well, well white people get it too and everything but, I just—And then they think they're bad and they're like—They should speak English too, just like stuff like that.

Brian

Interviewer: Why do you think there are relatively few Hispanic and African-American doctors?

... well, they're probably discriminated against, but, but it's not really as bad as—as people think it is, or that it once was. Because, uh, I was watching this thing on T.V. about this guy that's trying to—How colleges and and some schools have made a limit on how many white students they can have there, and a limit—and they've increased the limits on how many Black and Hispanic students they have to have. So, a bunch of white people [rising intonation] are getting—even if they have better grades than the Black or Hispanic student, the Black or Hispanic student gets in because they're Black or Hispanic so. So, I think that that kinda plays an effect into it.

Karin

Interviewer: ... just say that it's a really really poor neighborhood um or a ghetto school, and, um, do you feel like somebody who goes to school there would have a chance, um, to succeed or become what they want to become?

Not as good as they would in a good school system. It depends on—I know that they probably don't. If they don't have enough money, they might not have enough to put into the school system and not—may not be able to pay the teachers and, um, the good supplies and the textbooks and everything. So maybe they wouldn't—they probably wouldn't have the same chance. But, I believe that every person has equal chances, um, to become what they want to be.

Jeremy (working class) personalizes his response and subordinates his argumentative "facts" to his by no means distanced viewpoint on minorities. Brian does not, at first, seem to personalize his response in the same way. However, in an interview replete with worries about "making it" in terms of going to a top college and having a successful career, there is little doubt that Brian's response is quite personal nonetheless (note also the rising emphatic intonation on "a bunch of white people"). While he most certainly could have stated his concerns as directly related to his own fears of affirmative action negatively impacting on his plans and desires, he chose not to.

Karin (upper middle class), after having spent a good deal of time discussing how good her school is and how important this fact is to her future, is then asked about the connection between poor schools and success. She first offers an argument, consistent with her views on her own school and future, that such schools will lower children's chances of success. However, she then contradicts her own argument when she says that she believes that every person has equal chances to become what they want to be. Given the fact that Karin spends a great deal of her interview talking about her hopes and fears for a successful future, it is easy to interpret her remark "they probably wouldn't have the same chance" as meaning "the same chance as ME." Karin's "distanced" argument has come too close to rendering the grounds of "worth" and "distinction" (of the sort she seeks) a matter of "chance," or, worse yet, injustice.

In fact, the upper-middle-class teenagers (as they all say in their interviews) have little actual experience with cultural diversity, too little to talk about it in the personal way in which Jeremy and Maria do. The educational sociologist Basil Bernstein would say that Jeremy and Maria are speaking in a "restricted code." But, ironically, this is so because their experience of social and cultural diversity is *not restricted* and the upper-middle-class teens' experience is. In fact, the upper-middle-class teens' language appears more "elaborated" in large part because they distance themselves from "everyday" social inter-action, mediate almost everything they say through their relationship to (and fears about) achievement and success, and sometimes "cloak" or "defer" their "material interests" with abstract argumentative talk in which they fail to directly mention their own personal interests and concerns.

Building Meaning in Narrative

Narratives are important sense-making devices. People often encode into narra-tives the problems that concern them and their attempts to make sense or resolve these problems. We turn now to how situated meanings and Discourse models work in narratives to build socially situated identities. We talk yet more about narratives in the next chapter, as well. We can get a start here if we turn, at last, to why there are two sets of numbers listed for Brian in Table 10.1 above. The first set of numbers is for Brian's interview as a whole. The second set is the numbers Brian receives when we remove the only extended narrative in his interview. We have seen above that the upper-middle-class teens narrativize much less than the working-class teens. The difference in Brian's numbers is illuminating when we see that his single extended narrative, without which his interview patterns move yet closer to those of his fellow upper-middle-class teens, is precisely about moving from being an "outsider" to being an "insider" among those very teens.

Below, I print Brian's narrative, followed by some of the interviewer's follow-up questions and Brian's answers. I have bolded Brian's repeated use of the habitual aspect marker "used to." Since it will not play a role in our analysis, I do not place Brian's interview into its lines and stanzas (we will use lines and stanzas in an analysis in the next chapter):

Interviewer: ... did anything happen that changed your life significantly?
Oh um, when I was in like fifth and sixth grade, I **used to** take like hyper-spasms at recess. Like I **used to** get like mad and run around like a freak. And I was like the most hated kid in the grade, because I was such a spaz and I **used to** run around, and I **used to** be like—I **used to** be like—Like I'd play tetherball at recess. So whenever like I lost, and somebody like cheated, I **used to** get so mad
I **used to** run around and everybody **used to** gather around like laughing at me and stuff. But then—but then like—then after a while, I just like realized why the hell am I doing this, everybody hates me, so then I stopped. And then—and then, it's not really any problem now. I'm just kind of—I dunno.

Interviewer: Did it kind of come to a head, where like it went really bad one time, and it was after that you just realized that –
No, not really, I just—in fifth grade I was pretty bad, but in sixth grade I just slowly, slowed down. And then seventh grade I didn't have any and then I haven't had any this year.

Interviewer: So, did you feel like it was cause you just—you hate losing? I mean when—I mean you were younger and –
No, no, the thing I hate is, I hate unfairness in games, and I just really hate it.

Interviewer: If somebody cheats?
Yeah and I got so mad, because whenever I played, they knew that I would take like, hyper-spasms, so they all gathered around and then when I—and then when I tried to hit the ball, they would like grab my shirt or something. So I was like [burned???].

Like many narratives that attempt to make deep sense of very real concerns, Brian's narrative is not "logically" consistent. In deep narratives, people do not focus on logical consistency; rather, they focus on the theme they are attempting to instantiate and develop. Brian describes himself as a pariah ("hyper-spasms," "get like mad and run around like a freak," "most hated kid," "a spaz"). His repeated use of the habitual aspect marker "used to" stresses that his pariah behavior and status were an enduring and ingrained trait, part of his "habitus" in Pierre Bourdieu's terms ("habitus" means one's habitual way of being in the world as embodied social being). He was driven to a state of frenzy by "cheating" or "unfairness in games."

Brian's "redemption" is described as a moment of sudden, personal, individual, rational realization. All at once, based on his personal effort, he "stopped" (note that the "unfairness" need not have stopped). But when the interviewer asks if, indeed, Brian's transformation was so sudden, he indicates that it was not (it appears to have taken a year or two).

We have seen that Brian, in his interview, is, like our other upper-middle-class teenagers, deeply invested in assessment of self and others, the connection between today's activities and tomorrow's success, and movement through "achievement space." Brian's narrative is his "origin" story, how he transformed himself through his own individual efforts and through rational calculation into an "acceptable" and "worthy" person (with the "right" *habitus*). Such "redemptive moments" are, in fact, typical of many male autobiographical stories in Western culture (Freccero 1986). In stressing individual effort and rationality overcoming emotion, Brian is enacting classic values of U.S. middle-class, capitalist culture.

At the same time, the "old Brian" (the one that "used to") learns that one cannot show too much emotion in the face of competition, even in the face of unfair competition. In middle-class, Anglo-centered culture, the person who shows heightened emotion, or too much emotion, "loses." And, yet, if one has learned to let go of one's anger at unfairness in competition, it is not likely that the larger inequities of our society (things such as racism, classism, and sexism) will engender much passion in Brian, and, indeed, they do not in his interview. Brian's transformation story—his only extended narrative—is, then, too, the story of an upper-middle-class child rationalizing (in several senses of the word) his assumption of an upper-middle-class *habitus*, a process that actually took extended norming and socialization.

Readings

Bourdieu, P. (1985). *Distinction: A social critique of the judgement of taste*. Cambridge, MA: Harvard University Press.

Freccero, J. (1986). Autobiography and narrative, in T. C. Heller, M. Sosna, & D. E. Wellbery, with A. I. Davidson, A. Swidler, & I. Watt, Eds. *Reconstructing individualism: Autonomy, individuality, and the self in Western thought*. Stanford, CA: Stanford University Press, pp. 16–29.

Gee, J. P. (2000). Teenagers in new times: A new literacy studies perspective. *Journal of Adolescent & Adult Literacy, 43*, 412–420.

Gee, J. P. (2002). Millennials and Bobos, *Blue's Clues* and *Sesame Street*: A story for our times, in Donna E. Alvermann, Ed. *Adolescents and literacies in a digital world*. New York: Peter Lang, pp. 51–67,

Gee, J. P. (2006). Self-fashioning and shape-shifting: Language, identity, and social class, in D. Alverman, K. Hinchman, D. Moore, S. Phelps, & D. Waff, Eds. *Reconceptualizing the literacies in adolescents' lives*. Second Edition. Hillsdale, NJ: Erlbaum, pp. 165–186.

Gee, J. P., Allen, A.-R., & Clinton, K. (2001). Language, class, and identity: Teenagers fashioning themselves through language. *Linguistics and Education, 12*, 175–194.

Gee, J. P. & Crawford, V. (1998). Two kinds of teenagers: Language, identity, and social class, in D. Alverman, K. Hinchman, D. Moore, S. Phelps, & D. Waff, Eds. *Reconceptualizing the literacies in adolescents' lives*. Hillsdale, NJ: Erlbaum, pp. 225–245.

CHAPTER ELEVEN
Sample of Discourse Analysis 2

A Case Study: Sandra

In this chapter I turn to a closer look at just one of the teens in the study discussed in the last chapter. The girl we will meet in this chapter is "Sandra" (not her real name), one or our working-class teenagers. Sandra is an active and resilient participant in her environments, with no "special" problems untypical of those environments, though those environments present plenty of very real problems for teenagers like Sandra. The interviewer was a middle-class white female graduate student earning a PhD in psychology. She was known to Sandra to be interested in teenage girls' lives at home and at school.

My main concern with Sandra's interview will be to analyze one of the many narratives she tells. But I want to set the analysis of this narrative in the larger context of Sandra's whole interview. I want to stress the ways in which an analysis of the rest of the interview and of the narrative can mutually support each other, helping us to achieve some degree of validity in terms of criteria like coverage and convergence (as well as linguistic detail, as we draw on a variety of different aspects of language).

We will start our analysis of Sandra's interview by considering the whole interview and reflecting on two of the building tasks we discussed in Chapters 2, 7, and 8, namely the Connections Building Task (no. 6) and Sign Systems and Knowledge Building Task (no. 7). Let us start with Connections:

6. Connections: In any situation things are connected or disconnected, relevant to or irrelevant to each other, in certain ways.

Our first step was to look across the whole interview for themes, motifs, or images that co-locate (collocate) with each other, that is, themes, images, or motifs that seem to "go together." Such related themes connect diverse parts of the interview together and give it a certain overall coherence and "texture." In doing so, they render certain things as connected and relevant to each other in Sandra's world as depicted in her talk and other things as not as closely connected or relevant to each other.

There are three related motifs that run through Sandra's interview. All three of these motifs have to do with how Sandra sees things in her world as connected or disconnected, especially the latter. In fact, the notion of connection and especially disconnection is a major overall theme in Sandra's interview and worldview. In each of these cases, Sandra uses many words and phrases that appear to share certain aspects of situated meaning with each other. Below, I list some examples of each of these under the labels "Disconnection," "Not Caring," and "Language and Laughter." These are Sandra's three major motifs. It is apparent that "Not Caring" is also a form of disconnection, and many of the "Language and Laughter" examples involve affective language, nonsense, noise, or laughter as ways to disconnect from authority and hurtful (judgmental) language. These three motifs constitute connected threads that run throughout Sandra's interview:

Motif 1: *Disconnection*. Examples: Sandra's boyfriend is blamed for things, but "like nothing happens, he don't get punished"; Sandra tells her father to "shove it," but "I don't get punished" (there is "no point since they are getting a divorce"); Sandra's best friend is punished by her father "for nothing"; her best friend's father makes her friend clean up a mess she didn't make; Sandra's boyfriend refuses to clean up a mess he made, but goes on to clean up the whole yard unasked; Sandra is "always in trouble for what she didn't do"; drunken neighbors give her too much money for baby-sitting; Sandra "forgets to forget" a baby-sitting appointment that had been canceled and shows up anyway, and the people go out anyway; Sandra emotionally "freaks out" at night, but doesn't really know why; Sandra wants no relationship with her parents because too good a relationship would be "weird"; Sandra was "supposed to have been a boy," but the adoption agency failed to tell her parents she was a girl; mother punishes sister without knowing what really happened; a friend tells her one of her favorite dresses is ugly and offers to take it to the Salvation Army only to keep it for herself; Sandra's grandmother is the "thing she holds onto," but "she is kinda flaky lately"; Sandra's friends laugh at her at a party, but she can't understand what's so funny, she doesn't "get it at all."

Motif 2: *Not Caring*. Examples: Sandra's boyfriend swears and smokes and his "mom doesn't care"; he smokes weed and "nobody cares"; he was "on house arrest and he went out anyway"; Sandra and her friends blame her boyfriend for everything, but "he don't care"; Sandra "doesn't care" that "nobody likes him [her boyfriend]," nor that her father "hates" him [her boyfriend]; Sandra's best friend is adopted, but "she doesn't care"; Sandra's best friend writes on mirrors "and she doesn't care"; if people say she's a "slut," "it doesn't bother her."

Motif 3. *Language and Laughter*. Examples: Sandra's sister's fiancé says he hates her and then gives her a diamond ring; Sandra's sister's fiancé threatens her, but he "is only fooling around"; Sandra blurts out "shut up, you fart smellers" at a wedding party when people are looking at her and she doesn't know what to say; Sandra often says things like "pool pilter" instead of "pool filter"; people she cares about give her "the answer I want to hear, that sounds right, with my problem"; Sandra's grandmother says "weird funny" things to make her laugh, like "I smell you" rather than "I love you"; Sandra's oldest sister says something good "and then ruins it"; Sandra's best friend's mother is "cool" and "we talk to her" because she "buys cigarettes for people" and "she won't say nothin'"; if someone says something to hurt her feelings, Sandra shakes until "someone says something to make me feel better"; Sandra's boyfriend and grandmother hold her to make her feel better, but her mother "says stupid things"; when Sandra confronts a white girl who "thinks she's black" and who has insulted Sandra, the girl puts her fist to Sandra's face and says "Talk to the hand, my face don't understand" and Sandra replies "If your hand had a mouth I'd talk to it"; Sandra likes her boyfriend because he's "funny" and "makes me laugh"; her best friend makes her laugh when she does funny stuff she doesn't realize she's doing; her best friend makes her laugh by making funny noises; her best friend makes her laugh by pretending to smoke in a way she really doesn't.

There are various things we could do with these motifs, in terms of worries about the validity of our analysis. For example, we could get "inter-judge reliability" in regard to the words and phrases within these themes, or in regard to similar or different themes independent judges might come up with. While there is certainly nothing wrong with this, my interest in these themes is in using them to begin to form hypotheses about some of Sandra's situated meanings and figured worlds, hypotheses that I can then check by further consultation of this and other data.

Ultimately, the validity of the analysis will reside in how the ideas we can generate from the above motifs help to illuminate other data (coverage), data that we hope will lead us to similar conclusions (convergence). I will also appeal, below, to the details of linguistic structure, and I have had a number of other discourse analysts go over this data with me, checking my conclusions with them and being sure that they do not see important motifs I have missed (agreement). Remember, validity is never "once and for all." Other people working on our data, or similar data, will discover things that support, revise, or challenge our own conclusions. Validity is social.

So we see that Sandra uses a large number of words and phrases that take on, in her interview, situated meanings that cluster around the three motifs we have listed above. In turn, these motifs are all integrally concerned with building connections and disconnections in the world as Sandra sees it and portrays it in her interview. However, Sandra's third motif, the one we have labeled Language and Laughter, also relates to Building Task 7, Sign Systems and Knowledge:

> 7. Sign Systems and Knowledge: In any situation, one or more sign systems and various ways of knowing are operative, oriented to, and valued or disvalued in certain ways.

In Motif 3, in particular, Sandra seems to disavow the *representational* function between words and the world, the very language function that others (e.g., schools) take to be of primary importance. By "representational function," I mean the idea that language connects directly and straightfor-wardly ("objectively") to the world "out there" ("re-presents" it), and that this has little to do with how people feel, what their needs are, or what their personal opinions, based on their own lived experiences, are. Sandra sees words said only because they are "true" or are "facts" backed up by some authority figure (e.g., her sister, her mother, her father, or, by extension, her teacher) as "stupid" and as a way to "ruin" things.

In turn, Sandra celebrates the social, bonding, and affective functions of language. Language that is silly or funny, but that "feels right" and that is intended to make one feel good is the only truly efficacious language. Sandra wants to relate only to those who tell her "the answer I want to hear, that sounds right, with my problem." She wants a relationship with an adult only if they "won't say nothin'" (i.e., engage in judgmental language or tell on her) or if they speak "silly," but endearing, talk to her, like her grandmother.

In terms of Building Task 7, Sandra is privileging one form of language, namely affective, caring language, and disprivileging another form, namely objective unemotional fact-giving authoritative language. Of course, this also relates to ways of knowing the world and other people, as well as relating to them, that Sandra either prefers or disprefers. Both from how Sandra carries out her work with this building task, and from many other aspects of her interview, we eventually drew the hypothesis that she was operating with a figured world something like:

Sandra's Figured World about Language:
Objective, fact-giving language, especially objective, fact-giving, judgmental language, is the preserve of "authority" figures, who are uncaring and untrustworthy. In contradistinction to such language, language that is used primarily for social bonding and which speaks to people's emotional needs, and is not used primarily to give facts or make judgments, is the preserve of friends and people who are caring and trustworthy.

Sandra disavows "authoritative representation" (whether adult control or the authority of asocial "factual" language), both in terms of how her world is and in terms of her ways of being in that world. This disavowal is coupled with a celebration of social interaction outside of or opposed to such authoritative representation. Once we have hypothesized this figured world as operative in Sandra's interview, we can gather more data about how far and widely it functions in her world. It would be particularly interesting, for example, to see if and how it operates in her relationship to teachers and school. Evidence we connected on this score showed that, in fact, Sandra liked teachers who showed they cared about the students personally (e.g., one who knew a student was asleep in class because she had been working at a job the night before) and disliked those who stressed academic content, but not caring.

Figured worlds do not belong to just one person. They are shared by a social group whose reality and experience they seek to capture in a useful, albeit oversimplified way. Thus, we would hypothesize that Sandra's figured world is shared by some or many of her peers and others in her world. We would, thus, need to extend our data collection (or look through the data from our other working-class kids) and check this hypothesis out. And, indeed, we found that Sandra's figured world ("cultural model") above holds across a number of her peers and reflects their view of authority figures.

The anthropologist John Ogbu has argued that, in his studies of students in urban classrooms in the United States, there are two different figured worlds at play about the relationship between teacher and student. Some students (among whom he argues are those from immigrant families that freely chose to come to the U.S. to improve their lives) operate with a "pragmatic, utilitarian" model that stresses that what is important about the relationship between teacher and student is that the teacher has important and useful knowledge and skills to transmit to the student. Whether the teacher likes or cares about the student or his or her family or cultural group is less important than the knowledge and skills being transmitted.

Other students (among whom Ogbu argues are those from families whose ancestors came by force to the U.S., for example African-Americans, and Native Americans and some Latinos whose ancestral lands were taken by the U.S.) operate by a "caring" model that stresses that what is important about the relationship between teacher and student is that the teacher likes, respects, and cares about the student and his or her family and cultural group. The transmittal of knowledge and skills, on this model, should operate within a caring relationship. These students tend to disaffiliate from teachers and schools whom they see as uncaring, disrespectful, or untrustworthy.

Sandra, though she is a lower-socioeconomic white girl whose ancestors, long ago, came freely to the U.S., clearly operates by Ogbu's caring model, one he attributes to many African-American students. In fact, we have argued that she holds a yet more general caring model—one that applies across the board to authority figures—and also ties it to forms of language in interaction (authoritative, fact-giving language vs. affective, social, caring language).

Let me give a final brief example that captures the figured world we have attributed to Sandra. In response to the interviewer's question "Is there someone … who you feel really doesn't understand you?," Sandra breaks into a long story about taking a drive with her sister after she (Sandra) had been punished by her mother, where her sister clearly wanted to offer Sandra "authoritative" advice and to know "facts" about her life (e.g., in regard to boys and safe sex) outside of any ongoing social interaction ("She's never talked to me like that before"). While there are other parts of Sandra's interview where she talks freely about sex with her friends, her response here is "Wow! That's weird."

The understanding Sandra wants from her sister—or anyone else, for that matter—is based on words that consider her affective (not cognitive) perspective, that are part and parcel of ongoing egalitarian social interaction, and that are used to heal and bond. Words outside such a context, "authoritative words," make "no sense." Thus, she says of her sister: "… she'll give me a right answer, like the answer that I want to hear, … but then we'll keep talking about it, and it will make no more sense, no more sense." By this, Sandra means that the sister will start to answer in an empathetic and affective way, but then switch to more authority-based talk seeking facts and offering adult advice.

Sandra's Narrative

My main interest in this chapter is to see how our data and ideas about Sandra's motifs can illuminate and get illuminated by a close look at one of her narratives. Turning to one of Sandra's narratives allows us to get much closer to the details of her actual language and "voice."

At the beginning of her interview, Sandra brings up her boyfriend, and the interviewer asks "What kind of boyfriend is he?" Sandra responds with what sounds like a series of only loosely connected stories. However, Sandra's approach to narrative is classically "oral." Once we carefully consider the features of such storytelling, it becomes apparent that Sandra's seemingly multiple stories constitute one tightly organized unified story.

Sandra's story is reprinted below. I label its sub-stories and sub-sub-stories in terms that will become clear in the analysis to follow (the story is printed in terms of its idealized lines and stanzas, see Chapter 9):

STORY: THE RETURN OF THE TABLE
FRAME
Stanza 1
1. [Sighs] He's nice.
2. He's, he's, he like he's okay, like
3. I don't know how to explain it.
4. Like, say that you're depressed, he'd just cheer ya up somehow.
5. He would, he'd make ya laugh or somethin
6. And you can't stop laughin, it's so funny

SUB-STORY 1: BREAKING THINGS
SUB-SUB-STORY 1: BREAKING THE FAN
EXPOSITION
Stanza 2
7. Like he does these, like today his mom hit the, she she, he was, he was, he was arguing with his mom,
8. He swears at his mom and stuff like that,
9. He's like that kind of a person
10. And his mom don't care.

Stanza 3
11. He smokes,
12. His mom don't care or nothin,
13. He smokes weed and everything and nobody cares.
14. Cos they can't stop him,
15. He's gonna do it anyway
16. Like on house arrest he went out anyway.

START OF SUB-SUB-STORY 1 PROPER
Stanza 4 [Started]
17. So they're like so yesterday he was arguing
18. And she held a rake
19. And she went like that to hit him in the back of the butt,

Stanza 5 [Expository Aside]
20. Like she don't hit him,
21. She wouldn't hit him

22. She just taps him with things,
23. She won't actually like actually hit him

Stanza 4 [Continued]
24. She just puts the rake like fool around wit' him,
25. Like go like that,
26. Like he does to her.

Stanza 6
27. Like he was, and like she was holding the rake up like this
28. And he pushed her
29. And the rake toppled over the um, fan.
30. It went kkrrhhh, like that.
31. And he started laughing,

Stanza 7 [Expository Aside]
32. And when he laughs, everybody else laughs
33. Cos the way he laughs is funny,
34. It's like hahahahah!
35. He like laughs like a girl kind of a thing.
36. He's funny.

Stanza 8
37. And then his mother goes, "What are you doing Mike?"
38. And she's like going, "What are you doing? Why are you laughing?"
39. And she goes, "Oh my god it broke, it broke!"
40. And she's gettin all, she's gettin all mad the fan's broken
41. And she trips over the rake,

Stanza 9
42. And she goes into the room
43. And she's like, "Don't laugh, don't laugh,"
44. And he keeps laughin.
45. It's just so funny.

SUB-SUB-STORY 2: BREAKING THE TABLE
EXPOSITION
Stanza 10
46. And he'll knock down the table
47. And he'll, like we'll play a game,
48. It's me, Kelly and him and Kelly's boyfriend,
49. It's just kinda fun
50. Cos it's just weird,

Stanza 11
51. We like don't get in trouble,
52. Like he gets blamed for it,
53. Like nothing happens.
54. He don't get punished.

Stanza 12
55. So we always blame him for everything.
56. He don't care,
57. He says, "go ahead, yeah, it doesn't matter."

START OF SUB-SUB-STORY 2 PROPER
Stanza 13
58. So we were pulling the table
59. And he was supposed to sit on it, jump on it and sit on it
60. And he didn't,
61. He missed

Stanza 14
62. And the table went blopp! over
63. And it broke.
64. Like it's like a glass patio thing
65. And it went bbchhh! All over everywhere.

Stanza 15
66. He's like, "Oh no!"
67. Well Kel's like, Kelly goes, "What happened, What happened? What did you do now Mike?"
68. He goes, "I broke the table,"
69. She's like "[sigh]," like that.

SUB-STORY 2: MONEY FROM WINDOW FALLING ON HAND
Stanza 16
70. He just got money from his lawyers
71. Because he slit, he slit his wrists last year,
72. Not on purpose,
73. He did it with, like the window fell down on him,

Stanza 17
74. Well, anyway, it came down and sliced his hand like right um here
75. And has a scar there
76. And um, it was bleeding
77. So they had to rush him to the hospital,
78. It wouldn't stop,
79. He had stitches.

Stanza 18
80. And they said that he could sue,
81. And they got five grand.
82. So they just got it two weeks ago
83. So he just bought her new table.

FRAME
Stanza 19
84. He's okay.

85. He's, he's nice in a caring,
86. He's like really sweet

Sandra organizes her oral text in terms of "the principle of the echo," that is, later parts of the text echo or mirror earlier ones, a key device in oral storytelling in many cultures. This lends—to switch to a visual metaphor—to a "boxes within boxes" shape to her text. Below, in Figure 11.1, the structure of Sandra's oral text is outlined, notating but a few of its most salient echoing features (for some readers, Figure 11.1 may be distracting until they have read the analysis of Sandra's story—feel free to skip it, if that is the case, and come back to it later).

Sandra's whole oral text is bracketed in Figure 11.1 by a repeated frame: the boyfriend is nice. The main story is composed of two sub-stories. The first ("sub-story 1") is about losses caused by the boyfriend accidentally breaking things. The second ("sub-story 2") is about the boyfriend gaining money because a thing (i.e., a window) has accidentally "broken" him (i.e., injuring his wrists). This "inverse accident" leads to one of the "lost" things being restored (i.e., the table), yet another sort of inversion. And, of course, "restoration" of a "lack/loss" is a classic narrative closing device in oral-based cultures. The first sub-story ("sub-story 1") is itself composed of two stories. The first ("sub-sub-story 1") is about the breaking of the fan; the second ("sub-sub-story 2") is about the breaking of the table.

There are large amounts of parallelism between the two breaking narratives (the fan and the table). Both begin with expository stanzas saying that the boyfriend's actions always go unpunished. These stanzas are followed, in both cases, by "fooling around" involving the boyfriend. Then, in each case, an object falls and makes a noise. The accident leads, in the first case, to the boyfriend being asked "What are you doing?," and, in the second, to his being asked "What did you do now?" These questions both go unanswered. The fan story closes with the mother issuing a verbal command to the boyfriend to stop laughing, a command which goes unheeded. The table story closes with the boyfriend's sister issuing no verbal command, but merely an unverbalized sigh. The boyfriend's laughter in the first story is echoed by his sister's sigh in the second.

These two breaking stories are both about "accidents" involving the boyfriend that lead to loss (fan, table). They are followed by a story (sub-story 2) about another accident involving the boyfriend—only this accident is not play, but a serious injury; a person rather than a thing breaks; and the accident leads not to loss, but to gain (money) and restoration (the table). In the fan story, the boyfriend will not heed his mother when she asks him to stop laughing. In the window story, the boyfriend restores the table to the mother without being asked to do so. Such "reversals" and "inversions," are, of course, powerful integrative or connection devices. Additionally, this sort of parallel structuring lends a certain "equivalence logic" to the text. Different stanzas are equated either through direct similarity or through reversals, a looser sort of similarity.

Frame: S1: Boyfriend is nice

STORY: Replacing the table

Sub-story 1: Breaking things

Sub-sub-story 1: Breaking the fan

S2–3:   Exposition: Boyfriend does things, nobody cares

S4:   Mother fooling around with boyfriend leads to:

S6:   Fan falls and makes noise: kkrrhhh
            Boyfriend laughs

S7:   Boyfriend laughs
            Boyfriend makes noise: hahahahah!

S8:   Mother asks: "What are you doing Mike?"

S9:   Mother tells boyfriend not to laugh
            Boyfriend keeps laughing

Sub-sub-story 2: Breaking the table

S10–12:   Exposition: Boyfriend does things, doesn't get in trouble

S13:   Boyfriend fooling around with the girls leads to:

S14:   Table falls & makes noise: blopp! bbchhh!

S15:   Sheena asks "What did you do now Mike?"
            Sheena makes a noise: sigh

Sub-story 2: Boyfriend gets money from window falling on his hand

END OF STORY: Boyfriend replaces table ("So he just bought her new table")

Frame: S19: Boyfriend is nice

Figure 11.1 **The structure of Sandra's oral text**

One of my interests, as a linguist, in Sandra's story is this: it is now well known that many African-American children, teenagers, and adults can tell extremely well-formed "oral style" stories (which, by no means, implies they are not perfectly literate, as well)—though this style of storytelling is not usually "successful" in school, especially in the early years. These stories share aspects of the style of Western oral-culture "classics" like Biblical stories and Homer's epics (not to mention a great many non-Western oral-culture "classics"), as well as aspects of literature such as some poetry and the prose of "modernist" writers like James Joyce and Virginia Woolf. They also incorporate some features unique to African-American culture, as well as features rooted in African cultures.

We know much less—next to nothing—about the "natural occurring" (i.e., non-school-based) narrative abilities of white working-class people, especially children and teenagers. What little has been said is often pretty negative. I would hope that Sandra tempts a reassessment.

Sandra's story encapsulates many of the themes and motifs we have discussed above: disconnection (no direct consequences to boyfriend's acts; table restored unasked); disavowal of authoritative language as efficacious (the mother's command goes unheeded, her question and the sister's go unanswered; the sister/peer only sighs); a world of laughter, noise, and physical and social action interaction; a world of accidents and play, not facts, well-connected happenings, and knowledge; a world in which what counts is the affect (e.g., laughter) you effect in others.

We can see that the sorts of hypotheses we drew from our study of Sandra's motifs, hypotheses which are illuminated by and draw further support from a study of Sandra's first-person statements (not discussed here), help, in turn, illuminate the deeper sense of Sandra's narrative. At the same time, our analysis of that narrative gives us further support for the sorts of hypotheses we can draw from Sandra's motifs. What we are gaining here, then, is coverage (ideas inspired by one part of the data extend to and illuminate other parts) and convergence (ideas from new parts of the database continue to support ideas we have gotten from other parts of the database). Further, we have begun to support our ideas with a variety of different linguistic details in the data (linguistics).

Ultimately, what we see is that Sandra thematizes an opposition between "authoritative representation" and "sympathetic social interaction" as part and parcel of her "identity work." Since the realm of "authoritative representation" is quite likely to be associated with schools, Sandra's very identity work will (and, in fact, does) work against her affiliation with school, unless the school comes to know, understand, and adapt to her language and identities.

Readings

Gee, J. P. (1997). Thematized echoes, *Journal of Narrative and Life History,* 7, 189–196.

Gee, J. P. (2006). Self-fashioning and shape-shifting: Language, identity, and social class, in D. Alverman, K. Hinchman, D. Moore, S. Phelps, & D. Waff, Eds. *Reconceptualizing the literacies in adolescents' lives.* Second Edition. Hillsdale, NJ: Erlbaum, pp. 165–186.

CHAPTER TWELVE
Sample of Discourse Analysis 3

For a final sample of discourse analysis I want to return to some data in Chapter 2, namely the history project where university academics and school teachers were working together. In this chapter we will look beyond the data in Chapter 2 to see how later events can give us yet deeper insight into what was going on in our original data. Once again, my goal here is simply to show some of the sorts of questions and issues that can arise in the course of analyzing the building tasks we have discussed and using the tools of inquiry we have introduced.

The data in Chapter 2 concerned a university history professor ("Sara Vogel") who wanted to work with middle-school teachers to get students engage in doing oral history. She wanted the children to interview their relatives and neighbors to gain information about the history of their local neighborhoods and the city in which they lived. At the same time, she was working towards writing a grant to gain federal funding for a longer-term and bigger project of the same sort in the local schools.

The university at which the professor taught ("Woodson") was a small elite private university in "Middleview," a largely working-class industrial city that had, in recent years, lost a good deal of its heavy industry to overseas competition. There were historic town–gown tensions between the university and the city and, in particular, tensions between people who taught at the university and people who taught in the public schools, tensions over status and commitment to the city. The university faculty were not born in the city and often did not stay there, moving on to other jobs in other cities; the public school teachers were invariably born there and intended to stay there.

The data we looked at in Chapter 2 came from the first official meeting of the project. This meeting was attended by the university history professor, two of her undergraduate research assistants, a representative of a group that was helping to the fund the collaboration between the professor and the teachers (who we will call "Ariel" and who was an advanced graduate student), two curriculum consultants, and the teachers. The curriculum consultants were professionals who worked for a local historical museum. They were specialists in designing history curricula for children and were hired by the funders to help the university history professor and Ariel, neither of whom knew much about curricula in schools. The data we looked at in Chapter 2 was talk from one of the teachers ("Karen Jones"). Karen had been asked by Ariel, who was chairing the meeting, to give those at the meeting some background on what had transpired prior to this first official meeting.

As we saw earlier, the history professor had called the curriculum coordinator at Karen's school—"Mary Washington"—to ask for help on her project and to gain access to the school. A curriculum coordinator in a school, though usually a former teacher, is often viewed more as an administrator than as a teacher by the teachers in the school, at least this was so in Middleview. I repeat the data below:

1. Last year, Mary Washington, who is our curriculum coordinator here, had a call from Sara at Woodson
2. And called me and said:
3. "We have a person from Woodson who's in the History Department
4. And she's interested in doing some research into Black history in Middleview
5. And she would like to get involved with the school
6. And here's her number
7. Give her a call"
8. And I DID call her
9. And we BOTH expected to be around for the Summer Institute at Woodson
10. I DID participate in it
11. But SARA wasn't able to do THAT

From just this data we might guess that Karen Jones is bothered by the fact that Prof. Vogel contacted her school's curriculum coordinator and not Karen herself directly. Karen's language makes it sound as though she was "ordered" by Mary Washington to help Prof. Vogel. We pointed out in Chapter 2, as well, that Karen's talk emphasizes that she acted (making the call and attending the institute) even when "ordered" to, while Prof. Vogel failed to act (i.e., to attend the Summer Institute) even when she had initiated the original events. Thus, too, Karen makes herself seem reliable and Prof. Vogel not.

Note here, even in my own description, that it is hard to name the protagonists without notating status and power differences, an issue that we saw in Chapter 2 was relevant in the data itself. I have referred to the history professor as Prof. Vogel and to the teacher as "Karen Jones" or just "Karen." Partly I have done this to make clear who is who, but, nonetheless, it is a problem that becomes an issue to the participants themselves in terms of how status and power do and will function in the project. Hereafter I will refer to everyone by their first names and hope readers will remember that Karen and Jane are teachers, Sara is the historian, Mary the curriculum coordinator, Ariel is the chair of the meeting and the representative of the funders, and Shirley and Cynthia are the curriculum consultants (specialists from the history museum).

After the group had met for several weeks, a meeting occurred where direct evidence appeared that Karen and the other teachers were, indeed, bothered— and had been bothered from the outset of the project—that Sara had gotten to the school's children through the curriculum coordinator (Mary) and not through the teachers themselves. The teachers started the meeting by saying that they were no longer sure what the project was about; it seemed to them confused and unfocused. They went on to point out that Sara had, some time ago, given a draft of a grant proposal she was working on to the curriculum coordinator, Mary, not to the teachers themselves. The grant proposal was intended eventually to go to a federal agency to seek funding for continuing the current project or one like it. The teachers had not seen the grant and had noticed that, as a teacher we will call "Jane" (a good friend of Karen's) said: "there is no mention of the teachers as an actual component in the grant program." The grant proposal proposed to pay others, but seemed to take it for granted that teachers would work on the project without pay. Jane went on to say:

> You talk about um grant funding for curriculum planners, but I presumed that was the Shirley and Cynthia position. You talked about graduate students or even undergraduates, you know, funding those positions, but there was nothing that incorporated the actual classroom teachers in the grant proposal

Shirley and Cynthia are the curriculum consultants from the historical museum. Sara replies that "it's good for me to hear your concerns" and acknowledges that there "needs to be a committee made up of teachers as well as curriculum planners in terms of figuring out what resources are necessary or what ideally we would like to ask for in a grant." Sara's response elicits the following lengthy reply from Jane. In this reply Jane clearly returns to Karen's story about being told to call Sara, the data we looked at in Chapter 2. The text below is printed in terms of stanzas that I label in such a way as to help guide the discussion below (I will explicate the numbering system below):

JANE:
STANZA 1
TEACHERS NOT CURRICULUM COORDINATORS NEED TO BE ASKED
1a.   Well I think
1b.   one thing you need to recognize
1c.   about the structure of the Middleview schools
1d.   is that if Joanne, Linda, Karen, and I
1e.   or any combination thereof
1f.   are involving our classrooms
1g.   we are the people who need to be asked
1h.   and to be plugged into it.

2a.   Joe [a curriculum coordinator from another school] does
2b.   um as curriculum coordinator for Freeland Street
2c.   does not have the right to commit Joanne Morse.

3.   Nor Lucy Delano.

4a.   Nor does Mary [Washington]
4b.   have the right to commit
4c.   or structure the grant for us.

STANZA 2

THE TEACHERS IN THE AREA OWN THE KIDS

5a.   Uh it becomes a question
5b.   like Karen said
5c.   this isn't her priority area
5d.   that she wants to be in.

6a.   If it is mine
6b.   or someone else
6c.   we are the direct people.

7.   In a sense we own the kids.

8a.   If you want the children to be doing the work
8b.   you've got to get the classroom teacher
8c.   not the curriculum coordinator or

CYNTHIA:

STANZA 3

DIRECTION FOR FUTURE

9a.   But Jane
9b.   that's why we're doing this project
9c.   right?

10a. This this is a way to see what possible direction there is
10b. for the future
10c. and that's why in a sense
10d. we need to work through this.

STANZA 4:

THIS IS A FINITE PROJECT

11a. Now this is a finite project

JANE:

12.   Right.

CYNTHIA:

11b. Um that has some funding
11c. but is supposed to end
11d. and at the end of the school year.

STANZA 5

INITIAL CONCEPTION WAS WRONG

13a. Um and I think initially
13b. it was conceived

14a.   and and this was this was an error
14b.   that was corrected.

15a.   It was conceived
15b.   uh as something that would be fairly easy
15c.   to do in the school

16a.   Um that outside outside could've
16b.   resources come in
16c.   and give you'd the stuff you need
16d.   and then you could teach it.

17.   But you know that you can't do that.

STANZA 6
CURRICULUM DEVELOPMENT IS MURKY
18a.   There's a there's a big complicated process
18b.   of working through the materials
18c.   figuring out how to teach it
18d.   which is called curriculum development.

19a.   And that's what we're involved in now
19b.   and it's very murky
19c.   and it's very complicated
19d.   and we we don't know where we're going
19e.   but that's an innate part of curriculum development
19f.   unfortunately
19g.   especially when you work with a group of people
19h.   and you're not just doing it yourself.

STANZA 7
CURRICULUM DEVELOPERS AS HIRED GUNS
20a.   Um so
20b.   and that's where Shirley and I were hired
20c.   as sort of the hired guns
20d.   to come in and help facilitate it
20e.   because we know you don't have the time

21a.   um and and um Sara and Ariel [the representative of the funder chairing the meeting]
21b.   didn't don't have the experience
21c.   of working in the classroom
21d.   and they teach in a different structure
21e.   which is very different.

22a. And so
22b. so we're there as the helping hands to give you
22c. to to help you where you need
22d. and to act as sort of the interpreters
22e. and the shapers
22f. but in response to what is necessary.
23a. I mean
23b. we're not coming in to do something that we want to do.

24.   We're trying to facilitate what you want to do.

STANZA 8
PROJECT IS SOMETHING SMALL
25.   So but we also don't want to put any pressure

26.   I mean there shouldn't be any pressure.

27a. There should be something that's fun to do
27b. and what works works
27c. and what doesn't work goes by the wayside.

28a. And um that's all it can be
28b. you know something small
28c. that accomplished by the end of the semester.

STANZA 9
THIS IS PILOT FOR FUTURE PROJECT
29a. But if it goes into something that is exciting
29b. and has potential
29c. and should be continued next year
29d. and should be given to other teachers
29e. and should maybe affect other schools in Middleview
29f. then that's where Sara's working towards something more long term
29g. where this could be maybe funded by NEH
29h. and to pay teachers
29i. and to pay for release time
29j. and pay for materials
29k. and pay for resources to come in
29l. and make it work on a larger scale.

30a. So this is like a little pilot project that is
30b. I agree
30c. it's very murky
30d. and it's very frustrating

30e. but I see that as sort of inevitable
30f. and we can make that work for us
30g. instead of against us.

In the transcript above, every line is an "idea unit" (micro-lines, see Chapter 9). Everything with the same number (e.g., 5a–d) is a (however loosely connected) syntactic unit akin to a sentence, though, of course, what constitutes a sentence in speech is a more varied and less tightly integrated unit than in much writing (macro-lines, see Chapter 9). A period stands for an intonation contour that sounds "final" (rather closed off with the implication of what is to follow will not be syntactically integrated with what has just been said).

The stanzas above represent claims about how topics are organized in the data, claims that are supported (or not) in the discourse analysis to be offered. In that sense, the above transcript is not "raw" data, but is already "theoretical," that is, it already represents aspects of our analysis. I have discussed the notion of validity in Chapter 8 and will not discuss it further here. We could also engage in psycholinguistic research (e.g., investigating pausing, hesitations, intonation, and listener judgment of stanza boundaries) to support the way in which we have divided up a text into stanzas. However, here the stanzas are meant mainly as a guide for the reader to see how I have "read" (understood) the text and its flow of meanings. My discourse analysis is my defense of this "reading" and rises or falls according to the criteria of validity we discussed in Chapter 8. Of course, here I cannot engage in a full discourse analysis of the text above, but can only hope to give some indications of what such a full analysis might look like.

The data above makes it clear that in the first meeting—in the data we looked at from Karen in Chapter 2—Karen was indirectly castigating Sara for contacting the curriculum coordinator and not the teachers. In that first meeting, the teachers were unwilling to express this concern directly. Indeed, even in this later meeting, when the group members know each other much better, there had been much indirection and hedging prior to Jane's more direct statement.

We have now put out a fairly long piece of data. So how do we begin (though we have already begun in the sense that we demarcated the text into lines and stanzas and labeled them)? We could start with any building task or any tool of inquiry. Remember, these exist only to help us formulate questions and hypotheses to be tested against data. So, let's start with situated meanings, that is, the specific meanings words take on in specific contexts of use. In this case, as in so many others, people interactively negotiate, even contest over, what situated meanings words are to have in talk.

Consider the word "structure" in the phrase "structure of the Middleview schools" in line 1c. "Structure" here could meaning any number of different things, two of the most likely being "the official hierarchical structure of the schools as a law-governed bureaucratic system" or "the informal structure of the schools in terms of how people actually operate in practice day-to-day." Jane is telling Sara that she (Sara) operated, in going to the curriculum coordinator (Mary Washington), by the first meaning of "structure" when she should have, if she really wanted the teachers' cooperation, operated by the second. Jane is bidding to have the second informal sense of "structure"—the sense in which the teachers have more power—honored both in the talk in this meeting and in the practices operating among the members of the group.

Or, consider the word "own" in line 7. This word takes on a specific situated meaning partly in relation to the situated meaning Jane has already given the word "structure" (the informal as opposed to the formal hierarchy). For Jane, "own" seems to mean that teachers, not administrators, control access to students. In using the word "own" she wants to contrast the relationship or control teachers have over their students (in terms of the informal structure of the schools) with the sort of relationship or control administrators have over those students (which is formal or bureaucratic).

Or finally, consider the word "project" in 9b. In this line, the curriculum consultant, Cynthia, refers to "this project," meaning the activities in which the group is engaged. In 11a she characterizes the project as "finite," meaning that it is meant to be short-term and come to an end. In 28b she says the project is meant to be "small." In 30a she goes on to call it a "little pilot project" that, if it "goes into something exciting," may continue as a long-term project funded by the grant Sara is writing. The curriculum consultant is probably stressing that the project is "small," "finite," "little," and a "pilot" because from earlier talk at the meeting she fears that the teachers think they are getting themselves into too much work. However, there is a danger that the teachers will hear this as belittling the importance of the project and their work in it. Since they are already concerned about issues of status and power, this is a real danger.

However, more to the point, Cynthia is building a situated meaning for "project" that makes the current project an experimental ("pilot") part of a larger project that is controlled by Sara and the grant that she is seeking to get funded. The current teachers may or may not be part of this larger project in the future (Sara has suggested a committee to decide on resources), but the current project is now in danger of seeming to be an experiment conducted by someone else (Sara and the curriculum consultants) outside the control of the teachers themselves (note "that's where Sara's working towards something more long term" in line 29f). This situated meaning for "project," of course, comports very poorly with the situated meanings for "structure" and "own" which Jane was developing. These latter situated meanings stressed teacher control and informal power structures rather than bureaucratic processes typical of large federal grants (especially a grant which initially left funding for teachers out) and "committees" to discuss "resources."

At issue in using the word "project" and seeking to give it a specific situated (contextualized) meaning in this meeting is the question as to whose project the project is. Is it the teachers' project, aided by the historian and consultants? Is it the historian and the consultants' project aided by the teachers? Is it collaborative and in what sense? In stanza 7 Cynthia seems to try to make "project" mean an effort where the teachers are in control, aided by others, when she talks about "helping" (line 22b) and "facilitate" (line 24). Yet, when in the same stanza she uses terms like "give" (line 22b), "interpreters" (line 22d), and "shapers" (line 22e) she seems to imply a more agentive and controlling role for the consultants than for the teachers.

Much more could be said about the word "project" here. But the issue is clear. What situated meaning the word will take on in the talk and practices of the group is up for negotiation and contestation. It is part of what the group is trying to work out in the meeting and, indeed, in the "project" as a whole. This is, indeed, a case where the situated meaning of a word is part and parcel of what the communication is about. And the resolution of this issue—if people come to a common acceptance of what the word means here and now in their talk and in their practices—is part of what will determine whether there will be a "project," what it will be, and whether it will be "successful" or not (and "success" for the "project" will be yet another term over whose situated meaning the group will eventually negotiate and contest in the end).

We also see clearly here how issues of "politics" (status and power, the distribution of social goods) are fully caught up with the negotiation over and use of specific situated meanings for specific words. So we see here, too, how one of our building tasks—namely politics—is taking shape as people use language to distribute social goods and negotiate and contest over them, social goods like who has control when and where and how people are allotted roles, respect, and responsibilities in a common endeavor.

Of course, all the building tasks—building significance, practices (activities), identities, relationships, politics, connections, and knowledge—are clearly at stake here. What is the *significance* of going to the curriculum coordinator rather than the teacher? What *practice* or *activity*—just what sort of "project"—are the members of the group involved in? What sort of *identities* are the teachers, academics, and consultants acting out in these meetings? What is and ought to be the *relationship* among these people and their identities? What is the *politics* of the situation, who has what status and power over when and where? What is the *connection* between having gone to the curriculum coordinator and having left the teachers out of the funding requests in the draft grant? When and where is teacher *knowledge* to be privileged over or beneath academic or consultant knowledge? All of these issues are worked out through talk in interaction.

Situated meanings can guide us to figured worlds, since often people are giving words specific situated meanings because they are operating with specific figured worlds. The situated meanings Jane is giving to words like "structure" and "own" can help guide us in our search for some of the figured worlds (theories, stories, models) Jane is using. But we have to consult other parts of the transcript as well.

In stanza 1 Jane says that if someone wants to involve a classroom they need to ask the classroom teacher, not some administrator. This is the stanza where Jane gives "structure" its situated meaning as an "informal, not a bureaucratic, hierarchy based on local practices." In stanza 2 Jane points out that since Karen teaches English, history is not her "priority area." Jane, on the other hand, does teach history and so it is *her* priority area. If you want school children involved in doing history (and not English) then you need to go to the teacher who has history (and not English) as her priority area (note Jane's remark that "we are the direct people"). Of course, Mary, the curriculum coordinator, had told Karen—not Jane—to call Sara thereby violating this "rule." Indeed, Karen had said in the first meeting of the group (part of which we looked at in Chapter 2) that she herself had gone to Jane and gotten her involved precisely because history was Jane's area and not hers (even though Karen had always had her students in English class engage in interviewing their relatives about the past, something that would be called "oral history" in a history class).

Thus, it is clear that when Jane says in stanza 2 "[i]n a sense we own the kids," she means that each teacher "owns" the kids in her own class, but that the person whose priority area is history "owns" all the kids involved in any history project, regardless of what specific other classrooms they are in. This is so, in fact, even if Karen has children doing English with her that are not actually in Jane's history class. If you come into the school to do history you need to talk to Jane directly. On Jane's view, Sara should have contacted Jane first, not Mary or even Karen, even if she wanted history work going on in multiple classrooms (as she did).

Considering all this data, we can hypothesize that Jane is operating with a figured world something like the one sketched out below:

> In the informal practices and procedures of the Middleview schools, teachers, not administers, control access to the children in their classrooms. A teacher's priority area gives her special rights and responsibilities in regard to students for any enterprise involving that area.

This figured world may actually be at variance with some aspects of official bureaucratic policies in the schools, policies which require permissions from various sorts of administrators. To the extent that such variance exists, someone like Sara would have to have sought out a relationship with Jane first—perhaps on a partly or wholly informal basis—and then sought official permissions from Mary Washington, the curriculum coordinator, and other administrators (e.g., the principal and administrators at the district level).

We cannot know how the figured world that we have attributed to Jane looks in her head. Indeed, she may never have consciously articulated this figured world in words. If and when she has done so, she may have articulated the figured world differently on different occasions. The figured world is Jane's informal "theory" of how her school and schools in her area work in practice. She, of course, has many other such theories covering other aspects of her school, schools, and schooling.

Figured worlds are "theories" by which people are operating on a given occasion—they may operate by different theories on different occasions. In this case, Jane has been pretty direct in her use of the figured world, partly because the theory or model itself has been challenged by this project's origin and how it has proceeded ever since. In other cases, we have to do more work to infer a figured world from a variety of things a person says and how he or she says them on a given occasion.

Another one of our tools of inquiry was "intertextuality," that is, the ways in which a piece of spoken or written language uses or reuses words from elsewhere by either quoting them or eluding to them in some fashion. At first glance, intertextuality does not appear to play a role in the above data. But on second glance there is something interesting to be said about intertextuality in this data. Consider stanza 6 repeated below:

18a. There's a there's a big complicated process
18b. of working through the materials
18c. figuring out how to teach it
18d. which is called curriculum development.

19a. And that's what we're involved in now
19b. and it's very murky
19c. and it's very complicated
19d. and we we don't know where we're going
19e. but that's an innate part of curriculum development
19f. unfortunately
19g. especially when you work with a group of people
19h. and you're not just doing it yourself.

The teachers have claimed that the project is unfocused and unclear. They have implied that people running the project—primarily Sara, the historian, but also the funders and curriculum consultants—are responsible for this. This claim about the project being unfocused and unclear has been the teachers' entry into discussing the fact they were left out of the draft grant proposal. In stanza 6, one of the curriculum consultants, Cynthia, attempts to *name* (define, label) the sense of confusion the teachers feel about the project as "curriculum development" ("which is called curriculum development"). She says "curriculum development" is "murky" and "complicated." The fact that "we don't know where we're going" is "an innate part of curriculum development."

Cynthia is saying that her field—curriculum development—has a name for this messy process, it's just called "curriculum development." This naming of the process removes the murk and complication from the realm of personal responsibility on the part of the leaders of the project (which is where the teachers sought to place it) to the realm of the professional practices of curriculum development. While Cynthia has not used any more words from her field (which would have involved her in direct intertextuality), she has used the name of her field to imply that her field has words for defining and explaining this whole painful process, where "we don't know where we're going," words that "trump" the teachers' words (which imply personal responsibility for failing to do a good job). Thus, though this is but barely an instance of intertextuality, it functions powerfully, nonetheless.

We can clearly see this naming process as carrying out several of our building tasks, not least of which is Building Task 7, Sign Systems and Knowledge. Cynthia bids to privilege the language and knowledge of curriculum consultants over the language and knowledge of teachers speaking out of their everyday sense of practice. But, of course, other building tasks are relevant, as well, such as: no. 1 Significance (i.e., the messiness is really significant not as failure but as "curriculum development"), no. 3 Identities (i.e., the identities of teachers versus curriculum consultants), no. 4 Relationships (i.e., what relationship the teachers ought to have with the project and its leaders, not to mention to "curriculum development"), no. 5 Politics (i.e., the social good of who does and who does not know what all this messiness really means), and no. 6 Connections (i.e., what is the connection between Sara's acts and the messiness that the teachers perceive in this project and how it should be characterized).

Another of our tools of inquiry was Conversations, that is, the debates and issues that are widely known to a social group or society at large. So what Conversations can we assume the participants in this meeting are privy to? How might those Conversations impinge on what they say and what they take others to mean? One Conversation everyone in the room is aware of is the debate over the status of teachers and college professors in terms of who are "really" teachers (college professors teach, but aren't seen as teachers) and whose knowledge is to be privileged in regard to schools and schooling (e.g., are Schools of Education or teachers the real experts about schools and schooling?). Another Conversation everyone in the room is aware of—a much more local Conversation—is the historic town–gown tensions in Middleview, that is, the long-running tension between the working-class town and its elite private college and between teachers born and raised in Middleview and professors who have come from the outside.

We could proceed now to investigate how these Conversations are shaping what the people in the meeting say and how they respond to each other. We would certainly want to consider stanza 7 where Cynthia, the curriculum consultant, says "so we're there as the helping hands **to give you**, to **to help you** where you need and to act as sort of the **interpreters** and the **shapers**." Here Cynthia switches from "give," which implies the agency and empowerment of the curriculum consultant and not the teachers, to "help," which implies more agency and empowerment on the part of the teachers as part of a more equal collaboration. Despite this switch, "interpreters" and "shapers" seem to pretty much stress the agency and empowerment of the curriculum consultants and not the teachers. Cynthia is communicating in a very sensitive area here because it impinges on issues germane to the Conversation (debate) about whose knowledge is to be privileged in regard to schools and schooling—that of teachers or that of professionals who don't actually work daily in classrooms.

We could relate almost everything in the data above to one or more Conversations floating "in the air," that is, to debates that people in the room know are going on around them in their local area or in their society at large. They can all draw on the words and different "sides" in these debates as resources with which to make meaning and they can all use these resources to help them (for better or worse) interpret what others mean to say.

Finally, another of our tools of inquiry is Discourses. Discourses are the different ways of being different "kinds of people" (Hacking 1986). They are the different socially meaningful identities that people can take on in different situations, using language (social languages) and ways of acting, interacting, valuing, thinking, believing and using various sorts of objects, tools, and technologies in specific places and at specific times. In the data above—as in much of the meeting as a whole—the teachers are acting, valuing, and talking out of their Middleview teacher Discourse, the historian out of an academic historian Discourse, and the curriculum consultants out of their specialist Discourse as curriculum specialists. But, of course, people, even in a meeting like this one, can switch to speak out of different identities or even try to speak out of two or more at the same time ("hybridity").

Discourses are social and historical. Ways of thinking, acting, interacting, and talking like a Middleview teacher or an academic historian (of a certain type) predate the people in this meeting, though by acting out these ways these people can gradually transform what counts as being a Middleview teacher or an academic historian. The interactions in the data we have discussed in this chapter reflect a number of historical tensions between teachers and academics locally and nationally. So a D/discourse analysis should bring these tensions to bear as part of the analysis. This would require a chapter in its own right.

Clearly one of the issues that would arise is what sort of specialist knowledge (teacher, professor, curriculum specialist) is to be privileged in which contexts (in regard to classrooms, research, building curricula). Another issue that arises is whether teacher knowledge based on practice is, in fact, to be viewed as specialist knowledge or to be dismissed as just practical anecdotes. Yet another issue is whether it is teachers or administrators who should control (officially or informally) various policies and procedures as they apply to classrooms and schools. These are debates (Conversations) that are going on in education and have gone on for some time. They are debates not just between specific teachers and university professors, for example, but among various Discourses (e.g., teacher Discourses, university professor Discourses, and School of Education Discourses, as well as various policy-maker Discourses connected to the government and other institutions that seek to "control" teachers). They are debates about status, power, and social control—they are, thus, debates with deep consequences for the distribution of social goods.

Each Discourse (Middleview teacher, academic historian, curriculum consultant) orients to these issues in talk, beliefs, values, and attitudes in different ways. So we can see our data, as we have said, as conversation not just among these specific people but among these Discourses, instantiated in a particular way in the local area, but reflecting larger national and historical issues (though in a particular way). In fact, one thing we are trying to do in D/discourse analysis—that we were already starting to do in this chapter—is to uncover some of the specific "on the ground" working interactions among these Discourses.

Let me close with an example, from the same meeting, where the local Middleview people switch Discourses to the detriment of the historian (Sara), who won't or can't switch out of her specialist historian Discourse. You will remember that we started with the problem that Sara had gone to a curriculum coordinator (Mary, an administrator) at Karen's and Jane's school and not to them directly. At the end of the meeting, after the group had been discussing the children doing local history by collecting oral stories from their relatives, the World War II period came up.

This triggered Karen, Jane, and a man named Joe to reminisce, based on their local knowledge, about a place called Bright City where people went to dance during the war. Joe is, of all things, a curriculum coordinator (at another school, not Karen's and Jane's), just the sort of administrator that Mary Washington is. But now the teachers and Joe have switched to speak out of their local Middleview Discourse as "everyday" citizens of the town, not their Discourses as teachers or administrators.

People like Karen, Jane, and Joe are typical of Middleview citizens. They were born there. Their families have been there a long time. They plan to stay there. Their children plan to stay there. Sara, the historian, is typical of many professors (and certain other professionals) in the town. She wasn't born there and did not stay there as she climbed her professional career ladder. This is, indeed, one of the core historical tensions between the town and the university. Though Karen, Jane, and Joe switch to their Middleview "everyday person" ("life world") Discourse, Sara pretty much stays in her Discourse as an academic historian. She cannot really join their local Discourse. So let's look at the data:

KAREN:
1a.   My mother used to talk about in the 40s
1b.   you'd hang around at Union Station

1c.   and anybody would just pick you up
1d.   because everybody was going down to dance at Bright City
1e.   whether you knew them or not.

JOE:
2.   Lakeside Ballroom.

JANE:
3.   Yeah definitely.

JOE:
4.   My father used to work there.

JANE:
5a.   And also, once you finally get into the war situation
5b.   because you have Fort Derby
5c.   everybody would get a ride in to come to Bright City
5d.   to the amusement park

6a.   so it was this influx of two, three cars' worth of guys
6b.   that were now available to meet the girls that suddenly were there.

SARA:
7.   Well actually street, street cars had just come in in this
8.   and as I recall um from a student who wrote a paper on this
9.   Bright City and Park was built by the street car company
10.   in order to have it a sort of target destination for people to go to
11.   and to symbiotically make money off of this.

JANE:
12a.   Because once you got there
12b.   you could take a boat ride
12c.   and go up and down a lake

13.   and there were lots of other ways to get the money from people.

Sara's "well actually" in line 7 seems to "correct" the teachers and Joe. She seems to contrast their knowledge, based on local knowledge, to the professional knowledge of the historian. Ironically, this meeting is part of a local oral history project. Yet here the historian counters this oral "data" with the historical data taken from studies and books.

Jane effortlessly incorporates Sara's contribution into the local knowledge. Sara's allusion to a conspiracy between the street car company and the park—the sort of thing that is often central to academic Discourses (an underlying structural relation that explains surface facts)—is ignored. Eventually, Sara grows uncomfortable with this conversation, which is taking place at the end of the meeting, and leaves. The teachers, Joe, and now the curriculum consultants, too, themselves natives of Middleview, continue to share their local knowledge. The tensions among their competing specialist Discourses (teachers, administrators, and curriculum consultants), have, for the moment, evaporated. They talk out of a Discourse they share and that Sara doesn't. Ironically, it's local history—local history of the sort the Middleview people can talk and Sara can't, not local history as an academic specialty—that ultimately, at the end of this meeting, divides Sara from the Middleview people.

D/discourse analysis is not just about achieving abstract (theoretical, academic) understandings. We hope we can also deal with practical problems in the real world. The sort of analysis that has just been started is meant ultimately also to help us carry out projects like the one we have been analyzing here in better, more fruitful, and humane ways. While such applications are not the focus of this book—they would require another one of equal length—we can leave the reader to meditate on how things might have been done differently in this project in order to get people from the different Discourses to be able to work together in a more fruitful and productive fashion. One way I myself would start would be by having people overtly focus on the different Discourses at play and on their histories and tensions. The next step would be to devise ways in which people can together form a new, however temporary, Discourse, or mixtures of Discourses, to get work done they all want to do.

Reading
Hacking, I. (1986). Making up people, in T. C. Heller, M. Sosna, & D. E. Wellbery, with A. I. Davidson, A. Swidler, & I. Watt, Eds. *Reconstructing individualism: Autonomy, individuality, and the self in Western thought.* Stanford, CA: Stanford University Press, pp. 222–236.

APPENDIX

Discourse Analysis for Images and Multimodal Texts

This book is primarily about language. However, we live in a digital age awash in images and texts that combine words and images. Texts that combine words and images are often called "multimodal texts," because they combine different modes like language, images, and music. Such things as ads, music videos, and video games are obvious examples. Even academic texts like science textbooks and professional publications today combine a great many images (e.g., pictures, graphs, and diagrams) with language.

The theory of discourse analysis in this book applies, in large part, to "texts" which are composed of just images and to multimodal texts composed of combinations of words, images, and other modalities provided these images and combinations are meant to communicate. The theory applies because, in fact, discourse is about communication and we humans can communicate via other symbol systems (e.g., mathematics) or via systems composed using modalities other than language or ones composed by mixing other modalities with language.

We have argued that discourse analysis starts by asking questions which are tools for doing discourse analysis. We have introduced building tasks and tools of inquiry all of which lead us to ask certain sorts of questions of texts. Suitably adapted, all of these questions can apply to studying images and multimodal texts.

Let me here use the word "image" to mean either a static image (like a painting) or moving images (as in a movie or video game). And let us, for a moment, forget about words. If we want to analyze an image (remember I am using "image" to mean a single static image or a set of changing or moving images), first we have to ask what constitutes a "word" or "phrase" in the image. That is, what constitutes a small unit of meaning which can be combined with other such small units to make bigger units of meaning?

When you want to analyze an image, start by asking yourself what are the "elements" (parts) in the image out of which it seems to be composed. Take any element that seems to be an important "part" out of which the whole image is composed. This will change for various images you choose and in terms of what you want to analyze. In one case, it might be colors and shapes and in another case it might be the objects that compose the whole image. There is a "grammar" of images in terms of which we could formalize what counts as an element and what are the "rules" for combining them. But we do not need to be fussy right here and now about what counts as an element.

As with language, any image communicates (has meaning) only in context and leaves much "unsaid," assuming it will be filled in by people's knowledge of the context, including their cultural knowledge and former experience with such images. For example, when we see attractive people associated with products in an ad (something that happens often), we fill in, from our background and cultural knowledge, the idea that the ad is trying to suggest that the product will make us more attractive or, at least, will make other people see us as associated with attractive people and an attractive lifestyle.

Video-game players do not need to be told to break crates and boxes in a game to look for "power ups" in games—they know this from their previous experience with games.

Images, just like communication in language, do not just "say" things (carry "messages"), but seek to do things as well. It is clear that ads want us to do something, namely buy the product being advertized. Video games want players to do certain things (play in certain ways). Posters and documentaries often want us to change our political views or change how we act in society.

Let's consider some of our tools of inquiry: situated meanings; social languages; intertextuality; figured worlds; and Discourses. For whatever you take to be an element, ask what situated meaning (contextually specific meaning) this element has in the context in which the image is being "read." For example, the images of petals and flowers are both elements of larger images and scenes in the video game *Flower*. In the game—which is really a sort of poem—the petals and flowers take on a situated meaning as "forces of unspoiled nature imperiled by industry and pollution."

Go on from situated meanings to ask yourself how the elements you have found fit together—form a pattern—to create a certain sort of style for the whole image. This is the equivalent of a "social language." Just as wearing a swimsuit, a tank-top, and flip-flops patterns together to create a "beach style," so, as we have seen, certain sorts of words, phrases, and structures can pattern together to create a certain sort of style of language (e.g., hip hop or the language of physics), what we have called a social language. So, too, in an image, the elements can pattern together to create a certain style.

For example, in many role-playing games (like *Dungeons and Dragons* or *World of War Craft*) the elements, and the images and scenes into which they combine, pattern together to betoken a fantasy medieval world (thus, we get things like elves, castles, knights, magic and mages, and so forth). This sort of medieval fantasy style ("social language") is often associated with and in many cases inspired by Tolkien's *Lord of the Rings*.

Just as with social languages, different styles are associated with different identities and activities (practices). The medieval fantasy style of many role-playing games is associated with a heroic identity and the activities of heroes and warfare. People in such games take on fantasy identities as heroes (and sometimes as mightily evil beings).

The elements in an image, alone or together with other elements, can make intertextual references to other images, texts, or media (just as we can do with words in language). Furthermore, just as we saw for language, we can also talk about textual mixing, where one text (here an image) mixes elements from different styles or sources. In fact, in modern media, intertextuality and mixing (allusions to other texts and media, mixing, and remixing of styles and sources) are often pervasive. For example, later I will analyze a television commercial for Hummers that uses characters that look and act like they are in an old-fashioned Japanese horror movie (where giant monsters attack cities). The commercial is referencing such movies to sell cars. Many anime films so mix Japanese and Western cultural values and images that it is better to see them as mixing these two than simply referencing or alluding to one or the other.

Images, and the elements of which they are composed, use and rely on figured worlds just as we do when we speak or write. Figured worlds are simplified models or stories that we take for granted and that help explain how things are or should be in the world when they are "typical," "acceptable," or "normal" or, in some cases, "good" (we easily slip from "normal" and "acceptable" to "good"). For example, there are a good many movies, especially made in the United States, that accept and play on the figured world that if you just try hard enough and don't give up (don't give up your dream!), then in the end you will win, a common variant of what we called the "success model" in Chapter 6. *The Karate Kid* movies or the *Rocky* movies would be good examples.

Finally, images, just like when we speak or write in language, are always part of Discourses, if the images are meaningful and communicative. Images are associated with words, settings, and other sorts of objects in the service of letting people enact or recognize different sorts of socially significant identities and activities (practices). Just as words need to be combined with other things (like ways of acting and interacting or using various sorts of objects or tools) to enact an identity, so, too, for images. A video-gamer uses the images in a game to trigger certain actions, strategies, and values and, in the act, enacts his or her identity as a gamer in the Gamer Discourse. Someone else—say, a politician—sees only the images as content he wants to ban in his role as a moral crusader in a certain sort of political Discourse. So we always want to ask how images help people to enact different Discourses, how they seek to get people to recognize different Discourses, and how they seek to get people to participate in different Discourses.

So far I have left out words. But many images contain words as well. When an image contains words, as in a typical ad or video game, the words play two roles. In one role they are elements in language that we can analyze along the lines of this book. In another role they are elements in the image and need to be analyzed as part of the image. We always want to ask what do the words add to the image (or its elements) and what does the image (or its elements) add to the words and how and what did combining words and image communicate that could not have been communicated (at least not in the same way) by images or words alone.

After you have found situated meanings, "social languages" (styles), inter-textual references, figured worlds, and Discourses at work (and play) in an image or multimodal text, then ask how these are carrying out our seven building tasks captured in our seven building tools. That is, how are situated meanings, social languages (styles), intertextuality, figured worlds, and Discourses being used to build significance, practices or activities, identities, relationships, politics, connections, and sign systems and knowledge?

As an example, let's consider ads, which are easy cases. It is clear that some ads seek to give significance to products beyond what people would otherwise give them. Ads are an activity, not just a communication: they are selling things. Ads often seek to get viewers to assume a certain identity, for example as the sort of rich and powerful person who would drive a Hummer (see below). Ads are often designed to appeal to a certain customer niche or demography, often defined in terms of lifestyles (e.g., young urban professionals or middle-class Latinos) and, thus, seek to use and even help create a sense of people being related in certain ways to others in certain ways. Ads, of course, seek to connect things that, in reality, may have little connection. For example, some car ads seek to connect sex and cars when they place a "sexy" woman next to the car in the ad. Finally, ads often privilege certain styles of communication and ways of knowing the world. For example, the commercial I will analyze below uses humor (humor is a distinctive communicational or sign system) to disarm viewers and ads are certainly part of our "sound bite" culture that privileges short and pithy messages as a way of knowing over sustained argumentation and reflective thought.

Now let me take a simple example to analyze along the lines I have suggested: a television commercial for a Hummer (a jeep-like vehicle based on High Mobility Multipurpose Wheeled Vehicle—HMMWV or *Humvee*—used by the military; see http://video.google.com/videoplay?docid=-6547777336881961043# for the ad). This ad shows two monsters (a giant robot and a Godzilla-like monster) that look like they are from an old-fashioned black-and-white Japanese horror film. They are wreaking destruction on a city that looks like New York or some other skyscraper-filled city. Eventually the monsters meet up, fall in love, and have a baby. The baby is a Hummer. The ad ends with the words (the only words in the ad): "It's a Little Monster." This ad was aired as a commercial during the 2006 Super Bowl.

The two monsters and the city are clearly elements (though, of course, composed of other smaller elements). Within the ad, the monsters take on a number of situated meanings, one of which is surely "tough, hard, destructive beings that transcend the human laws and constraints of a city." When they fall in love, we get a situated meaning like "they are more human-like and soft than we thought," which comes as a surprise after the first situated meaning.

The elements in the ad—the monsters and their destructive actions, the city, and the black-and-white film-like images—all create a pattern that resembles (perhaps in a "tongue in cheek" way) the style of an old-fashioned Japanese horror film. In fact, since there is no reference to Hummers at all until the end of the commercial, we viewers may be wondering why we are watching something that looks more like a grade B horror film than an ad for a car. This is the commercial's style or "social language."

Of course, the fact that the ad has used the style of a Japanese horror film is also a clear intertextual reference to such films and to the popular culture of which they are a part. Later the two monsters act out a number of scenes that are a clear intertextual reference to a typical boy–girl romance story of the sort we have all seen in many movies. Since this sort of story is not what we expect in a horror film (at least from the monsters), this causes surprise based on what the earlier horror film intertextual reference has communicated to us.

The romance part of the commercial relies on a common figured world about romance. A male-like being romances a female-like being. They both act like young people on a date and, indeed, act out stereotypical dating activities. The ad only needs quick shots here because so many viewers can fill in the whole story based on their figured world for romance (a figured world that ironically has been partly informed by movies, though not by monsters in horror movies).

It is impossible to understand this ad just on the basis of its images (and final words). Just as with language, we need to ask what Discourse or Discourses in society it is part of. What sorts of identities and activities (practices) is it trying to enact, get us to recognize, and asking us to participate it? How is it using, not just its images and words to do this, but "dancing" (coordinating) with other things to accomplish this?

This ad was shown during the 2006 Super Bowl (the U.S. professional football championship), one of the most expensive and most watched places to advertize in the world. Ads during the Super Bowl are expected to be entertainment and even "art" (at least popular art), not just a sales pitch. Such ads get a lot of publicity and are an attempt to position the company and its products as having a "cool," "modern," "with it" (in terms of popular culture) identity in a high-tech, global world. Such ads are trying not just to be in such a Discourse, they are trying to create it and adapt (even co-opt) it to sell their products.

Hummer—in this ad and in its other ads—is also associated with both a military Discourse (because Hummers came from and mimic military vehicles) and a Discourse of upper-middle-class wealth and power (because Hummers are very expensive and get very poor gas mileage; in addition to the fact they are much bigger than most cars and, thus, Hummer drivers are more likely to survive in a crash with other drivers driving smaller cars). The ad we are analyzing has clear references to the military Discourse (identity) through its warfare/destruction images. After all, the baby Hummer is the child of two destructive forces and the implication is that it could help in that destruction, the way all children might follow in their parents' footsteps.

The Discourse of upper-class wealth and power seems not to be referenced in the ad, other than through the association of a Hummer with such big and powerful objects as the monsters. However, the ad ends with the "daddy monster" (the robot) putting the Hummer down and watching it drive off in a way that looks to me just like a kid putting a toy car down, pushing it, and watching it move. This implies that Hummers are the "toys" or the "toy cars" of big and powerful "people." Their "toys" are bigger than regular people's cars, just as they themselves are bigger (richer, more powerful) than regular people driving "small cars."

To go further with Discourses we would have to study how people consume the Hummer ad to enact and recognize certain sorts of identities in the world. For example, I myself enjoy the ad, but as part of my values and actions in the world as someone who sees himself as part of a certain sort of environmental or "green Discourse." I see the commercial as both humorous in its own right, but also unintentionally (or is it really unintentional?) humorous in how it lets me read Hummers as destroyers of our environment and the people who buy them as "monsters." My response to the commercial allows me to enact this anti-Hummer Discourse, an irony given what General Motors (who owned Hummer in 2006, but no longer) spent on the ad. It is, of course, possible that the ad is "thumbing its nose" at people like me by saying something like "See, people who drive Hummers can destroy the environment and get away with it—people like you don't matter and wouldn't buy a Hummer anyway."

I have not dealt with the words in the ad: "It's a Little Monster." These words are an intertextual reference to a common "mean" thing parents say about the children but intend in an endearing way. This fits with the "human-like and soft romance" meanings and figured world in the second part of the ad. At the same time, it literally means the Hummer is, like its parents, a monster of the type that wreaks havoc on cities in old Japanese movies. This fits with the earlier part of the ad where we see the monsters as hard, powerful, and destructive. In the end, the images and words of the ad make us see a Hummer we own, or can own, as a child (or a "toy," when we consider the last image in the commercial) with the potential for great power. It appears the ad's "author" cares less that this power might be destructive than that it is mighty, "world shaking," and impressive, which is what I think Hummer owners must believe (given the damage they do to the environment) about their cars and themselves.

Even from what little I have said about the Hummer commercial, it is clear that situated meanings, social languages (style), intertextuality, figured worlds, and Discourses are tools that can be applied to images, as well as language. I have tried to hint how each of these theoretical tools is being used to engage in some of our building tasks, for example how the situated meanings, social language (style), intertextuality, figured worlds, and Discourses recruited in the ad or by its "readers" are building things like significance; activities/ practices; identities; relationships; politics; connections; sign systems and ways of knowing. I do not have time here to take up each building task in turn. Indeed, it would be good practice for the reader to do so. Also, I have left out our tool of inquiry (big "C") Conversations, though it is clear that many ads like the one we have discussed—and a great other many sorts of multimodal texts—play into large societal debates around issues whose poles many people in society know.

Readings

Gee, J. P. (2007). *What video games have to teach us about learning and literacy.* New York: Palgrave Macmillan.

Kress, G. (2010). *Multimodality: A social semiotic approach to contemporary communication.* London: Routledge.

Kress, G. & van Leeuwen, T. (1996). *Reading images: The grammar of visual design.* London: Routledge.

Kress, G. & van Leeuwen, T. (2001). *Multimodal discourse.* Oxford: Hodder Arnold.

Glossary

Academic Language
    Specialist styles of language associated with academic disciplines, fields, and domains, including the so-called "content areas" in school (e.g., mathematics, science, social studies, history, civics, etc.).

Activity
    See "Practice."

Big "C" Conversations (Tools of Inquiry)
    "Conversations" (with a capital "C") are debates in society or within specific social groups (over focused issues like smoking, abortion, or school reform) that large numbers of people recognize, both in terms of what "sides" there are to take in such debates and what sorts of people tend to be on each side.

Big "D" Discourse (Tool of Inquiry)
    Social languages (see below) are varieties or styles of language used to enact specific socially situated identities and activities (practices) associated with those identities. But people enact identities and activities not just through language, but by using language together with other "stuff" that isn't language. I use the term "Discourse," with a capital "D," for ways of combining and integrating language, actions, interactions, ways of thinking, believing, valuing, and using various symbols, tools, and objects to enact a particular sort of socially recognizable identity. If you want to get recognized as a street-gang member of a certain sort you have to speak in the "right" way, but you also have to act and dress in the "right" way, as well. You also have to engage (or, at least, behave as if you are engaging) in characteristic ways of thinking, acting, interacting, valuing, feeling, and believing. You also have to use or be able to use various sorts of symbols (e.g., graffiti), tools (e.g., a weapon), and objects (e.g., street corners) in the "right" places and at the "right" times. You can't just "talk the talk," you have to "walk the walk" as well. The same is true of doing/being a corporate lawyer, Marine sergeant, radical feminist, or a regular at the local bar. One and the same person might talk, act, and interact in such a way as to get recognized as a "street-gang member" in one context and, in another context, talk, act, and interact in quite different ways so as to get recognized as a "gifted student." And, indeed, these two identities, and their

concomitant ways of talking, acting, and interacting, may well conflict with each other in some circumstances (where different people expect different identities from the person), as well as in the person's own mind.

I elsewhere use the term "primary Discourse" for the Discourse people pick up through their initial socialization into life through their home and whatever counts as the group of people who socialize them early on in life. The Discourse that involves being a "person like us," where "us" is the primary socialization group of the person. This is the identity you take on early in life as a member of what counts as your family, group, or culture depending on how this is defined in your specific case.

I use the term Secondary Discourse for any Discourse—any way of being a certain kind of person through words, actions, interactions, values, and language—connected to larger public social institutions outside one's family or early socializing group, whether this be a church, school, government agency, workplace, or interest-driven group (e.g., gamers or anime fans). Secondary Discourses allow us to enact identities connected to more public sphere domains than our homes, families, or "home cultures." Some Secondary Discourses (e.g., some church Discourses and, for many middle-class families, schools) have close relationships with the primary Discourses of some people, people who engage in activities in the early socialization of their children that get them ready for later entry or allegiance into these secondary Discourses. This is a process I have called "borrowing."

Primary and secondary Discourses, as well as borrowing, are discussed in my book *Social linguistics and literacies: Ideology in Discourses*. Third Edition. London: Taylor & Francis, 2007.

Building Tasks

This book takes the view that people use language actively to build things in the world. Just as hammers and saws can be used to build buildings, so, too, grammar can be used to build things in the world or to give meaning and value to things in the world (think of this as a form of decorating or renovation). We use the grammar of our languages to build significance, practices, identities, relationships, politics, connections, and to build sign systems and claims to know, as well as to privilege certain sign systems and ways of knowing (see Glossary for each different building task). We can see each of these as a "task" speakers and writers take on when they speak or write beyond giving information or informing people. In fact, in most cases we give information (inform) so as to engage in one or more of these building tasks. Both speakers (writers) and listeners (readers) build, since listeners (readers) have to follow the speaker's (writer's) guidance to build what they want the listener (reader) to build.

Clause

In a rough and ready way we can define a "clause" as any verb and the elements that "cluster" with it. So in a sentence like "Mary left the party because she was tired," we have two clauses: "Mary left the party" and "because she was tired." The sentence "Mary left the party" contains only one clause. In a sentence like "Mary intended to leave the party," we have two clauses: "Mary intended" and "to leave the party" (where "Mary" is understood as the subject of "to leave"). Here the second clause ("to leave the party") is embedded in the first clause ("Mary intended") as the direct object of the verb "intend." These two clauses are so tightly bound together that they would most often be said as a single speech spurt.

In traditional grammar, a sentence is any clause that stands complete by itself (e.g., "The boys liked the cakes"). A non-sentential clause is any string of words with a subject and predicate that does not stand complete by itself (e.g., "John thinks that the boys like the cakes," where "the boys like the cakes" is a clause, but "John thinks that the boys like the cakes" is a sentence). Since linguists do not want to keep having to say "clause or sentence," they sometimes call anything with a subject and predicate a clause, whether it is a clause or a sentence in traditional terms.

Collocational Patterns

Any pattern of words or grammatical structures (types of words and phrases and clauses) that "hang together" to betoken a particular social language (and the identity associated with it) in the way in which sun hat, swimsuit, sunscreen, a towel, and flip-flops "hang together" to betoken a "sunbather."

Connections Building Task

Using language to make things connected or relevant to each other or to make then disconnected or irrelevant to each other.

Context

Context includes the physical setting in which a communication takes place and everything in it; the bodies, eye gaze, gestures, and movements of those present; what has previously been said and done by those involved in the communication; any shared knowledge those involved have, including shared cultural knowledge. However, context is both something "already there" and created by the way we talk. What speakers say keys people to construe the context in certain ways while, at the same time, people use how they view the context to interpret what is said. We called this the "reflexive property" of language and context. Listeners use only what they deem the relevant parts of context to interpret what was said (see "Frame Problem").

Conventions

Conventions are like rules, except that they are often unconsciously followed. Conventions are agreed-upon ways to act or interact, but, again, the agreement is often tacit or unconscious and has arisen because people follow or "imitate" what others have done. Conventions can be more or less rigid or flexible, that is, people following a convention can sometimes do things pretty much the same way every time or act with more flexibility and still be seen as following the convention. Language, meaning, and practices are all based on conventions. When you speak or act, if you are not, in some way, following a recognizable convention, then others would not be able to know what you were saying or doing. This does raise an interesting issue of how we ever do anything really new or how new conventions arise (both deep problems in social science), though clearly part of the answer is that we can combine conventions to make new ones or give old ones partially new meanings (sometimes based on other conventions). Since conventions are like rules and breaking them can lead to bad consequences in society (a "loss"), we can view speaking and acting in society as like engaging in games (which have rules and win and lose states).

Conversation (Big "C" Conversation)

See "Big 'C' Conversation."

Conversational Analysis

A detailed form of discourse analysis that sees conversation as the basic human communicational form and seeks to explicate how people produce and reproduce social order through talk and orientation to talk and each other in social interaction. The approach is almost always just spelled as "CA" and is a branch of sociology (one that gives up building grand sociological theories in favor of describing the order people actually create and how they create and sustain that order). Manny Schegloff at the University of California at Los Angeles is the best living practitioner of CA.

Critical Discourse Analysis

Any form of discourse analysis that seeks to engage with politics (see the Glossary entry for "politics"). Critical discourse analysis deals with whose "interests" are represented, helped, or harmed as people speak and write. When "critical discourse analysis" is spelled as "CDA" it often refers to the work of Norman Fairclough and his associates.

Dialect

A style of speaking and/or writing a language (and spoken and written language are usually different) associated with a given region, ethnic group, social class, or other social division. Dialects can vary by pronunciation ("accent"), grammar, or discourse (communication) features or all of these.

Discourse (Big "D" Discourse)

See "Big 'D' Discourse."

Discourse (Little "d" discourse)

With a little "d" ("discourse"), this word in this book means any instance of language-in-use or any stretch of spoken or written language (often called a "text" in the expanded sense where texts can be oral or written).

Discourse Analysis

The analysis of language-in-use whether spoken or written. Linguistic forms of discourse analysis pay attention to the details of grammar and how they function in communication. Other forms of discourse analysis pay attention only to themes and messages (sometimes this is called "content analysis").

Figured World (Tool of Inquiry)

A figured world is a theory, story, model, or image of a simplified world that captures what is taken to be typical or normal about people, practices (activities), things, or interactions. What is taken to be typical or normal, of course, varies by context and by people's social and cultural group. A figured world is a socially and culturally constructed way of recognizing particular characters and actors and actions and assigning them significance and value. Thus, we all have ways to construe what is a typical or "appropriate" bedroom, house, spouse, marriage, way of raising children, educated person, alcoholic, romance, student, and so on through an endless list. Figured worlds have also been called "folk theories" and "cultural models." When people simulate in their minds what counts as a typical or "appropriate" marriage or married couple (to take one example) they are creating or calling on their figured world of marriage or married couples. However, figured worlds are not just in people's heads, since they are often reflected in texts and media of various sorts as well.

Final Intonation Contour

An utterance said with a noticeable rise or fall (or rise-fall or fall-rise) of the voice on the information focus in the intonation contour. This sounds "final," as if a piece of information is "closed off" and "finished." In this book I have used a double slash ("//") to represent the end of the final intonation contour.

Form–Function Correlations (Tool of Inquiry)

Any correlation in terms of which a given word or type of word, phrase, or clause is associated with a given communication function. For example, subjects of sentences (as in "Mary" in "Mary got into Stanford") are corre-lated with or associated with the communicational function of being the "topic" of a sentence (the "topic" is what is being talked about or the thing that the speaker or writer is making a claim or assertion about or asking a question about).

Frame Problem

People interpret what they hear or read by considering both what was said or written and the context in which it was said or written. Speakers and writers can never put everything into words explicitly, so they must rely on listeners and readers drawing inferences about their meaning based not just on what they have said or written, but also on the context in which they have said or written it. But context (see "Context" in the Glossary) is indefinitely large and so listeners and readers must make judgments about how much of the context and what parts of it are relevant in interpreting what a speaker or writer means. It is always possible that considering more of the context would change what the listener or reader takes the speaker or writer to mean. So the question arises as to how we know when to quit and how we make judgments about what in the context is relevant to interpretation and when and how we choose to widen what we consider relevant in the context. This is called the "Frame Problem" (and it is something that computers are very bad at when they try to match human beings in making judgments about relevance).

Writing raises an interesting problem with context, since we can consider the context in which a text was written or the context (which may be hundreds or thousands of years later—witness the Bible or the Koran) in which the text is read, or both. People debate which context gives rise to the "right" meaning. But there is no answer to this question—it is a choice of what practices we want to engage in.

Functional Grammar

An overt description of grammar (the conventions people follow in speaking or writing a language) that pairs different types of grammatical structures (e.g., different sorts of subjects and objects, nouns and verbs, noun phrases and verb phrases, and clauses—e.g., relative clauses) with the one or more functions they typically serve or can serve in communication.

Grammar

The conventions having to do with word use and the construction of phrases and sentences that one follows in speaking and writing a given dialect, social language, or language. These conventions are often called "rules," but they are tacit and unconscious. People also write grammars, that is, they explicitly describe the rule system of a language. Such grammars can be purely descriptive in the sense that the grammar describes what speakers actually do. They can also be prescriptive in the sense that the grammar describes what the author takes to be "correct" or the way people "should" speak and write.

Hybridity

Hybridity refers to people, uses of spoken or written language, practices, Discourses, or cultures that combine or mix two or more different identities. Sometimes hybridity is hidden or denied (or its origins are forgotten) and people see what is really hybrid as uniform, single, or "pure." Very little in the way of people, language, practices, Discourses, or cultures is in reality "pure." At least historically almost everything is a mixture. (For example, English is a mixture of German, Latin, and early French, not a "pure" Germanic language.)

Idea Unit

See "Speech Spurts."

Identity

A word used for lots of different things. What I mean by it in this book is this: Different ways of being in the world at different times and places for different purposes; for example, ways of being a "good student," an "avid bird watcher," a "mainstream politician," a "tough cop," a video-game "gamer," a "Native American," and so on and so forth through a nearly endless list. I do not mean your core sense of self, who you take yourself "essentially" to be, though that is an important notion as well. I often use the term "socially situated identity" or "social identity" instead of just the word "identity" to make clear I am talking about how we recognize and act out different social roles or different social positions in society.

Identity Building Task

Using language to enact specific socially situated identities or to project such identities onto others, or to privilege or disprivilege such identities.

Information Focus

See "Intonation Contour" and "Stress."

Intertextuality (Tool of Inquiry)

When we speak or write, our words often allude to or relate to, in some fashion, other "texts" or certain types of "texts," where by "texts" I mean words other people have said or written. For example, *Wired* magazine once printed a story with this title: "The New Face of the Silicon Age: Tech jobs are fleeing to India faster than ever. You got a problem with that?" (February 2004). The sentence "You got a problem with that?" reminds us of "tough guy" talk we have heard in many movies or read in books. It intrigues us that such talk occurs written in a magazine devoted to technology. This sort of cross-reference to another text or type of text I refer to as "intertextuality." In instances of intertextuality, one spoken or written text alludes to, quotes, or otherwise relates to another one.

Intonation Contour

The pattern of length, loudness, and pitch changes across an utterance (see "Stress"). The intonation contour is "how we say" what we say in terms of the way we lengthen words, use various degrees of loudness on different words, and the ways in which we change the pitch of our voice on different words and across a string of words. In English, the intonation contour signals attitude, emotional meanings, emphasis, and various nuances of meaning. It is hard to describe such meanings, but they are crucial to communication and whether a communication goes smoothly or offends people.

Life world

A term used in different ways in different scholarly sources and not used at all by "everyday people." Your "life world" (sometime spelled as "lifeworld") is composed of those places or spaces where you communicate as an "everyday person" and make claims based on "common sense" and "everyday knowledge" and not specialist or expert knowledge. People use their vernacular when they are communicating in their life world. The concept is useful because it allows us to reflect on the fact that in our modern high-tech, science-driven global world, the life world (the space where people can comfortably claim to know things based on non-expert knowledge) is shrinking.

Line

A line is what I, in this book, call an idea unit or a tone unit (see "Speech Spurts").

Macro-lines

It is often said that, in speech, there are no such things as "sentences," that the sentence as a linguistic unit is a creature of writing only. I do not believe this is true. What is true is that sentences in speech are much more loosely constructed, much less tightly packaged or integrated, than in writing. Nonetheless, people often use the syntactic resources of English to tie together two or more lines into something akin to a sentence. I will call these "sentences" of speech *macro-lines*, referring to what we have so far called "lines" (i.e., intonational units, idea units, tone groups) as "micro-lines" when I need to distinguish the two. So by "macro-line" I mean "what counts as a sentence in speech."

Macrostructure

Larger pieces of information, like a story about my summer vacation, an argument for higher taxes, or a description of a plan for redistributing wealth, have their own characteristic, higher-level organizations. That is, such large bodies of information have characteristic parts much like the body has parts (the face, trunk, hands, legs, etc.). These parts are the largest parts out of which the body or the information is composed. They each have their own smaller parts (ultimately body parts are composed of skin, bones, and muscles, and the parts out of which a body of information is composed are ultimately composed themselves of stanzas and lines). The setting to a story is a piece of the larger organization of a story. It is a "body part" of her story. Stories are often composed of the following parts: Setting, Catalyst, Crisis, Evaluation, Resolution, and Coda. Other sorts of language are composed of different parts. The larger "body parts" of a story or other language genre as a whole can be called its "macrostructure," as opposed to its lines and stanzas which constitute its "microstructure."

Meaning

Meaning arises when any symbol (which can be a word, image, or thing) "stands for" (is associated with) something other than itself. So the word "tree" stands for trees in the world. A picture of a tree could be treated in the same way. So could a line drawing of a tree. What a symbol stands for is called its "denotation" or "reference." People use certain information or conventions to identify what a symbol stands for. This information or these conventions, which are often talked about in terms of a concept or idea in the head, are called the symbol's "connotation" or "sense." (We can see that the connotation or sense is not really just in people's heads as a concept. Since the connotation or sense is based on conventions people follow, connotation or sense is also in people's social practices, since conventions are social practices.) So the word "unicorn" is associated with the connotation or sense of "horse-like animal with a horn" (and other things, as well) and this concept and/or set of conventions allows us to understand that the word stands for (refers) to unicorns (which happen not to exist in the real world, but do "exist" in people's stories, fantasies, and images). People can treat an object—say babies—as symbols so long as they agree on the concept (idea, interpretation, conventions) that ties them to what they stand for (designate, denote, refer to), say "innocence" in the case of babies.

Non-Final Intonation Contour

An utterance said with only a small rise or fall (or rise-fall or fall-rise) or a level pitch of the voice on the information focus in the intonation contour. This sounds "non-final," as if more connected information is to come. In this book I have used a single slash ("/") to represent the end of a non-final intonation contour.

Politics

The word is used in many different ways. In this book, it means any situation where social goods or the distribution of social goods are at stake. Any case where we talk, write, or act in ways that give or withhold social goods or say or imply how social goods are or should be distributed is political in my sense. This often involves speaking, writing, or acting in ways that say or imply what is "appropriate," "normal," "natural," "good," or "acceptable" (or their opposites) in regard to certain people, things, or activities. All of these are almost always associated with social goods (for example, many people do not want to be seen as "unacceptable" or "incorrect" English speakers, not least if they are, in fact, native speakers of English who speak a different dialect of English than "Standard English").

Politics Building Task

Using language to give or take away social goods or projecting how social goods are or ought to be distributed.

Practice

A word used in many different ways. In this book, "practice" means a socially recognized and institutionally or culturally supported endeavor that usually involves sequencing or combining actions in certain specified ways. Encouraging a student is an action, mentoring the student as his or her advisor in a graduate program is a practice. Telling someone something about linguistics is an action (informing), lecturing on linguistics in a course is a practice. Sometimes the term "activity" is used for what I am calling a practice.

Practices (Activities) Building Task

Using language to enact specific practices (activities) alone or with others.

Recognition Work

The work we humans do through talk and interaction to seek to get recognized as having a specific socially situated identity. The factors that go into getting so recognized or failing to. All the contestation, negotiation, and ambiguities around such identities and the ways in which we humans "bid" for them (try to get them recognized and accepted) and relate to and contest with each other over them.

Reflexive Property of Language and Context

See "Context."

Relationships Building Task

Using language to create or sustain social relationships or to end or harm them.

Semiotics

A term for the study of sign systems.

Sign

Any word or symbol (which could be an image or object) that has meaning (stands for something else thanks to a given concept, interpretation, and convention which relates to the sign and the thing it stands for).

Sign System (or Semiotic System)

Any system of signs that are related to each other to allow communication (meaning giving) in a given domain or area. Language (a system of words and their various possibilities for combination) is the most important sign system, but there are many others (e.g., mathematics, road signs, or insignia in the military). One could, for example, treat a system of buildings—as in Washington, DC—as a sign system in the sense that they communicate messages about power and status, for example. The "author" of this communication is of course not the buildings by themselves but their designer and the people who sustain them in part because they communicate such messages.

Sign Systems and Ways of Knowing Building Task

Using language to create, sustain, revise, change, privilege or disprivilege any language or sign system or characteristic way of knowing the world or making knowledge claims about the world.

Significance Building Task

Using language to make thinks significant or important in various ways or to lower their significance or importance.

Situated Meanings (Tool of Inquiry)

The specific meanings words and phrases take on in actual contexts of use. Speakers and writers construct their utterances or sentences to guide listeners and readers in constructing these specific meanings based on what was said and the context in which it was said. Of course, speakers and writers can never be sure listeners and readers have constructed the specific situated meanings they intended and, too, listeners and readers can choose to be uncooperative (or "resistant") and construct specific situated meanings without full (or any) regard for the intentions of speakers and writers.

Social Goods

Anything a person or group in society wants and values. Some things (like status, money, love, respect, and friendship) are taken by nearly everyone in society as social goods. Other things are social goods only to small groups (e.g., having seen a rare bird and having it on one's life list—though this is, of course, a source of status among a relatively small group of people—i.e., birders—a widely sought-after social good).

Social Language (Tool of Inquiry)

Any variety or style of speaking or writing associated with a socially situated identity of any sort (this identity may be associated with a social group, profession, culture, practice, social role, or interest-driven activity like video gaming). The term "register" is sometimes used in the same or similar way. Social languages include dialects and all other styles or varieties of language associated with distinctive social identities and their concomitant practices (activities).

Specialist Language

Any style of language (which may involve special words, special uses of grammar, or special discourse features, or special pronunciations, or all of these) used when one is speaking or writing (and these might well be different) as a specialist or expert of a certain sort. People who share a specialty or expertise often develop their own "ways with words." These people might be doctors, carpenters, criminals, anime fans, video gamers, soldiers, biologists, bird watchers, and so on through a very large and ever-growing list.

Speech Spurts

Thanks to the way the human brain and vocal system are built, speech, in all languages, is produced in small spurts. Unless we pay close attention, we don't usually hear these little spurts, because the ear puts them together and gives us the illusion of speech being an unbroken and continuous stream. In English, these spurts are often, though not always, one clause long. These spurts contain one piece of information (and, thus, are often called "idea units") and contain one intonational focus (one major pitch change), creating either a final or not final intonation contour (and, thus, are called "tone units").

Standard English

A term with lots of different meanings or at least nuances. By "Standard English," in this book, I mean the way English is typically spoken and written (and these are different) when it is used for public sphere purposes (e.g., job interviews, mainstream media, political speeches) and does not display regional, ethnic, class, or other social variation. This really is a fiction, since variation is always present in some form in language use. But it is an important fiction nonetheless, since there can be negative consequences for being perceived as not using Standard English in some circumstances. Standard English is taken by many in society to be the way educated people speak and write (keep in mind, though, that spoken and written forms of Standard English are different), though when such educated people are speaking informally to friends they often use forms that would not be used in more formal settings.

Stanza

A stanza is a group of lines about one important event, happening, or state of affairs at one time and place, or it focuses on a specific character, theme, image, topic, or perspective. When time, place, character, event, or perspective changes, we get a new stanza. I use this term ("stanza") because these units are somewhat like stanzas in poetry.

Stress

Stress is a *psychological concept, not a physical one.* English speakers can (unconsciously) use and hear several different degrees of stress in a word, but this is not physically marked in any uniform and consistent way. Stress is physically marked by a combination of increased loudness, increased length, and by changing the pitch of one's voice (raising or lowering the pitch, or gliding up or down in pitch) on a word's primary ("accented") syllable. Any one or two of these can be used to trade off for the others in a quite complicated way. Thus, in the word "wonderful" people hear the first syllable (the accented syllable) as having more stress than the next two and they hear the third as having more stress than the second: WONderFULL. In an utterance composed of several words (say a clause like "I think you are wonderful") each word will carry a different degree of stress in comparison to each other depending on what the speaker wants to mark as new and/or important and as old and/or less important. This pattern of stress on different words is called the intonation contour of the utterance. The word with the most stress in the intonation contour of an utterance is marked by a noticeable movement in the pitch of the voice (a rise, fall, rise-fall, or fall-rise) and is said to be the "information focus" or just the "focus" of the intonation contour. Thus, if I say "I think YOU are wonderful," I make "you" the new or important information, while if I say "I think you are WONderful," I make either "wonderful" or the "you are wonderful" or "I think you are wonderful" the new or important information (when the focus is on the last word, then the new or important information can be that word or any phrase or clause it is part of). When one word in an utterance is given extra stress this is called "emphatic stress" and gives extra emphasis to this word, as in "**MY** daughter is a real STAR" (where I have used bolded print for the emphatic stress and regular print for the focus). Often emphatic stress is taken to imply a contrast—as here, a possible contrast between, say, my daughter and yours.

Theory

A theory is a set of claims about what exists in a given sphere of reality (e.g., language, cells, evolution, the environment, society, etc.), how these things should be described, and how these things are related and interact with each other and with what results (outcomes). The claims in a theory are hypotheses (guesses) until substantive evidence is collected for them. When such evidence is collected the theory is held to be "true" (a representation of reality), though open to revision by the normal processes of scientific or empirical investigation. (Even though empirical theories are always open to revision, ignoring well-supported theories is usually dangerous and stupid and can cause much harm.)

Tone Unit

See "Speech Spurts."

Tools of Inquiry

This book introduces form–function correlations, situated meanings, social languages, Discourses, Conversations, and intertextuality as "tools of inquiry" (see the Glossary for each of these). They are tools of inquiry in the sense that they lead us as discourse analysts to ask specific sorts of questions about our data.

Utterance-Token Meaning

Another term for what I have called "situated meaning" in this book.

Utterance-Type Meaning

The general meaning or range of meanings, or meaning potential, of a word or phrase considered outside of actual contexts of use.

Vernacular

The word has different meanings and if you look it up in a dictionary it will be given meanings irrelevant to how I use the word in this book. In this book, "vernacular" means the style of language people use when they are seeking to communicate as "everyday people" and not as experts or specialists of any sort (though they may speak as such specialists and experts in other settings). It is the form of language people have learned in their early socialization into language within their homes or communities. A person's vernacular will vary with his or her social and cultural background, though as people engage with each other in a cosmopolitan society they will often converge on styles of the vernacular that are more similar to each other. People will vary in how they use their vernacular style depending on how informal or formal they want to be in given contexts (that is, people do not speak to their spouses in bed the same way they do to a stranger in a bar, but in both cases they are probably using their vernacular [non-specialist] style of language).

Index